Fugitive
Empire

Fugitive Empire

Locating Early American Imperialism

ANDY DOOLEN

UNIVERSITY OF MINNESOTA PRESS

MINNEAPOLIS • LONDON

Chapter 1 was originally published in slightly different form as "Reading and Writing Terror: The New York Conspiracy Trials of 1741," *American Literary History* 16, no. 3 (2004): 377–406; reprinted by permission of Oxford University Press. Chapter 4 was originally published in slightly different form as "Snug Stored Below: The Politics of Race in James Fenimore Cooper's *The Pioneers*," *Studies in American Fiction* 29, no. 2 (Autumn 2001): 131–58; reprinted by permission of *Studies in American Fiction* and Northeastern University.

Published by the University of Minnesota Press
111 Third Avenue South, Suite 290
Minneapolis, MN 55401-2520
http://www.upress.umn.edu

Library of Congress Cataloging-in-Publication Data

Doolen, Andy, 1968–
  Fugitive empire : locating early American imperialism / Andy Doolen.
     p. cm.
  Includes bibliographical references and index.
  ISBN 0-8166-4453-5 (hc : alk. paper) — ISBN 0-8166-4454-3 (pb : alk. paper) 1. Imperialism—History—18th century. 2. Slavery—United States—History—18th century. 3. Imperialism in literature. 4. American literature—Colonial period, ca. 1600–1775—History and criticism. 5. American literature—1783–1850—History and criticism. 6. United States—Race relations—History—18th century. I. Title.
  E179.5.D66 2005
  325'.32'097309033—dc22   2005013947

Printed in the United States of America on acid-free paper

The University of Minnesota is an equal-opportunity educator and employer.

12 11 10 09 08 07 06 05   10 9 8 7 6 5 4 3 2 1

Contents

Acknowledgments

In attempting to acknowledge those who provided guidance, helpful commentary, and support, I confronted the perils of genre. How was I to distinguish among the contributions made by mentors, colleagues, friends, and loved ones, so I could then place them in separate paragraphs? After several drafts, I decided to surrender and find comfort in convention. Over the course of writing this book I have enjoyed the friendship and intellectual camaraderie of a number of wonderful people, and with great pleasure I now thank them publicly. My only regret is that my words will fail to convey my deep sense of gratitude.

I thank the following people who read and commented on parts of this manuscript: Joan Dayan has been there for me every step of the way, giving me unstinting support and helping me to understand, in her own brilliant way, how the histories of slavery left their imprint on early American culture. Ed Dryden, Annette Kolodny, and Charles Scruggs provided expert advice and incisive commentary. Their genuine passion for literature and critical inquiry is inspiring and abundantly evident in their teaching and in the examples of their scholarship. Dana Nelson, Dale Bauer, and Gordon Hutner were indispensable readers and colleagues. Dana read the entire manuscript and then some. Her criticism, scholarly expertise, and encouragement were crucial when I began to revise and to articulate the connections between British and U.S. imperial culture. Dale was my main writing partner for a year and improved this manuscript in innumerable ways. I have benefited from her generosity, intellectual energy, and weird sense of humor. Gordon was an invaluable reader and resource. Hours of conversation with him about literary history and scholarship were an enormous benefit when I began to think about the larger implications of my work. Michael Eliot read the entire manuscript twice and gave me careful and thorough criticism, which thankfully honed in on areas that needed more attention. Maja Lisa Von Sneidern was constant both in her encouragement and in her attendance at the Home Den, and Sharon Harrow read portions of this manuscript at a minute's notice. Finally, I owe a special debt to Alex Macleod, who read countless drafts written in the ugly stages, never pulling his punches and always challenging me to earn my conclusions. I can begin to repay him for this debt by acknowledging that if an eloquent sentence unexpectedly appears in these pages, Alex probably had something to do with it.

I have received financial support over the years, providing me with both the funding to conduct archival research and the free time to write this book. I thank the dean of arts and sciences at the University of Arizona, the English department at the University of Arizona, the English department and Art Young at Clemson University, and the College of Arts and Sciences at the University of Kentucky. I wish to express my gratitude to the helpful support staff at the New York Public Library, the New York Historical Society, the Newberry Library, and the library at the University of Arizona.

Thanks to Richard Morrison at the University of Minnesota Press, who was unflagging in his support and good humor at each stage of this process. His skillful advocacy made this book a reality, and his confidence in it kept me motivated and excited. I also wish to thank Nancy Sauro for her expert copyediting.

During the course of writing this book, a number of friends and colleagues generously shared ideas, creativity, and vision. I wish to thank Daniel Cooper Alarcón, Susanna Ashton, Virginia Blum, Ann Brigham, Mary Cappello, Lauren Cathcart, Dave Correia, Michael Crutcher, Jack Daniels, Kristine Dorame, Janet Eldred, Denise Fulbrook, Jyllian Gunther, Gregory Jackson, Kristen Kennedy, Craig Kleinman, Toni Kuehn, James Lilley, Donald McNutt, Jim Minton, Lee Morrisey, Angela Mullis, Michael Neal, Ben Nye, Catherine Paul, John Peacock, Yolanda Pierce, Armando Prats, María Laura Hernandez Reyes, Ellen Rosenman, Kendra Scott, Matt Sheehan, Dan Snyder, Jeff Stone, Jean Walton, and Jerry Williams.

My extended family has become even more extended during the time it took me to write the book. I thank them for their patience, their interest, their sense of adventure, and our island histories. I owe special debts to Jackie Bogan, for having a special relationship with Saint Jude, and to Vincent Curley, for sharing his passion for history with me; to Jim Bogan, for his example of academic freedom; to Kevin Greer and Daniel Stolar, for their friendship and for allowing me to discuss this book while on interminable road trips through Mexico; and to my sisters, Gina, Sheila, and Katie, for being my oldest friends and biggest supporters. Finally, I thank my father, Carl Doolen, for being a model of kindness and integrity, and my mother, Mary Doolen, for teaching me how to enjoy life. I dedicate this book to them.

Introduction

When I first conceived of this book, my aim was to write about the way slavery disrupted expressions of U.S. identity in the late colonial and early national periods. Intending to focus on the anxieties surrounding the "domestic" institutions of slavery, I soon found this convenient category was an illusion. I realized that slavery was a phenomenon of empires that collapsed national borders, and my study would need to find novel ways to comprehend how early Americans made sense of the many linkages between foreign and domestic worlds. To capture these linkages, *Fugitive Empire* begins in the year 1741, not 1776. In 1741 colonial officials in New York City discovered an alleged conspiracy among their slaves to burn Manhattan to the ground. Described as a classic witch hunt by many historians, the New York Conspiracy trials resulted in the execution of thirty suspected slave conspirators and four white ringleaders. But what prevailing historiography defines largely as a local crisis, I view as a global confrontation between European empires that played a badly underestimated role in forming American nationhood. England and Spain were fighting the War of Jenkins's Ear in the West Indies at the same time the New York Conspiracy trials were proceeding. It became clear to me that imperial conflict reached far beyond the waters of the Caribbean and in fact generated sufficient fear of a Spanish invasion that, even before the first fires broke out, the fear experienced by white colonists distorted, if not produced, the evidence of insurrection. Conditioned to see their enemies as imperial foes threatening the home front, white colonists looked at their slaves, prized for their seeming loyalty and submissiveness, and saw Spanish insurgents.

While military campaigns occurred primarily on the Caribbean frontier, New York City, an important British port, was rightly seen as a potential Spanish target. The patriotism of empire surrounding the War of Jenkins's Ear heightened the public feeling of vulnerability and led many English colonists to suspect all foreigners, including their slaves, of planning sabotage. Indeed, there seemed to be some truth to a nightmare scenario of a massive uprising when, at the outset of the war in 1739, over a hundred slaves along the Stono River in South Carolina rebelled. They collected weapons, killed whites they deemed unfriendly, and made a valiant, if unsuccessful, run for Saint Augustine, Florida, and, it was believed, the protection of Spanish forces. To colonial officials in New York, the connections between this internal uprising and the Caribbean conflict were all too clear. The fires of 1741 broke out at the height of the war, just as the colony rushed to organize and send a volunteer militia to fight in the West Indies; rather than read their own domestic failings in the multiplying fires, officials ultimately apportioned blame conveniently beyond their borders. Initial assessments that the fires were triggered by accident or by a local crime ring immediately gave way to panic, fears of a Spanish insurrection, and the court's violence.

One of the colonial magistrates, Justice Daniel Horsmanden, wrote the only contemporaneous history of the New York Conspiracy trials. If scholars were still in the business of pronouncing a "classic," then this text would undoubtedly qualify as one. Like our familiar canon of authors who stumbled over the obstacle of racial difference when they defined a universal American character, Horsmanden told a quintessential protonational story that narrated the consolidation of white racial solidarity in terms of British empire. In a moment of patriotic enthusiasm for the defense of English freedoms, disaster hit the home front in the form of a terrifying slave conspiracy. In Horsmanden's account, the court emerges as the city's savior; the magistrates, thankfully recognizing Spanish designs in the fires and acting vigilantly, even heroically, delivered a swift and necessarily brutal reprisal against the city's foreign conspirators: the slaves. Following the fires, thirty-four executions carried out by the authorities confirmed Justice Horsmanden's position that the court was the conduit for a civilized and just England. In many ways, therefore, the events of

1741 anticipate the dynamic and logic that brought about the violence and tyranny inherent in what would soon become the national ideology of American republicanism. In both cases the ideals of freedom and justice are invented in the face of an imaginary enemy, and those ideals, as constructed by the state, are inextricable from what seem to be antithetical principles: brutality and terror. Both the imperial court and the Founding Fathers produced and protected a white national identity while converting blackness into a foreign threat to the republic.

A closer look at the events of 1741 reveals, I argue, an embryonic stage of U.S. imperialism. Military conflict abroad and the trade in slaves at home guaranteed that even if the days of the British empire were numbered, the exercise of a characteristically imperial network of power would long survive the Revolution. The critical paradigm of *American exceptionalism,* which reaffirms the fundamental ideals of the age of revolution, has long denied the existence of imperial authority in early America.[1] This critical perspective proliferates the myth that the American Revolution extirpated the force and logic of empire with the irresistible and heroic dream of egalitarianism and freedom. But rather than stipulating that such national myths and republican ideals are historical givens, *Fugitive Empire* identifies empire and the logic through which it operates as fundamental to the formation of the new United States. It argues that the republican rhetoric of liberty and equality for all not only obscured but, more insidiously, legitimized the operations of imperialism. My title has, therefore, a double reference: on the one hand, it invokes the heretofore hidden imperialism, reputedly antithetical to republican values, that shaped our culture and institutions in America's formative years; on the other hand, it directs our attention to the histories of slaves and the institutions of slavery that make manifest precisely how U.S. imperialism has imprinted its racial geographies on our nation. Republican ideals very well might have inspired the Founding Fathers and their vision of national institutions; nevertheless, their own investment in the operations of empire ensured that the new nation-state could only be constructed from within the shell of the old empire.[2]

While American imperialism was until recently viewed as a contradiction in terms, the idea and nature of an American empire has become a common topic in public discourse after the collapse of the Soviet Union and two wars in Iraq.[3] There is bipartisan agreement between otherwise warring political factions of neoconservatives and liberals that acute global crisis has made it necessary for the United States, as the world's lone superpower, to act like a civilized empire.[4] As the subject appears in public discourse, the only distinction between neoconservative and liberal conceptions of empire is that the former embrace an aggressive unilateralism, while the latter wish for a more globally sensitive multilateralism. Neither doubts that it is only the United States that has the moral and military authority to prevent the spread of global anarchy at the beginning of the twenty-first century. Missing from public discourse, of course, is the question of history; this is a significant omission, since an awareness of omnipresent imperial power in U.S. history would cast doubt on those who argue that a changed world requires preventive military strikes. Naturally, neoconservatives will forever muster the chimera of Rome as proof that the imperialism they advocate is a kinder, gentler, more compassionate imperialism, while "liberal interventionists," as Amy Kaplan describes them, will object weakly that recent imperial adventures are incompatible with revolutionary liberalism and threaten the very fabric of our republic.[5] But these turns toward history are mere rhetorical gestures. Actual historical critique of American imperialism reveals the full shape of U.S. power: it was never either republican or imperial, but always an unstable mixture of idealism, force, and pragmatism, which took distinct forms at distinct historical moments. And yet one element has always remained constant: since its inception, the American state has consistently crafted, wielded, and justified imperial power in the name of freedom.

Reexamining the historical complexity of American imperialism can open up new lines of inquiry into contemporary events and help us understand the effects of imperial power on culture in the United States as well as abroad. As John Carlos Rowe notes, American studies has been at the forefront of challenging the absence of empire in U.S. historiography. Emerging from the Vietnam era was a distinguished group of scholars, such as Richard Slotkin, Annette Kolodny, Reginald Horsman, Richard Drinnon, Ronald Takaki, and Michael Rogin, who cast the problem of colonialism in nineteenth-century America in a new light. Their internal colonization thesis directed critical attention to the workings of imperial power within the United States: continental expansion and Indian dispossession, slavery and the imposition of racial hierarchies, and white power and the changing conceptions of the American subaltern. Among others,

Rowe, Amy Kaplan, and Shelley Streeby have recently broadened the scope of this investigation. Viewing histories of continental expansion, internal colonization, and war in a global framework, they have developed ways of reading the influence of empire on U.S. culture.

My work builds on recent theories and studies of U.S. imperialism that repudiate the standard European model of a central government reigning over extensive and far-flung colonies, and identifies a more ambiguous and terrifying *process* of power consolidation across borders rather than derived from a single geographic *place*.[6] What I will call the historical trinity of U.S. imperialism—war, slavery, and territorial expansion—was a process of imperial domination that bridged the British empire and the new United States. The historical trinity was a vast network of power tied to the global economy, institutions of slavery, the U.S. Constitution, the forced dispossession of American Indians, and military power. Fundamental to my study is the idea that this system of racial domination was the primary characteristic of early American imperialism, setting it apart from models of imperialism deriving from histories of European and Roman expansion. Giving evidence of a residual imperial authority at the heart of republicanism, the practices of racial domination foreground the role the American state played in waging wars over trade and territory, in expanding state power throughout the hemisphere for the sake of controlling foreign markets, and in dominating cultural relations at home.[7] I am interested less in the theoretical concept, and more in the actual practices and cultural expressions of U.S. imperial power.[8]

My interest in imperialism has much in common with recent efforts in American studies to rethink an older developmental narrative of U.S. imperial power, which begins with nineteenth-century continental expansion into western territories and is closely followed by a pivotal shift to overseas expansion at the beginning of the twentieth century. The most fruitful scholarship insists on building a critical historical project that identifies the continuity of imperial power from British North America to the formation of the United States. For example, Kaplan searches for new "multiple historical trajectories of the anarchy of empire"; the historical trinity of war, slavery, and territorial expansion is central to her rethinking the "imperial crucible" of U.S. nation-building.[9] One important consequence of her interest in the "anarchic routes and irrational workings of empire" is the putative anomaly of 1898. Arguing against the notion that the U.S. imperial ventures into the Caribbean and Pacific islands at that time were atypical, Kaplan converts that event into merely a "middle chapter" of U.S. imperialism, while positing the continental conquests of the 1840s as her new (and, by nature, flexible) starting point.[10] To this end, my book investigates even earlier chapters of U.S. imperialism, concentrating on structures of empire traditionally overlooked in U.S. historiography and questioning the main developmental narrative that charts the progression from republicanism to democracy. I begin in 1741 in order to rethink the origins of U.S. culture within the British empire's expanding geopolitical boundaries. While 1776 may mark the birth of an independent nation, the republic would eventually be joined to a previous imperial network that preceded the American Revolution and the Constitutional Convention.

From such a perspective, slavery can no longer be seen simply as America's dirty secret, giving the lie to the founding ideals of liberty and justice for all. For while at first glance slavery certainly seems to expose a fundamental hypocrisy within the system, I contend that slavery is so thoroughly a part *of* the system that it is both the logical effect of American constitutionalism and its sine qua non. The state's psychic and material investments in slavery ensured that, along with the change from colony to republic, the coercion and tyranny necessary to preserve such an institution were in fact built into the Constitution's very fabric, disguised and rationalized through appeals to new and enlightened principles. In the cruelest of ironies, then, the American rhetoric of equality was articulated not simply over and against an imperial logic of racial domination, but within that very logic. In the new republic, whiteness declared independence, using terror as its founding vocabulary.

Historically this irony is clearest when the Founding Fathers made the institutions of slavery a vital component of American constitutionalism. In doing so, they retained a valuable imperial institution, which only tyranny could safeguard, and exiled the new United States from its professed republicanism of merit and sympathy. Independence did not mean that the United States simply discarded its old imperial dress for republican garb. Remarkably, slavery—in colonial times the most unsteady and dangerous of institutions—was as much responsible for securing agreement between the states on a constitution as any of the grievances listed in the Declaration of Independence. Article I of the Constitution supported this framework by reducing each slave to three-fifths of a white citizen, which granted slave-holding interests—whether Virginia master class or New York investor class—a decided advantage in political affairs. The new United States clarified its investment in white power in a number of ways, all of which defined the new citizen as independent, American, white, and male. In 1790, the Naturalization Act limited citizenship to "free white persons," which effectively barred African-Americans from becoming citizens for eighty years. Three years later federal legislators passed the first Fugitive Slave Law, which strengthened Article IV of the Constitution. If one accepts the Constitution as a symbolic expression of the American character, then the age of revolution constitutes a founding moment when the framers secured slave property in the process of producing a free white America.

The apparent need to stipulate the moral authority of the revolutionary generation, and the implicit injunction that true patriots must believe in them, has unnecessarily obscured the issue of white power. While ambiguity about the issue of slavery has shrouded the Constitution and its framers, such efforts to construct white power and secure slave property are not always hidden from historical view. In fact, generations of historians have recycled the belief that these legislative actions were a necessary Machiavellian process of maintaining the states' "Great Compromise" on the issues of slavery and sectional power. Yet this prevailing perspective does not probe beneath declarations of order and unity. It does not consider how race became essential to both the articulation of a common U.S. identity and the normal functioning of national institutions. While no African-Americans participated in framing the Constitution, Ralph Ellison claims their presence in the liberated colonies influenced the creation of national ideology: "Despite their social powerlessness, Negroes would now be intricately involved in the use and misuse of a specific form of symbolic action, the terminology of Democracy."[11] To this end, one can begin to recognize how the state's "misuse" of race, as Ellison notes with exquisite restraint, goes beyond allegedly shrewd legislation. Many of these official acts were not always overt as federal laws and have long been forgotten; other acts appear as inconsequential nonevents in history or are simply inaccessible minerals lost in the sediments of our national archives and narratives. This is the fate of four fugitive slaves, who escaped to freedom in Pennsylvania in 1797 only to face expulsion, as well as Absalom

Jones's congressional petition to abolish the Fugitive Slave Law, written on their behalf. Their fate demonstrates how racial domination was part and parcel of the sound functioning of American constitutionalism.[12]

How can a critical framework shaped by recognition of imperial power transform an overlooked petition to abolish the Fugitive Slave Law into a major event in the formation of U.S. political culture? In the late 1790s, as we shall see in chapters 2 and 3, Federalists were guiding the United States into an undeclared war with France in the West Indies. Military conflict on the Caribbean frontier, as it had done in 1741, raised the specter in the imperial imagination of an invasion of foreign slave rebels that was equal parts truth and fiction. It was true that insurrectionary slaves both across the U.S. border in Spanish Florida and within the union itself threatened the master class and their Southern communities; however, it was fiction when Federalists, in order to build support for an expansive war program, warned that France would recruit America's own slaves in a massive conspiracy against the United States. Confronted with these Federalist fictions as well as a crippling factionalism, the Republican Speaker of the House James Madison took one look at Jones's petition and refused to schedule it for debate. Known for his skill at procedure, Madison based his refusal on a 1790 agreement that required Congress to suppress all petitions and legislation that posed a threat to slavery. Reluctant to open debate on African-American liberties, Madison claimed such an issue was too provocative in the anxious political climate. Judging by historical studies of the period, the defeat of the Fugitive Slave Law petition is a nonevent. Even James Roger Sharp's *American Politics in the Early Republic,* an indispensable aid to understanding the Federalist era, ignores it.[13] For Sharp, it would seem, racial issues were a negligible influence on U.S. political life: the book even fails to mention the suppression of Jones's petition. Even in the late twentieth century—when the future has supposedly opened the archives of the past to the historian—Sharp corroborates the systematic silencing of democratic resistance initiated by Madison's republican authority.

Narratives about race are essential to the formation of U.S. power, and the historical residue of Jones's petition on behalf of the four fugitives continues to contest our contemporary understanding of the "use and misuse" of race in early American culture. Removed from an imperial context, the petition's fate is seemingly little more than one representative case (out of

many), when a budding theoretical republicanism had not yet reached mul-
ticultural maturity. Thus, from a contemporary vantage point, the fate of
the petition is emblematic, an outdated historical curiosity that historians
dust off when needing to measure the progress of the American republic.
The petition, and Madison's suppression of it, I argue, matters because it
exemplifies the relationship between what Michael Rogin refers to as the
political and racial demonology that characterizes past and present U.S.
imperial cultures.[14] Just as Horsmanden perceived a vast slave conspiracy
in 1741 consisting of real slaves who were nightmarish metaphors for a
colony at war, federalist-authored conspiracies of slave terror served as an
essential adjunct to state power, republican in principle, imperial in practice. The political manipulation of real and imagined slaves was as critical
to the functioning of imperial authority in the eighteenth century as the
manipulation of "bad Muslims" in the twenty-first.[15] Madison may not
have believed in the insurrection stories invented by his Federalist antagonists, but he exploits an anxious climate, even encourages it, so he can
suppress the petition and maintain order in divisive times. Unlike the
passing of a U.S. law that theoretically represents true republicanism, and
thereby a powerful legal precedent that shapes the future, the state's insurrection story is not considered a relevant scene in the story of republicanism. Perhaps this is because it essentially invokes an antithetical imperial
power. For the African-American encountering this republican form of
government, armed with nothing but patriotic principles, there was no
separation of powers—only white dominion.

Jones and his petition on behalf of the four runaways to abolish the
Fugitive Slave Law played a significant, if forgotten, role in shaping the
practices of American republicanism—but only if that political system is
understood as a structure of empire. Like the Fugitive Slave Law itself, the
suppression of the petition upheld the border between chattel slavery and
personhood, free and slave states, white and black. In a revolutionary society of rebirth, where colonial subjects became citizens and colonies became
states, slaves were reborn as slaves. Both marking the visible border of civic
identity and constituting the real source of Southern authority, the slave was
essential to the imperial project. As we saw in 1741, the state relied on narratives about race as a strategy for wielding power at home and in foreign
territories. Particularly during conflicts with European states, the ambiguity of the slave's allegiance was believed to endanger national security,

which served to justify the state's military and commercial expansion into foreign territories. As I discuss in chapters 2 and 3, at the end of the eighteenth century the Federalist scenario of insurrectionary slaves poised to penetrate U.S. borders helped the government not only to build a military apparatus but also to bring the war home. While imperial aggression resulted in the notorious Alien and Sedition Acts (1798), it also contributed to the demise of a cross-cultural abolitionist movement by the late 1790s. Madison's refusal to debate the petition effectively labels the abolitionist movement, which had lost white support as the decade wore on, as a foreign faction falling outside the scope of legitimate American dissent. As a result, even such renowned "Friends of the Negro" as slaveholding Benjamin Rush distanced themselves from a model of racial reform tied to legitimate republican practices. As an alternative to petitions for racial reform, for example, the Pennsylvania Abolition Society issued a pamphlet that taught free African-Americans how they could help maintain social order through "nine steps to moral conduct." It would be another thirty years, with the rise of Garrisonian abolitionism, before white Americans would rejoin African-Americans in advocating abolition of the Fugitive Slave Law.

The effects of terror are embedded in colonial and national narratives, whether those narratives take the shape of documentary history, novels, law, the annals of Congress, or an article in the U.S. Constitution. The problem for the critic continues to be to discover ways of reading these textual effects of British and U.S. imperial practices. Yet I resisted the temptation, when exploring the interrelationships among terror, slavery, and American writing, to draw on recent theories of Gothicism in American literature. This decision might sound curious, particularly since, like theorists of Gothicism, I am also a firm believer in their key tenet: Toni Morrison's observation that the "Africanist presence" is at the root of our historical and literary traditions. That the African-American experience should be central to this project of rethinking our national traditions is no longer a critical apostasy, as it was only two decades ago. The focus of the best studies in gothic literary criticism—identifying moments when African-American writers, as Teresa Goddu says, "haunt back" or when writers become possessed by the horrors of slavery—has made what were once strange apparitions in our national consciousness appear familiar to us. Many studies of the American Gothic take this experience as both inspiration and object of study. For example, Goddu's guiding belief is Richard Wright's theory that the African-American is the "embodiment of the tragic past," of slavery, segregation, and racial violence, which American Gothic literature either attempts to avoid or refuses to ignore.[16]

Such progressive critical discourse, which requires the academic to write on behalf of the oppressed against the state's racist practices, has altered our historical understanding of American identity. A major critical notion of the American Gothic holds that its horror stories of violence and dispossession contradict cherished American myths of freedom, equality, and self-determination. As a cultural category, the American Gothic implies that the distortions and monstrosities that we admire in gothic fictions are extrinsic to national foundations, a destructive tumor residing in an otherwise healthy body. Accepting racial domination as a connecting thread of U.S. imperial culture, *Fugitive Empire* takes a different angle: the supposedly aberrant gothic effects are not misrepresentations or distortions of national myths but realistic representations of the smooth functioning of American constitutionalism. If we view slavery and the imperial past as constitutive to the foundation of both the United States and its republican principles, then there are no cultural contradictions for the American Gothic to expose.

I want to bring a differently elusive figure into focus, a white one, a fugitive imperial state that escapes from early American cultural studies and evades scrutiny. Like the more familiar African-American ghost, the fugitive state also haunts, also embodies slavery's tragic past, but it still appears invisible to historical analysis and retains the source of its power. I describe this force as "fugitive" because it constitutes an imperial power that, if we heed republican ideology, supposedly does not exist in early America. These practices occur when the state converts skin and blood into the legal justifications for slavery, when it polices racial hierarchies with a special class of penal laws, when it reinforces ideals of white racial purity through official rituals of execution and banishment, and finally when the state invents official narratives of insurrection and invasion as a strategy for reinforcing political authority.[17] These racial fictions—taking the form of the official discourse of law, policy, proclamation, and public ritual—constitute the logic of U.S. imperialism in the late colonial and early national periods, transforming the terror of white supremacy into a rational and permanent presence.

This presence of terror distinguishes narratives written during periods of war, territorial expansion, and heightened racial awareness. Since this book concentrates roughly on a one-hundred-year period when "literature" referred to a broad range of imaginative, political, public, and scientific writings, my understanding of the term is equally inclusive. For my specific measure, I welcomed texts into my consideration that help us understand the public and private moments of U.S. imperial culture, from state-authored racial fictions to embedded histories of slavery and political resistance. While I work to restore the political and historical character of race relations and white citizenship by demonstrating how the historical trinity of war, slavery, and territorial expansion is intrinsic to the evolution of U.S. imperial culture, this itself is a goal undermined by the legacy of empire. Since the fugitive state produces fictional histories that claim to be accurate and true, few stable contexts exist that even begin to contain the histories of racial domination. My sense of an elusive historical truth derives as much from studying practices of imperial power, such as its racial fictions, as it does from postmodern theories of historiography. For example, consider that slave revolts were perhaps the most significant acts in early American race relations. They not only represent resistance to imperial power and the institutions of slavery but, as I will argue, also expose the imperialist logic that informs American constitutionalism. And yet the archival memory of these moments is selective and its veracity unreliable. The evidence that historians possess to construct an interpretation of a particular revolt is almost always tainted by its close relationship to a master class bent on maintaining white power and privilege at any price. Coercion and torture produced the slave confessions and testimonies, recorded in the magistrate's or master's hand, that historians still try to read like tea leaves for signs of what really transpired.[18] In other words, when magistrates, prosecutors, and other representatives of white power pick up the pen to record slave defiance, the final insurrection story is necessarily more fiction than fact; truth itself has become a kind of fugitive in the archive.[19] The strength of the master class's authoritarian voice, seemingly speaking accurately and with lethal precision, initiates what Michel-Rolph Trouillot describes as a "cycle of silences" that hides fugitive histories; the differential power relations evident in the master's erasure of the slave's resistance informs all subsequent interpretations that return to listen to those first masters and magistrates speak. I return to those first interpretations and investigate how imperial authority creates an official archive. Each chapter of *Fugitive Empire* attempts to break the "cycle of silences" by uncovering the ignored or hidden histories of British and American imperialism and recognizing the representational strategies involved in producing white racial solidarity. If there is a ready-made context for these histories, then it must exist somewhere between what Carl Sandburg, after confessing his inability to tell a true history of the Civil War, called the "steel of fact" and the "fog of dream."[20]

In addition to empire studies, two overlapping discourses called whiteness studies and critical race studies began to emerge in the 1980s and 1990s; these three interdisciplinary schools of cultural analysis contribute to my study of U.S. imperial culture. Each chapter of *Fugitive Empire* both addresses the historical trinity of U.S. imperialism—war, slavery, and territorial expansion—and focuses on those special national narratives that appear in moments of acute social tensions in the late colonial and early national periods. A number of scholars share my view of the national narrative as a site of conflict rather than cohesion, of resistance rather than coherence, although I take special interest in how those national narratives can function in a wide imperial network of power. In that sense, the national narrative is also an imperial narrative.[21] Thus, *Fugitive Empire* joins a long, often contentious debate about empire in U.S. culture as well as slavery's place in the American historical and cultural imagination. My investigations trace the ideological connections among disparate national narratives, including Daniel Horsmanden's *Journal of the Proceedings in the Detection of the Conspiracy* (1744); Charles Brockden Brown's journal, the *Monthly Magazine,* and his novel *Arthur Mervyn* (1799); cross-cultural histories of the 1793 yellow fever epidemic; James Fenimore Cooper's novel *The Pioneers* (1823) and his fictional travel narrative, *Notions of the Americans* (1828); the annual reports of the American Colonization Society; William Apess's autobiography, *A Son of the Forest* (1829), and his history of the Mashpee revolt, *Indian Nullification* (1835); and William Lloyd Garrison's polemic against racial injustice, *Thoughts on African Colonization* (1832). In addition to these narratives, my study also incorporates more popular and partisan documents circulating in the late colonial and early national periods: court records, magazines, congressional records, official correspondence, personal narratives, and documentary histories, written by many hands, provide a fuller understanding of the different roles race played not only in the colonies' transformation into the new United States but also in the emergence of a national literary tradition.

Beginning *Fugitive Empire* with the events of 1741 makes it possible to view the connections between race, imperialism, and nationhood as a historical process that spans the eighteenth-century English empire and the new United States.[22] As we shall see, the convergence of the New York Conspiracy trials and the War of Jenkins's Ear was a turning point in the transformation of British colonists into revolutionary *white* Americans. I am interested in how imperial crisis shapes both Justice Horsmanden's history of the "Great Negro Plot" and public perceptions of the fires. More than a judicial record of the conspiracy trials, I argue, Horsmanden's history depicted the dangerous borders of the British empire, some of which the United States would soon inherit. Horsmanden evokes a dynamic by which imperial expansion in the West Indies endangers the center of English authority; imperial power, in turn, reconstitutes itself by imagining the foreign enemy moving into the heart of the colony. Waging war to expand the national domain in the hopes of controlling West Indian trade, and perhaps colonizing Spanish Cuba, led to confused geographical, political, and racial borders in New York. For colonists participating in their first imperial campaign, the ambiguity and perils of open borders produced simultaneous articulations of British patriotism and a counterdistinctive *white* American identity. Both the war and the conspiracy trials politicized cultural identity and racial affiliation in New York: to be black in 1741 was to be rendered a foreign threat. The imperial court, acting on the conviction that the colony's slaves had joined its Spanish enemy, committed egregious executions and banishments in order to consolidate white power and to repair the border between foreign and domestic geographies and peoples. Thus, recasting the events of 1741 so they celebrate a vigilant court, Justice Horsmanden inadvertently writes a history of U.S. imperialism in its first stages of development.

A two-chapter cycle rests on this foundation and explores how the unstable borders evident in 1741 reemerge at the end of the eighteenth century in the United States. I trace how the historical trinity of U.S. imperialism becomes integral to the cultural work of Charles Brockden Brown. Challenging the prevailing critical tendency to view the first half of his writing career as his more liberal and creative period, chapter 2 demonstrates how Brown's often overlooked literary and cultural journal the *Monthly Magazine* participated in the political and cultural clashes of the late 1790s. No political bystander, Brown and his journal disseminated a Federalist ideology grounded in a collective racial anxiety that aimed to garner support for war with France. Treating the *Monthly Magazine* as a cultural archive of U.S. imperialism, my chapter examines its political essays, reviews of Fourth of July orations and George Washington eulogies, fiction, and historical essays. I open with an analysis of how the racial fictions of Federalist militarism reappear in Brown's journal, then I consider how imperial culture might have shaped the journal's depiction of an imperiled nation beset by a restless free African-American and slave population. Reconstructing the decade's protest against the Fugitive Slave Law, and putting the dissent in dialogue with the vitriolic politics of the Alien and Sedition Laws, chapter 2 documents how the fear of threatening aliens quickly manifested itself as a virulent backlash against an African-American population increasingly figured as fugitives in a white America.

Brown is better known for his popular novels, which depict a United States threatened by French enemies, rebellious slaves, and vengeful Indians, among others. Building on Brown's support for Federalist imperial politics, chapter 3 locates the novel *Arthur Mervyn* in the global corridor that connected the financial and political centers of the eastern seaboard with the contested markets of the West Indies. I reconsider the standard reading of the yellow fever as Brown's attempt at realistic documentation in the tradition of Defoe's *A Journal of the Plague Year*. Instead, I outline an eighteenth-century discourse of contagion tied to the practices of American imperialism. My analysis shows how the historicity and political content of the yellow fever metaphor in *Arthur Mervyn* marks a prevalent fear in the United States that expansion into a Caribbean region unsettled by war and racial violence would infect the United States with the same disease. While the resolution in *Arthur Mervyn* is usually read as a utopian statement of a healthy city, to my eye, Brown's representation of a recovered Philadelphia appears as a fantasy of social and racial order.

Whereas previous chapters traced domestic racial anxieties to imperial expansion into the Caribbean frontier, the final two chapters consider how continental expansion rendered the racial threat internal and domestic. The economic resurgence of slavery in the first two decades of the nineteenth century, as well as growing concerns about an impure white republic, caused a shift in U.S. imperial culture. After years of speculation, two plans—African-American colonization and Indian removal—were designed to remove both free African-Americans and American Indians from a white America. Chapters 4 and 5 of *Fugitive Empire* examine how these twinned movements shaped the explorations of national identity in the work of two very different authors, James Fenimore Cooper and William Apess.

Cooper wrote *The Pioneers,* the first of the Leatherstocking novels, while white Americans openly debated solutions to the "race problem." While he allegorized the founding of America, legislators were negotiating the Missouri Compromise, the latest strategy for both expanding the United States and maintaining a system of racial domination in the North and South. At the same time, the American Colonization Society began relocating free African-Americans to the African colony of Liberia. For many critics, *The Pioneers,* characterized by legal drama, is a cultural touchstone for the evolution of a theoretical republicanism. Yet by extracting this major novel from its historical position within debates on race and nationhood, critics divorce it from the contexts of imperial power. Unstable racial identities, producing a climate of unrestrained white power, are at the heart of *The Pioneers.* Both the public airing of a slavery crisis and wide support for African colonization demonstrated a range of racial anxieties, from insurrection and miscegenation to suffrage and an increasing free African-American population. I show how the drama of these fugitive histories comes to shape the U.S. historical novel, which despite its desperate desire to lend credence to a republican fiction moving into the future, cannot conceal an imperialistic record of racial domination.

Finally, chapter 5 examines how American Indian writer William Apess confronted new formations of U.S. imperialism and white power in the 1830s, when President Andrew Jackson and Indian removal marked the acceleration of territorial conquest. Apess, a Pequot, political activist, revivalist preacher, and war veteran, published five works between 1829 and 1838, and taken collectively his writing against removal and for Native rights constitutes one of the most compelling arguments for racial justice in the antebellum period. Putting Apess in dialogue with William Lloyd Garrison, I consider how Apess borrowed from the anti-imperialist rhetoric of abolitionism and anticolonization, as codified in Garrison's influential *Thoughts on African Colonization.* In both his autobiography and his political writing on behalf of the Mashpee Indians of Massachusetts, Apess

joins the African-American and Native histories of resisting U.S. imperialism and exposes the state's fear of a racial uprising. Apess and Garrison
challenge what Dana Nelson calls the false promise of American constitutionalism, which "persistently draws our attention toward its containment
promise, its promise to manage democracy for us, toward a better future."[23]
Viewed together, Apess and Garrison work to claim an intercultural democratic theory that rejects the logic of constitutionalism, and its fantasy of
a racially exclusive popular sovereignty, as an inherently imperial and antidemocratic politics. Both Apess and Garrison went to jail for protesting
against U.S. imperial power and its crimes against humanity. *Fugitive
Empire* ends with their incarceration as a concise message about how new
formulations of a racially inclusive democracy called forth new methods
of policing and punishment. At the same time, crafting a politics of racial
justice and analyzing white racism, condemning imperial racial fictions as
oppressive and unenlightened, Apess and Garrison exemplify the possibil-
ities of achieving radical democracy in U.S. imperial culture.

While I call attention to important turning points in U.S. imperial culture, I am not suggesting that every text, every author, can be read in a
common way within such a framework. My critical interests led me to a specific set of texts and authors that addressed fundamental questions linked
to the historical trinity of U.S. imperialism. Nor do I construct a theoretical paradigm in which to view it in the late colonial and early national
periods. Perhaps the time will come after scholars recover and reconstruct
the fugitive histories of U.S. imperial culture in its first stages when such
a narrative can take shape outside the reach of American exceptionalism.
The patriotic belief that republicanism always trumps imperialism in U.S.
political development, except in irregular moments, is hegemonic, determining the production of knowledge across the disciplines. Faced with
such obstacles, not to mention imperial culture's own distorted archives, I
limit myself to locating specific historical trajectories of U.S. imperial culture, when the state either imagines its demise or goes out in search of new
enemies. Such excavation work of historical archives and memories is necessary to the larger project of rethinking the nature and progress of American imperialism across the centuries.

chapter 1

War for Empire and the New York Conspiracy Trials of 1741

The mysterious string of thirteen fires that ripped through and alarmed New York City in the spring and summer of 1741 began with a conflagration that turned Fort George, one of British America's strongest fortifications, into ashes. In the days that followed, each blaze contributed to the mystery until the report of a slave, spotted running from the scene of the tenth fire, persuaded the people of New York that the puzzling fires were really opening salvos in a massive slave insurrection. City officials acted quickly, interrogating more than two hundred people, black and white, and they soon uncovered what they believed to be a gang of dispossessed slaves and Irish indentured servants, who, it seems, had planned to burn New York City to the ground and kill their masters. Stunned by the boldness of the plot, authorities immediately began to investigate and to prosecute hundreds of alleged conspirators. Although authorities knew disgruntled indentured servants to be key conspirators, blame fell squarely on the city's large slave population. In the end, the colony of New York executed thirty slaves and four white ringleaders, publicly flogged seventy slaves, and transported over one hundred more to the Caribbean slave markets, never to return.[1]

Was there really a conspiracy to burn New York City in 1741? Unlike an uprising or rebellion, conspiracy was a crime of reckless speech rather than action, a verbal plan that threatened social order, and thus difficult to prove in any era. "Conspiracy lies in asserting and agreeing," Thomas Davis writes, "in 'loose talk' of doing a deed."[2] The recent controversy over the

Denmark Vesey conspiracy of 1822 reminds us that while Anglo-American conspiracy law might set the limits on prohibitive speech, none of the legal niceties mattered much when whites thought they heard "loose talk" coming from slaves.[3] When we read the official archive of a slave conspiracy, we encounter a written record authored by whites in a slave society, a culture of terror that defended white power at all costs. One method of defense was the mass execution of the alleged slave conspirators, almost always made possible by a special class of laws. For instance, during the conspiracy panic in New York, the court relied exclusively on the law of Negro evidence, which had been designed to prosecute potential slave uprisings. *Negro evidence* was defined as the incriminating testimony of one slave against another—the court needed no other proof than this to sentence a slave to death in 1741.[4]

Prosecutors went to great lengths to acquire such testimony. Often the inducement was the king's mercy: either testify against coconspirators and earn a lesser punishment or face a capital charge and certain execution. Prosecutors employed coercive tactics like the threat of the gallows and hanging the dead bodies of the condemned on gibbets; offered "immunity" or protection in the form of a general pardon; and conducted dragnets, sweeping slaves off the streets for interrogation with the presumption of guilt. As a result of these practices, our view of the conspiracy trials must necessarily pass through an archive distorted by this violence; and for the historian trying to sort out testimony according to degrees of coercion, connecting the dots in the ashes of 1741 is a treacherous, perhaps impossible, undertaking.

The search for a verdict based on unimpeachable evidence inspires the historiographies of slave conspiracies, even when we know how white authorities elicited such "facts." The historian who wishes to retry the New York Conspiracy trials is even further handicapped by a valuable missing archive, the Supreme Court records, destroyed with other judicial documents from the era, ironically enough, in a fire. Furthermore, there are few revealing letters, journals, or poems about the trials or executions, and colonial newspapers simply reported the plot's existence and then kept track of executions. A single "eyewitness" account remains, *Journal of the Proceedings in the Detection of the Conspiracy,* written by Daniel Horsmanden, the city's recorder and one of the three judges at the trials. He compiled his documentary account from the prosecutors' notes, his memory of the suspects' examinations, addresses to the court by prosecutors and defendants, and both his firsthand reflections on the motivations of particular suspects and his proud commentary on the court's timely vigilance. His "official" record of the proceedings has always been the heart of all investigations into what really took place in 1741. Publishing this record in 1744 as a way to silence public criticism of the court, Justice Horsmanden wanted to justify the court's verdicts and punishments. To put it simply, this deeply flawed text—which Philip Morgan calls an "exercise in post-hoc justification of a controversial prosecution"—is the key piece of evidence in all subsequent historical examinations of the New York Conspiracy trials.[5]

Thus, although even the finest historians readily regard this mine as contaminated by the court's practices of intimidation, coercion, and torture, they still descend into it to extract raw materials for interpretation. Some historians believe that no slave conspiracy occurred in New York in 1741 but there may have been a conspiracy among the prosecutors, whose deep-rooted racism and fear of African-Americans escalated the violence into a witch hunt. A second perspective holds that what prosecutors saw as a vast conspiracy to overthrow English authority was actually loosely affiliated gangs, who set fires to cover their crimes. A third, and related, perspective claims that a vast conspiracy did exist, although leaders were not interested in establishing their own government. Instead, disgruntled slaves desired personal freedoms and reacted against the master class by joining whites in stealing from the rich and setting their homes on fire. Finally, a fourth perspective believes that there was a conspiracy in 1741 to overthrow the imperial administration and take over the colony. No matter which perspective, the historian must find a way to resolve the problem of tainted evidence. There is only Horsmanden's problematic text; there are no bodies of murdered white people, no organized escape to the northern frontier, no slave caught with a torch, and most important, no confessions from those thought to be the principal conspirators. Davis resolves the lack of reliable evidence by choosing to write a historical fiction that necessarily takes its dialogue, central characters, and motivations from Horsmanden's account. Marcus Rediker and Peter Linebaugh create a fascinating narrative of heroic slaves carrying their knowledge of insurrection into all parts of a fluid Atlantic world, a "Caribbean cycle of rebellion" that reached New York City in 1741.[6] Even if one considers this a possible *cause* for a revolutionary conspiracy, the only proof of its *effects* were mysterious fires, forced confessions, and a suspect historical text. Finally, Peter Charles Hoffer, swayed by Horsmanden's insider perspective, simply decides to accept the representation of events as "at least partially true" and avoids the troublesome facts of coercion, torture, and false confessions.[7] Like other historians before them, they can construct their case only from circumstantial evidence. Sooner or later everybody returns to Justice Horsmanden's understanding and memory of the critical evidence, the conspirators themselves, and their confessions and motivations.[8]

This chapter, then, goes in a different direction and elects not to sift through the evidence in the hope of convicting the true culprits or determining the extent to which a conspiracy existed. On the contrary, I am interested less in the planning of conspiracy, more in how the events of 1741 converge with an imperial conflict known as the War of Jenkins's Ear. Positioning Horsmanden's documentary history in this international context, my investigation considers how white panic, caused by conspiracy and war, shaped public perception of the fires. Two years before signs of a plot appeared in New York, the colony embraced this imperial war fought between England and Spain over "American" trade routes in the West Indies; from the beginning, a bellicose patriotism of empire, sweeping England and her colonies, characterized the War of Jenkins's Ear. By the time of the first fire in 1741, rumors of slave insurrections in other colonies had already alarmed New York, while war hysteria made many colonists suspicious of the slave population's loyalty to England. Many wondered if their slaves were covert enemies who might join forces with Spain upon an invasion.[9]

Read alongside the War of Jenkins's Ear, Justice Horsmanden's text becomes something more than a prosecutor's dubious justification of the trials and, instead, offers us an unforeseen opportunity to understand the effects of England's global ambition on colonial identity. In New York, the war led the prosecutors to suspect the city's slaves—approximately 20 percent of the population in 1741—of being involved in an international conspiracy to overthrow the colony. Instead of a documentary history of the trials, I want to suggest that Horsmanden's text is a war narrative; it tells a story about how an evil Spanish empire, enticing the enslaved with promises of freedom, turned New York's once loyal, obedient, and dutiful slaves into fierce enemies of the state. In my reading, the war and the conspiracy scare work together to reinforce white racial solidarity in New York.

My investigation of this dynamic will begin with an analysis of the conceptual strategies Justice Horsmanden uses as he composes his official record of the conspiracy trials. How does Justice Horsmanden attempt to stabilize a racial hierarchy unsettled by the war and charges of conspiracy? How does historical writing define, support, and/or escalate the terror that rules all slave cultures, particularly one mired in an acute crisis? The next two sections investigate how the War of Jenkins's Ear might have shaped Horsmanden's historical understanding of the conspiracy. Vexed by what it considered to be a war on two fronts—Spain on the Atlantic frontier and slave rebels within the colony—New York experienced a militarism that made a white identity the only safe identity. How did New York's own imperial fantasies of Caribbean colonies help to transform the local conspiracy scare into a geopolitical crisis connected to the fears of a Spanish invasion? How did the war's Caribbean theater of action shape racial formation in New York?

These strands come together in the final section, "War and Conspiracy: State of Emergency," which explains why Horsmanden's history is left open, unfinished, the threat of insurrection still hovering over the city. The refusal to end the narrative, to claim a world free of conspirators, is the political content of the form itself, the action of a colonial official attempting to rebuild social order by warning the public of imminent disaster. This crafted insecurity is our own cautionary tale. It is a sign of a fractured colonial discourse that, once threatened, will work compulsively toward a single aim: to govern the shadowy territory between fact and fiction, innocence and guilt, white and black, and in the process, reconstitute its dominance. While Horsemanden attempts to construct a history of the trials that monopolizes the "facts" and evidence, this chapter explores his failure to tell a story of a colony safe from future threats.

ARTFUL CHRONICLE

During New York's political wars of the 1730s, Horsmanden rose to prominence because he was skilled at using the written word to defend Governor Cosby's imperial administration against a rival group led by Lewis Morris, chief justice of the provincial court. When the administration grew irritated with the opposition's criticism, it charged the opposition's public voice, the *New York Weekly Journal,* and its editor, John Peter Zenger, with publishing seditious material. Governor Cosby appointed Horsmanden to a council as a political attack dog, "to point out . . . the particular seditious paragraphs" in the opposition press.[10] Zenger's eventual acquittal made the trial a milestone in defining the legal freedom of the press as well as the limits of imperial power. Despite the acquittal, Horsmanden established a reputation as a skillful partisan and was handsomely rewarded with a special license from the governor to purchase six thousand acres along the Hudson River near Albany.

Nobody considers the New York Conspiracy trials to be a milestone on the grand march toward American constitutionalism, perhaps because of the court's unprecedented assault on the colony's slaves; nevertheless, both cases reveal the new power of print in the American colonies. As Michael Warner remarks, official documents "metonymically represented the aura of imperial administration" and opposition could potentially disrupt the "networks of power uniting the colonies and deriving from the English courts."[11] At the height of the conspiracy trials, there was no public resistance to either the prosecution or the administration, but as the sense of panic diminished during the two years following the trials, critics began to question the court's actions. Attempting to reinforce their political authority, the imperial administration enlisted Justice Horsmanden to publish a spirited defense and strengthen colonial authority.

After Zenger, the conspiracy trials accelerated Horsmanden's rise to prominence. Appearing before the common council in April 1741, he was one of the first public officials to argue that the random fires were actually a conspiracy to overthrow the city; while sitting on the Supreme Court, he directed the prosecution, interrogated defendants, and sentenced those found guilty. His partisanship poses a problem for Horsmanden, the author. Attempting to put to rest any doubts that his personal involvement might unfairly influence his opinions, Horsmanden reassures the reader that he will represent the proceedings in an objective, neutral form. "[A] *journal* would give more satisfaction," he writes, "inasmuch as in such a kind of process, the depositions and examinations themselves, which were the ground-work of the proceedings, would appear at large." Lacking a controlling narrator, the chronicle form (what he refers to as a "journal") promises the reader a clear view of the evidence. Simply by exhibiting the "ground-work" of depositions, testimony, confessions, and summations in chronological order, Horsmanden believes the chronicle will unfold the "most natural view of the whole" and make skeptics "undeceived."[12]

More than any piece of evidence, the chronicle's narrative condition persuades Horsmanden's readers that justice was done in 1741. A prominent narrator, such as Edward Gibbons, Francis Parkman, or Lewis Mumford, defines the "history proper," a form of history writing that Horsmanden calls "historical relation." Consequently, the chronicle form is often viewed as possessing fewer signs of narration or fiction making. This objective pose, however, can be the chronicle's most swaying feature because the narrator's apparent neutrality works to conceal the artfulness of the narrative's construction.[13] With this in mind, one can see the outlines of the coherent story that Horsmanden's chronicle fashions out of a murky historical field. Every culture cultivates particular story types that help a people make sense of the past. In the eighteenth-century colonial world, the insurrection story captured white fears of a slave uprising. In New York, the insurrection story resonated in historical memory, beginning with the 1712 slave uprising, dotted with the many real episodes of slave insurrections and failed plots in the North American colonies as well as the many rumors and half-truths, and capped with the puzzling fires of 1741. Like contemporary reports by government officials and media outlets about terrorist attacks, and the semiotic range of color-coded alerts, it hardly mattered if the slave conspiracy was *real* or *imagined*—this ambiguity, and the sensation it evoked of imminent danger, gave the story its explanatory effect. The insurrection story, with its gripping story line of racial antagonism and terrifying imagery, helped white colonists rationalize an inchoate fear caused by both the fires and the war.

Fiction making was precisely what critics accused the courts of doing, which explains why Horsmanden stresses his role as the dutiful city recorder. He gathers the prosecutors' notes, transcribes the court's official statements, and creates a simple calendar for the events. Yet underlying his judicial realism is the insurrection story, and we see signs of it in his first step in composing the chronicle. With the unproven fear of insurrection driving the court's interpretation, he takes control of historical time, a move that also has the effect of inscribing the court's disciplinary power. The most basic element of the chronicle form—the mere act of selecting and propelling details through a chronological cycle—compromises his neutral stance by sowing the first seeds as well as the first impressions of a plot: the first day, second day chronology is the flashing red light of a conspiracy that inevitably grows into a security threat with each passing day. Because Horsmanden aims to identify the origins of the plot, the first detail also happens to evoke the final threat of a potential slave conspiracy. A group of slaves walk down the street after yet another mysterious fire in the spring of 1741, and a white woman, Mrs. Earle, looking out her window, overhears one of them boast "with a vaporing sort of an air, 'Fire, Fire, Scorch, Scorch, A LITTLE, damn it, BY-AND-BY,' and then [he] threw up his hands and laughed."[14] The sequential ordering of events is fundamental to the chronicle's rhetorical effectiveness; as the curse is presented as evidence, it acts as a secret code in the narrative, something the testimony that follows will inevitably decipher. Beginning with this first suspicion of a plot and tracing the gradual accretion of rumors as they become verifiable truth, the chronicle has the effect of re-creating and highlighting the suspense felt by the public during the year of the trials.

At this point, the sequence has already signaled the chronicle's polemic because local culture possesses knowledge of the underlying story type; no narrator needs to interrupt and explain the curse's meaning. Fire may have been a handy weapon for the insurrectionary slave, but it was legendary in the white imagination. A mysterious fire could often appear to whites, even if only a nagging doubt, as the first assault in a race war. The curse of "Fire, Fire, Scorch, Scorch" was particularly alarming to New Yorkers because arson had been the slaves' weapon in the 1712 revolt. Thus, the curse does not prophesize a swift inferno but a city terrorized in degrees, bit by bit and day by day, heightened by the curse, "damn it, BY-AND-BY," a terrifying threat precisely because of its ambiguity. Moving beyond the temporality of a threat realized immediately, in a little while, or in the future, the "by-and-by" also suggests that the threat may never come, that it resides solely in an overwrought imagination. Because the trials lacked both confessions from the alleged arsonists and direct physical evidence, this opening narrative is critical for Horsmanden because it provides an interpretive frame for the court reports that follow.

Like any good storyteller, Horsmanden lets the reader hear as well as see the symbolic origin of the conspiracy, and he allows the image of the slave rebel Quack's resistance to remain. He goes as far as to punctuate Quack's curse with the unnerving sound of his laugh. Laughter, like the torch, constitutes a sign of resistance to white power, precisely the effect Horsmanden is aiming for in these early pages. At this point, he is content to allow the image of resistance to remain without contesting it and robbing Quack of his temporary agency. "Laughter is a free instrument in their hands," Mikhail Bakhtin declared famously about medieval peasants, and for the sake of his plot, Horsmanden will let the sound reverberate.[15] The narrative's opening requires the sensation of three slaves dreaming of burning the city, and then reveling in it, a folkloric image bent on massacring the city's white people.

WAR AND CONSPIRACY: PATRIOTISM

If indeed the conspiracy really happened, then Justice Horsmanden's chronicle was undoubtedly written by the court and for an anxious public. The problem of context is a fundamental issue for historians studying the New York Conspiracy. Rediker and Linebaugh's recent interpretation is based on their conviction that slave resistance made the 1730s a pivotal period in slavery's history: "The magnitude of the upheaval was, in comparative terms, extraordinary, encompassing more than eighty separate cases of conspiracy, revolt, mutiny, and arson—a figure probably six or seven times greater than the number of similar events that occurred in either the dozen years before 1730 or the dozen after 1742."[16] On the other hand, Morgan believes that the ideology and practice of white supremacy in a slave society should make us feel less certain about our accounting of racial unrest. He cites the "near-hysterical proportions" of whites when faced with rumors of rebellion, suggesting this history of conspiracy scares "may well reveal less a 'cycle of rebellion,' as Linebaugh and Rediker would have it, than a time of acute social tensions when rumors fed on themselves and whites."[17] Although we can be fairly certain about an insurrection, like the one that occurred along the Stono River in South Carolina in 1739, how do we determine the *real* from the *imagined* conspiracies or judge degrees of truth in a coerced confession?

Doubts about the New York Conspiracy have made it a minor and neglected event in our national history. Set in a Northern colony with no real slave hero like Denmark Vesey or Nat Turner, lacking all original trial transcripts, and influenced by war hysteria, the New York Conspiracy has been classified as a minor historical case. Although some might view New

York's incomplete archive as a serious disadvantage, the Vesey Conspiracy illustrates how court records can constrict historical investigations. New York's missing archive may be an advantage, particularly since we can never forget, when encountering Horsmanden's portal to the conspiracy, the imaginary component of his history. Thus the New York Conspiracy affords us the opportunity to understand how white power transformed an inchoate fear of a slave uprising into a narrative that terrified the public. In Charleston, as in New York, some part of the "upheaval" occurred in the white public's imagination; as Davis ultimately concludes, it is on the "various perceptions of that peril on which the historian may fruitfully focus."[18]

The insurrection story itself organized these perceptions of racial unrest; although each story type is generic in a fundamental sense, in New York in 1741 the presence of Spanish sabotage became part of the emerging plot. Depicting the city's crisis as a guerilla battle in a war for empire, Horsmanden represents the magistrates as true patriots, whose vigilance saved the city. This dominant motif celebrates patriotic union and white solidarity simultaneously, both as overall effects of the war, unusual because wars between England and other European powers rarely fostered solidarity among North American colonies. In fact, over a century of colonialism, competing for precious export markets, and fighting countless Indian wars, the English colonies were often pitted against each other in competition for Native allies, land, labor, settlers, and resources. American participation in the war effort marked the first time England had called on her colonies to contribute money, troops, and other support to a foreign war away from their homes. For the first time in a generation, the North American colonies experienced an emerging sense of solidarity as they went to war against a rival empire.

The first years of the war produced a constant flow of information in North American newspapers, private correspondence, combat reportage, and government documents that intensified the common purpose against the Spanish. The War of Jenkins's Ear came at a pivotal moment in the British empire, when English merchants at home and in the colonies were pushing into new markets and antagonizing the Spanish Guarda Costa. On the North American mainland, colonists peered into the glow of this "American" war and imagined fertile islands, like Cuba, that they would transform into free English colonies. While having the tactical aim of controlling

Spanish markets and trade routes, British imperial ideology interpreted every open market, every commodity exported to England, as physical extensions of English liberty. English patriots proclaimed that Spanish tyranny, which encompassed all the evils of a long-detested rival, undercut these essential freedoms. Indeed, for over a decade Whig patriots had characterized such depravity as the "death of liberty," and talk of seizing Spanish islands became a remedy for reaffirming the nationalist ideals of "honor, justice, Property, and Laws."[19] Construed within the crucible of war, English hawks translated liberty as freedom of trade in the Caribbean, a freedom they accused Spain of attacking. For many mainland supporters of the War of Jenkins's Ear—whether driven blindly by profit, a firm belief in English imperialism, or a combination of the two—taking Spanish warships and territories would strengthen the empire by removing Spanish corruption while expanding English liberty to the edges of the American frontier.[20]

This new patriotism of empire transformed the racial climate in New York City; when the fort burned to the ground, followed by the governor's home, people were conditioned to see a Spanish-led conspiracy rather than an accidental overturning of a lantern, a homegrown group of disgruntled slaves, or a local gang of thieves. For example, one potent image circulating in reports was of slave forces fighting on both sides, reports that surely caused many New Yorkers to worry about the war's potential effects on their slave population. The Caribbean practice of using slave militias in armed conflict made mainland observers fearful that the example of organized, fighting slaves might spread to plantations and colonies.[21] This fear appeared to come true when authorities in South Carolina reported that the slaves involved in Stono's Rebellion, before their capture, were making their way toward the Spanish outpost at Saint Augustine. Despite the long distance from the border war between South Carolina and Spanish Florida, New York worried about a Stono-style rebellion spreading to their city, particularly after authorities suspected a plot in New Jersey in 1740, and the *New York Gazette* published new reports of yet another outbreak of a slave uprising in South Carolina that same year. Finally, one wonders if colonists were thinking about their own efforts at undercutting Spanish rule; the English imagined many "schemes of liberation in Spanish America," most of which involved inciting racial groups, such as the Creoles, Africans, Indians, or mestizos, against each other or directing them against the Spanish government.[22]

The particular insurrection story that emerged from this context was not regional but international in scope, including a scenario in which slaves would rise up when Spain's ships appeared on the horizon.[23] When Horsmanden reports on the early signs of the conspiracy—the overheard curse of "Fire, Fire, Scorch, Scorch"—he refrains from direct commentary. But as Wayne Booth remarks, "authors often [conceal] their commentary by dramatizing it as scenery or symbol," and the chronicle's setting of a curse delivered in a peaceful cityscape forecasts violence.[24] The three original conspirators walk below Mrs. Earle's window on the Sabbath, a sacred and patriotic day that also contains within it the promise of a fateful reckoning: "This Sunday as three negroes were walking up the Broadway towards the English church, about service time."[25] The sequence expresses the peacefulness of the community, gathering as families in faithful worship, but the movement of the three slaves divides the scene into black and white. Sunday was the day colonists feared vengeful slaves would choose for insurrection, and the three advancing black figures appear bent on massacring the white people, defenseless in the church. The inaugural motif of a peaceful city about to be attacked by fanatics masked in blackness, servitude, and feigned loyalty forecasts the conclusion of the courts that the religious fanaticism of Spanish Catholics had directed the slaves down Broadway that morning toward the seat of English Anglican authority.

The rhetoric of delayed coding often conceals authoritative discourse; when used to evoke a setting it is particularly effective in revealing the bloodshed buried beneath a pastoral scene. The curse initiates the threat, which is fully disclosed in the chronicle's next significant sequence. After relating the mysteriousness of the rash of fires, the chronicle reports on an accelerating series of images. Yet another fire, then a public cry to "take up the Spanish Negroes," and soon after, in the "by-and-by," the Spanish slaves are "rising."[26] The prophesy of "Fire, Fire, Scorch, Scorch" has become evident, pointing to a Spanish plot, precisely what American colonists feared during the war. Weaving conspiracy together with war, Horsmanden's chronicle ultimately ends up channeling the colony's surging patriotism in ways that support colonial authority. "Fire, Fire, Scorch, Scorch" is a warning, given by Horsmanden, that reminds citizens that their lack of vigilance had almost let the original three conspirators slip free. Not yet arrived at the point in the narrative when legal documents will outline the "facts" of conspiracy, the audience must face the most persuasive evidence—the suspense and vulnerability created with the elements of a patriotic fiction.

The real meaning of Horsmanden's warning only becomes clear when it is viewed within the context of the war and juxtaposed with its first hero, Admiral Edward Vernon, who guaranteed his superiors that he could take the Spanish stronghold of Porto Bello, Panama, with only six ships. Admiral Vernon's bold prediction and improbable victory began the war for the colonists and made him the symbolic figurehead for regaining English honor. (So much was Captain Lawrence Washington impressed by the admiral's valor that upon returning home from the war, Washington named his plantation after Vernon.) Horsmanden's opening story of the vengeful slaves gradually mixes the geopolitical with the domestic; it becomes just as much about imperial war as about a slave conspiracy and converts the slave's secret code into the complete outlines of the conspiracy. Before Horsmanden can conclude this plot, however, he must first revisit his earlier representation of Quack's resistance and establish interpretive control over him.

Quack had been in "confinement for some days," Horsmanden writes, before prosecutors, busy with other interrogations, returned to press him for an interpretation of "Fire, Fire, Scorch, Scorch."[27] Mimicking the colonists' patriotism, Quack claims he and his mates were simply paying tribute to Admiral Vernon's heroism. Colonists could not see the conspiracy through this ruse, Horsmanden suggests, because of their enthusiasm for the war: "But it being soon after we had news of admiral Vernon's taking Porto Bello, he [Quack] had contrived a cunning excuse, or some abler heads for him . . . that they were talking of admiral Vernon's taking Porto Bello; and that he thereupon signified to his companions, that he thought that was but a small feat to what this brave officer would do *by-and-by,* to annoy the Spaniards, or words tantamount; so that it happened Quack was enlarged from his confinement for some time."[28] Horsmanden finds this is the key moment, when colonists could have stopped the conspiracy before it started. In one sense, Quack embodies the anti-imperial practices of the colonial subject who deploys his own power against the state's attempts to dominate him. Refusing to recognize the colonizer's ultimate authority and claim on truth, indeed mocking it with his laughter, Quack defeats his interrogators by posing as a British patriot. In the process, his strategy reinscribes the signs of white power, reinterpreting his laugh as a

cheer for English victory in the "by-and-by." White power is heavily invested in the stereotype of an insurrectionary slave who waits to wage war
on behalf of Spain, but in professing his admiration for England and disregard for Spain, Quack's hybridity, at once slave and patriot, confounds
it. Horsmanden says as much, suggesting that Quack's mimicry of the
English colonists had prevented them from detecting the conspiracy that
Quack conceals behind his fugitive word play.

Yet this same play frees him for a time. When no narrator surfaces to
contest Quack's laughter, unlike earlier in the chronicle, Horsmanden
moves to undermine the earlier representation of the rebel's subversiveness. As evidence of Quack's cunning, Horsmanden points to the slave's
calculated use of the "by-and-by" and counters it with a claim that is actually a temporal space of reckless plotting. However, a rash of new fires
removes the ambiguity and for Horsmanden reveals the lie. The court's
opinion moves against Quack, and now they "were apt to put a different
construction upon Quack's words and behavior; that he thereby meant,
'that the fires which we had seen already, were nothing to what we should
have *by-and-by,* for that then we should have all the city in flames, and he
would rejoice at it;' for it was said he lifted up his hands, and spread them
with a circular sweep over his head, after he had pronounced the words
(by-and-by) and then concluded with a loud laugh."[29] The lingering impression of Quack's resistance to colonial authority is short-lived. The narrator's
authoritative voice meets Quack's antagonistic rhetoric, camouflaging what
the narrator deems his true intent. Unlike the earlier representation of
Quack's resistance, Horsmanden now intrudes and provides the correct
interpretation of "by-and-by." Lacking a confession from Quack, Horsmanden mimics the slave in a way that conveys to the reader what Quack
"thereby meant" by the curse. Benedict Anderson stresses these moments
of "reversed ventriloquism" in colonial discourse, when nationalists desire
to speak for the dead.[30] These moments are integral to the self-conscious
construction of a national narrative that must wrest control of Quack's
cryptic prophesy, find meaning in it, and explain the "silence of the dead."
Horsmanden not only tells us what Quack really meant but also increases
the sound of his laughter ("loud" this time) and adds ritualistic details of
Quack lifting up his outstretched hands and making a diabolical "circular
sweep over his head" in anticipation of celebrating the city's destruction.

Finally, Horsmanden's reversed ventriloquism highlights the paradox of national identification that was taking place in New York in 1741 in two interrelated ways. As Bernard Bailyn and Morgan point out, global wars were a "primary crucible in forging British national sentiment" in the colonies, but patriotic fervor often increased along with acculturation, when colonists began to feel its distance from England.[31] Despite Horsmanden's refutation and Quack's execution, the residue of his antagonism remains in the text. He is a figure of mimicry, and, as Homi Bhabha and other postcolonial theorists have recognized, such an antagonistic figure problematizes racial and national priority. The slave talking the talk of patriotism turns the nationalist discourse of 1741 into a crisis of belonging. Faced with the slave's ironic patriotism, the colonizer no longer feels secure in his English identity because the war brings to the surface the anxieties of national identification. Consequently, Horsmanden's ventriloquism both gives an inside view of Quack's state of mind and garners sympathy for a prosecution faced with such dissimulation; perhaps even more important, he substitutes the invented dialogue for a missing confession. At a time when all identities must be secured—none more so than the guilty slave rebel—the slave's attempt to appropriate a national identity threatens the colonizer's foundational narrative of whiteness. In the words of Bhabha, the "'national' is no longer naturalizable."[32]

WAR AND CONSPIRACY: RACE TRAITOR

In mid-eighteenth-century New York, everyday acts of slave resistance happened along Manhattan's wharfs, where many slaves labored alongside soldiers and Irish laborers. Notorious for criminal activity, the waterfront was also a place of interracial and international exchange, since Africans, Irish, English, West Indian, and Dutch met in taverns to drink drams of rum, fraternize, gamble, and fence stolen goods. Not surprisingly, public officials first interpreted the fires of 1741 as the deeds of a conspiracy of criminals whose only aim was to steal from the rich. In the beginning of the investigation, prosecutors focused on a tavern owner named John Hughson, well-known both for selling rum to slaves and for running a brothel. When prosecutors questioned his employee, a sixteen-year-old indentured servant named Mary Burton, about goods stolen from the Hoggs' residence, she said that "she would acquaint them with what she knew relating to the stolen goods from Mr. Hogg's but would say nothing about the fires."[33]

Determined to discover what she was concealing, prosecutors took aim at her resolve with promises of freedom from her master, a £100 reward, and the king's mercy; when bribes didn't work, they threatened her with imprisonment and the gallows. She became the star witness for the prosecution, accusing Hughson of being the ringleader in a vast conspiracy to burn the city to the ground, free the slaves, and install himself as king. Burton also testified that two slaves, Caesar and Prince, were the leaders of Hughson's "black guard," and that Hughson had promised them the opportunity to murder white people, to loot their homes, and to serve as commanders in what would be their colony's new military. In addition to Hughson, Caesar, and Prince, the prosecution charged Hughson's wife, Sarah, and Margaret Kerry, who worked the brothel at Hughson's tavern. She was also known as Peggy, the "Newfoundland Irish beauty," and "Negro Peg," a nickname stemming from her relationship with Caesar.

The two slaves, Caesar and Prince, were executed for theft. To try them for conspiracy would take too long, the magistrates determined, and they gambled that a swift and terrifying execution would break the case open: "[It] might break the knot, and induce some of them to unfold this mystery of iniquity, in hopes thereby to recommend themselves to mercy."[34] As an additional inducement, their rotting corpses were hung in chains well into the summer, but their example failed to coerce any of their supposed confederates to "break the knot" of conspiracy. A little over a month later, John and Sarah Hughson were executed, and his body was displayed next to his "black guard." Peggy was executed next, much to her surprise, since she believed that her cooperation with the prosecution had earned her a pardon; but Arthur Price, a jailhouse snitch exchanging information for leniency, implicated Peggy as a key conspirator. The pace of executions accelerated. In an attempt to inspire more "Negro evidence," the court condemned Quack and Cuffee to be burned alive, an extraordinary punishment in the mid-eighteenth century; on their way through the crowd and toward the stake, they screamed for mercy, claiming Burton knew even more than she had testified to. If the condemned offered to confess, they might earn a lesser punishment. Perhaps Quack and Cuffee considered this way out when they were being chained to the stake. As the fire burned around their bound bodies, an official recorded their last words but did not stop the execution. Prosecutors then took their testimony to Burton, who produced even more *white evidence*—what prosecutors conveniently labeled testimony given by white colonists—so much that the court authorized a mass arrest of the city's slave population.

Six weeks into the trials, the prosecution was having trouble extracting confessions; when the jails became overcrowded and the city's slaves learned of their precarious situation, one incriminating statement away from execution, Governor Clarke announced a proclamation offering pardon and transportation to those who confessed to the conspiracy. Clarke's proclamation produced sixty-seven more slave confessions.[35] The confessions contained inaccuracies, contradictions, obvious falsehoods, and a willingness to please the magistrates so they might remain alive. Clarke's proclamation of general pardon on June 19 was designed to bolster a flagging investigation with evidence of a merciful and just court, as well as to restore the public's confidence in the imperial administration.

It would be difficult to exaggerate the important role that confession played in an eighteenth-century capital case, particularly in the public's acceptance of the verdicts. In an era predating forensic sciences, confession sanctioned the guilty verdict, reflected praise on the magistrates, and justified the punishment. Thus the court's failure to obtain confessions from the principal conspirators led to a remarkable episode in which the public wondered whether the dead bodies of Caesar and Hughson were protesting against the court's verdicts. Rotting in their chains that summer, their black and white corpses appeared to exchange colors. Hughson's features had taken on, Horsmanden writes, a "deep shining black, rather blacker than the Negroe placed by him," his hair curling up, his face displaying the "symmetry of Negroe beauty; the nose broad and flat, the nostrils open and extended, the mouth wide, lips full and thick . . . his body swelled to a gigantic size." On the contrary, Caesar, "one of the head Negroe conspirators" had his face turn "somewhat bleached or turned whitish."[36] This apparent metamorphosis of white man to black, black man to white, posed a serious danger to official authority, since the bodies potentially communicated innocence to spectators. Justice Horsmanden would have to find a way to counter this alternate knowledge of the plot.

In the eighteenth century, public execution was an event in which the crowd actively participated by bearing witness, interpreting signs, and, if the punishment was deemed unjust, empathizing with the victim. It also turned the criminal into the central actor in the production, the stakeside declaration of guilt a chance to earn God's forgiveness and to initiate deliverance for a community afflicted by the criminal's sin. Horsmanden remembers Hughson as a puzzling text: showing no remorse, he walked to the gallows like a prizefighter, predicting the miraculous appearance of a sign that would prove his innocence, all of it a bold performance against the court. The crowd marveled at the red spots suddenly appearing on both his cheeks (was it a miracle?) and took note of his body language as he neared the stake, holding one arm up in the air, palm outstretched, expectantly.

Yet he wasn't saved, offered no dying confession as proof of his guilt, and his corpse became less the universal judgment delivered by the magistrate than a text of dangerous uncertainty. Rotting on the gibbet, his body began to signify and drew curious New Yorkers to the scaffold: "It occasioned a remark, that Hughson and he had changed colors. The beholders were amazed at these appearances; the report of them engaged the attention of many, and drew numbers of all ranks, who had curiosity, to the gibbets, for several days running, in order to be convinced by their own eyes, of the reality of things so confidently reported to be, at least wondrous phenomenons . . . many of the spectators were ready to resolve them into miracles; however others not so hasty, though surprised at the sights, were willing to account for them in a natural way, so that they administered matter for much speculation."[37] Penal torture provided the same moments of speculation as an execution. The spectacle of Hughson and Caesar hung on gibbets, never having given a confession of guilt, produced interpretations that endangered popular belief in the court's actions. The scene forces the state to lose control, if only temporarily, of the enunciatory power of a standard form of torture.[38] Writing after the fact, Horsmanden offers two interpretations of the metamorphosis of Hughson's body, the miraculous and the natural. Forced to reject any belief that might question the court's authority or honor, Justice Horsmanden intervenes to *expropriate* (precisely, the action taken by a state to deprive one of property) Hughson's ambiguous racial identity.

Remarkably, this gallows scene represents Horsmanden's tacit admission that Hughson's execution had cast suspicion on the court's legal authority and its power to create believable fictions of guilt and innocence. Whenever his control over the narrative slips, Horsmanden relies on the power of the court and colonial slave codes. Hughson's corpse transforms the gallows, a stage the court believed would showcase proof of its final authority, into a dangerous site of racial ambiguity, and Horsmanden's interpretive work must duplicate the racial fault line on which the entire prosecution has built its case. In her genealogy of the civil body in colonial America, Joan Dayan claims that ideologies of white supremacy took the dead as seriously as the living, effectively reducing a living person to a "civil body" that was no more than a "fabricated" corpse. I want to draw on this insight to explain how Horsmanden supplements penal torture with a critical explanation of the white criminal's intrinsic blackness. This fiction of white supremacy, as Dayan suggests, is "threatened by what one could not always see but must always fear: the black blood that would not only pollute progeny, but infect the very heart of the nation."[39] Outside the courtroom, Justice Horsmanden attempts to stabilize political and legal authority by fabricating the white criminal's transformation into a legally powerless slave.

Here Horsmanden's narrator stakes a claim for authority. In this crisis of interpretation, he must counter the sudden resistance to the court's authority; what had been the narrator's more subtle signs of his intrusion give way to a controlling presence. Horsmanden must reject the gallows' racial ambiguity with his own summation to this extralegal episode. He rejects outright the popular belief in supernatural intervention because he hopes to convince the audience of reasonable inference, that poison has blackened the body, a devious plan by conspirators to die in silence as martyrs to their cause. In other words, denied a confession, Horsmanden argues that Hughson's new color is the exact physical evidence the court had suspected but failed to uncover during its prosecution of the conspirators. Because of the popular belief in the body's supernatural or miraculous metamorphosis, he fixes it in the physical world by accusing a free African-American doctor from Long Island of providing Hughson and other prominent conspirators with lethal doses of poison to be ingested if captured by the English.

If the chronicle form is supposed to provide a regular order of events without commentary by a narrator, this unusual imposition is revealing. Justice Horsmanden has drawn on a legend told in histories of popish plots that explains away the absence of any real evidence, the missing confessions, with a convenient story of a fanatic who will die as a martyr for the cause rather than confess the truth. Similar to the use of DNA in contemporary trials, the poison in Hughson's interpretation becomes universal; it explains all—the blackness, the red spots on Hughson's cheeks, and his monstrous corpse, seemingly alive as it grows bloated and putrid underneath the late summer sun. As a result, Horsmanden's summation, its attempt to reposition the reader within the state's jurisdiction, rides on the narrator's "realistic" representation of Hughson's body. The historical account is hostile to the crowd's belief in mystery and, by implication, in the conversion of Hughson's body. It is the inevitable moment in all chronicles when a silent narrator, confronted with the disintegration of the very authority that sanctions his voice, insists on his right to speak.

By exorcising the supernatural, Justice Horsmanden restores the chronicle's verisimilitude, but this requires him to raise, and then answer, a contradiction implicit in his quasi-judicial summation: why would Hughson take poison if he expected to be rescued on his way to the gallows? Unable to give an answer based in the workings of the physical world, Horsmanden resorts to a false racial symbolic that represents blackness as evil. In fact, he claims that Hughson's prophesy was fulfilled and had affirmed the trials' facts. Hughson predicted that "some remarkable sign would happen to him, to shew (or signify) his innocence; and if his corpse becoming monstrous in size, and his complexion (for once to use a vulgar similitude) as black as the d——l, can be deemed remarkable signs or tokens of his innocence! then some may imagine it has happened according to his expectation."[40] In other words, a sign had indeed arrived, and it was the color of Hughson's corpse, black as the devil, that, ironically, has displayed his true colors to the public. Horsmanden has introduced the metaphysical, exactly what he'd been denouncing, but his mocking tone announces his summation over the metaphysical as nothing but a rhetorical flourish. He combats Hughson's prophesy with irony, interpreting *innocence* not as freedom from guilt but a benign condition when one no longer possesses the ability to injure.

Moreover, the literary construction of Hughson's metamorphosis into a "black devil" relies on the trope of metonymy; also operating along this figurative axis was the concept of Negro evidence, the linchpin in the prosecution's use of the conspiracy law. Rather than classifying Hughson from above—the realm of the symbol, the royal and divine—the proof of Hughson's blackness results from his contiguous relationship with Caesar. Hughson has to be more than a metaphorical "black devil"; the effect of conspiracy with slaves has to make him appear black, since his whiteness protected him from the law of Negro evidence. This scene's metonymic play of racial signifiers—the white man slowly turns black, in parts, his straight hair curling up, his face acquiring black "symmetry," the thin nose "broad and flat"—produces a racial hybrid that fractures the identity of the colonizer and challenges its power to represent and judge.

As judge and author, Horsmanden both denies the condemned the opportunity to signify on the gallows and presumes, in a moment of crisis, the right of categorization. With Hughson and Caesar seemingly exchanging colors, Horsmanden hopes to depict the confusion in a way that will defuse an explosive situation. If he tries to save or recuperate Hughson's whiteness, then the "mirror" would reflect a state power threatened by a dangerous coalition of disaffected white colonials and slaves, so he expropriates Hughson's whiteness and turns him black. For additional support Horsmanden includes a passage from prosecuting attorney William Smith's summation: "John Hughson, whose crimes have made him blacker than a negro: the scandal of his complexion, and the disgrace of human nature!"[41] Arguing against a type of racial ambivalence that endangers national loyalty and white supremacy, Horsmanden teaches white colonists, particularly those of the laboring ranks, about the dangers of being a race traitor. Only a white skin could free you from the arbitrary power of the law of Negro evidence.

Horsmanden's concern with the colony's unstable racial hierarchy has much to do with the War of Jenkins's Ear and public anxiety about the colony's vulnerable port and borders. When rumors of Spanish involvement in the conspiracy began to spread in early June, prosecutors turned their attention to five Spanish sailors—Antonio de St. Bendito, Antonio de la Cruz, Pablo Ventura Angel, Juan de la Sylva, and Augustine Gutierez—captured the previous year. Ignoring the sailors' protestations that they were free and sovereign subjects of Spain, the court of admiralty declared them slaves, which made them a valuable prize rather than prisoners of war. There was no mention of them in the preliminary stages of the conspiracy trials until one day a witness testified about inflammable "black stuff" that the Spaniards supposedly possessed. A few days later, on June 17, prosecutors asked Burton, the star witness, if she wished to add anything to her original testimony. Her memory seemingly prompted by this new concern, she now remembered that Hughson and Quack talked of their

Spanish partners, who were to be the vanguard of the Spanish invasion. That same day, perhaps spying a chance at freedom, two slaves—Jack and Bastian—repeated the same story, and the magistrates rewarded them with a pardon.

Taken together, the conversion narratives of Hughson and the five Spanish sailors enable Horsmanden to dramatize the legal machinery, but the set of narratives also function in the public sphere of colonial identity formation. His representation of Hughson's corpse makes a political metaphor out of Negro evidence so that he can convince readers of the criminal's guilt and just execution. In the case of the Spanish sailors, the narrator again falls silent, and in his place, Horsmanden simply records the court's charge to the jury. Their indictment is "grounded upon an act of assembly, supposing them to be slaves, by which act the testimony of one negro slave shall be legal evidence against another. But it has been made a question whether these prisoners, now before us, are slaves or not; and the prisoners themselves pretend to be free subjects of the King of Spain, with whom we are now at war, and from whom they have been taken and made prize."[42] Whereas the function of Hughson's conversion was to help rebuild the city's shattered racial hierarchy, the story of the Spanish sailors introduces a new dynamic in the formation of white supremacy. The passage comes at a critical point in the history since, hereafter, interrogations begin to produce evidence that Spain has organized the conspiracy. Precisely at this juncture the official voice of the court is substituted for the narrator. The voice both shifts the site of identity construction to the Caribbean frontier and connects racial and national belonging. Without the war, perhaps they would have been Spanish gentlemen, "free subjects." But war imports the threat on the Caribbean frontier into the city, making their claim on freedom, in the court's point of view, a weak pretense. It remains unclear in the jury charge whether it was their color, nationality, or a combination of the two that transforms them into prize slaves and, eventually, into living corpses. Aware of the Spaniard's racial ambiguity, the court informs the jury that only by seeing them as black can they sentence them to death: "if you take them . . . to be slaves, all the negro evidence which has been given upon this trial against them, is legal evidence."[43] The case of the five Spanish sailors cuts two ways: it highlights the effects of imperial war on colonial race formation and it demonstrates how racialized identities occupied multiple frontiers.

WAR AND CONSPIRACY: CUBA, "LAND OF PROMISE"

British imperial fantasies of an easy victory over a hated rival dominated the early stages of the War of Jenkins's Ear. The conflict had been more than eight years in the making: in 1731 the Spanish Guarda Costa had cut off Captain Robert Jenkins's ear after seizing and searching the vessel he had illegally piloted through Spanish territorial waters. Long frustrated by Spain's tightly managed mercantilism, English merchant vessels, hunting for new markets and consumers, constantly came into conflict with the Spanish forces. Over the course of the 1730s, prosperity in the North American colonies declined when productive power on the mainland began to outstrip West Indian consumer demand; worried by this development and eager to acquire new market incentives, British merchants and investors grew frustrated with an English peace policy with Spain that restricted their "free trade." For Whig patriots war appeared as the only option for protecting national honor and expanding English freedoms. In 1738 Captain Jenkins's severed ear became the *causus belli* for war. As a way to garner support, war hawks staged a national emergency; appearing before Parliament, Captain Jenkins removed his mutilated ear from his handkerchief, held the symbol of Spanish depravity high above his head, and was showered with approving shouts of "No search! No search!" As Francis Berkeley remarks, "Spanish outrages became the rallying cry," and Jenkins's performance "stirred [England] to a high pitch of excitement."[44]

In England, Rutman claims that "[t]he frenzy of delight which took possession of the nation was almost un-English and certainly unmatched since the days of the Spanish Armada's defeat."[45] English colonists also embraced the war effort, particularly after reports of Admiral Vernon's improbable victory at Porto Bello; they sang songs and wrote poems about Vernon's valor, celebrated English vessels and sailors in the harbor, and reveled in newspaper reports about captured Spanish "prizes" and gold pieces of eight. During the war's first two years, many colonists turned their eyes to Spain's Caribbean colonies and speculated about riches to be gained by conquering Cuba. Talk of possessing the territory was so intoxicating during the first year of the war that Admiral Vernon wrote to the Duke of Newcastle that North American colonists already looked on Cuba as the "land of promise."[46] This was more than idle dreaming; the imperial administration planned for occupation. Governor Clarke envisioned a future Cuban settlement that would bail out New York's sinking economy, a colony that might "take off more of the provisions of these northern provinces than all the other islands in the West Indies."[47]

By focusing on Governor Clarke's involvement with the war effort, one can see how perceptions of conspiracy in 1741 were tied not only to war but also to speculations about a future Cuban colony. In New York, Governor Clarke was responsible for raising volunteer troops to serve alongside British forces, and he drummed up support for the war by holding up Cuba as the central prize.[48] On July 14, 1740, the *New York Weekly Journal* published an official proclamation in which Governor Clarke pronounced that victory over Spain would secure West Indian shipping lanes; then he guaranteed that once England had taken hold of Cuba, "a door will be opened for a large consumption of provisions the staple of this province whereby the farmer as well as the merchant, may be greatly enriched."

Clarke enjoyed a reputation as a stellar recruiter, a reliable official who could marshal his money and connections in attracting forces when military commanders called for them. There were incentives for volunteers. The king's declaration of war, published in the *New York Weekly Journal,* made Cuba and other legendary spoils a reality for even the middling members of the volunteer militia:

> [They] are to have the King's clothing and the King's pay and their share of the plunder taken from the Spaniards and when they have taken the Place which are designed to be attacked (the Rich island of Cuba is said to be one of the places they design to take). . . . In this great undertaking these Parts of America will be at no Charge, the King Pays and Clothes all. And it may reasonably be supposed that this great Armament and large squadrons of Men of War, will occasion a great Demand of all forts of Provisions in these parts. (April 14, 1740)

The declaration addressed the concerns of merchants, politicians, and farmers, the obvious beneficiaries of spiked demand for all types of commodities, as well as the property-less volunteer, who can opt to have Cuban "land given to them." During the war's first two years, the *New York Weekly Journal* and the *Boston Gazette* published countless firsthand reports from the front: anecdotes, foreign reportage, and rumors that told extraordinary tales of rich Spanish ships captured by the English. Furthermore, it was well-known that Admiral Vernon would target Havana, the harbor where treasure-laden ships of the annual *galleon* gathered each year before departing for Spain. The *galleon* was the biggest prize of all—admirals, sailors, and pirates dreamed of capturing the flotilla of treasure ships—the aim of the British navy in the War of Jenkins's Ear.[49]

All of these stories acted as powerful advertisements for Governor Clarke when he tried to recruit colonial volunteers to join the English forces.[50] However, when it came time for volunteers to join in 1741, at the height of the conspiracy scare, colonists feared leaving their homes and loved ones unprotected; Clarke found it increasingly difficult to meet his quota. Explaining his case to the Duke of Newcastle, Clarke reported that "the fort was burnt, having wonderfully distracted the mind of the people throughout the province, who are in continual apprehensions of having their houses set on fire, in consequence of an horrid conspiracy of the negroes."[51] He worried that no enticement could counter the white colonist's fear of a slave insurrection.[52]

By the middle of June 1741, the conspiracy trials were in high gear, and officials were certain of Spanish involvement. Clarke, his reputation diminished, wrote a series of letters to his superiors that constitute the first "official" interpretation of the fires. In a letter to Newcastle, Clarke depicted himself as a heroic figure whose courage and foresight saved the king's city. While Justice Horsmanden's account, written three years later, depicts the Supreme Court as the city's savior, Clarke represented himself as the hero, in part because the war effort and the conspiracy were harming his prestige and costing him money. When five houses burned down in a single day, Clarke decided it was no accident, telling Newcastle that "I soon changed my thoughts and set myself heartily to work to find out the villainy." Clarke's narrative contrasted a picture of a distraught people (better than panicked leaders) with a poised official, cool under pressure, moving quickly to "appease their fears and secure them from danger." Clarke's mere presence seemingly restored order: "I went constantly to every fire to give directions and animate the people, and by my care and activity" contained the flames and obstructed the conspirators' plan to overthrow the city the night Fort George burned. That night, while the townspeople returned to their homes to sleep, Clarke represents himself as the city's guardian angel. Watching over them as a northwest wind ripped across the smoldering remains of the fort, he keenly observed that "sparks [had] begun to fly," and "I thought it necessary to alarm the people."[53]

Foucault's remark that "the least glimmer of truth is conditioned by politics" is especially suitable for trying to decipher Governor Clarke's interpretation of events. A staple of Whig rhetoric in the 1730s was the man of action, a "genius of Britain" like Admiral Vernon who advanced English liberty with a "militant zeal."[54] Clarke represented himself as New York's Vernon, a vigilant, courageous hero, but an unusual plea for compensation in the final paragraph tainted this self-portrait: "The loss I have sustained by the fire is greater than at first it appeared to be, and too heavy for me to bear without being supported by Your Graces' protection which I most humbly beg leave to ask."[55] When his superiors failed to respond to his request, Clarke made sure that subsequent reports from the colony reminded Newcastle and the Lords of Trade of his personal misfortune. As a result of the conspirators' attack against his home, Clarke wrote, "my loss sits very heavy upon me," and he worried that his sudden deficit would diminish his reputation as a dutiful servant of the King.[56] In a letter dated June 20, after repeating yet again that the plot might hinder efforts to recruit volunteers, Clarke reminded the Lords of Trade of his skill as a recruiter, a humble affirmation of loyalty for the King, and his support for the war effort.

Meanwhile, in New York, the initial perception of a local conspiracy had broadened; public officials were proclaiming that the fires were actually the first offensive in a foreign war, a conclusion that strengthened Clarke's petition for damages. In his June 20 letter to the Lords of Trade, Clarke included new intelligence sent by Governor James Oglethorpe of Georgia, a colony long tormented by border skirmishes with Spanish Florida. Oglethorpe had information that Spain had sent secret agents into English North America "to burn all the magazines and considerable towns . . . and thereby to prevent the subsisting of the great expedition and fleet in the West Indies."[57] Many colonial officials ignored Oglethorpe's warning, especially since the governor often cried wolf when it came to Spanish plots, but Clarke advanced his unsubstantiated theory as proof of a foreign hand in the fires. It was not as clear-cut as Edgar McManus would have it, claiming that Oglethorpe's letter "not only revived the conspiracy scare but gave it much more sinister dimensions."[58] Given a choice to weigh all types of evidence as either a local or international crisis, Clarke made sure his superiors understood that the fires were acts of war against the colony and that his losses hindered the war effort. The new intelligence from Georgia provided critical support for his agenda. New York in flames, the "confusion" that afflicted the townspeople, the men's reluctance to go to war and leave their families defenseless, and his own misfortune: Clarke used all of these scenarios both to protect himself in case he could not meet the King's demands and to justify his plea for compensation. He assured his superiors: "I will use my utmost application to raise recruits when the General writes for them, for as I did last year raise a greater proportion of Troops than any of our Neighbouring Colonies."[59]

Because other colonial governors were not dealing with a potential insurrection, Clarke rightly believed that they possessed an unfair advantage in raising troops for the war effort. Consequently, Clarke never wavered in his conclusion that the fires were part of an international conspiracy against England rather than the plotting of disgruntled slaves. He wrote report after report that affirmed the belief that New York City was a battlefield in the War of Jenkins's Ear. To what degree profit drove his interpretation is difficult to determine, but there is ample evidence to suggest that Governor Clarke was preoccupied with his own fortune. He was a prodigious land speculator, who used his office to get around the two-thousand-acre limit on land grants and to acquire over one hundred thousand acres in the Mohawk Valley. When George Clinton replaced him as governor in 1743, Clarke retired to a sizable estate in England. He had made his fortune in the American colonies.[60]

For other colonists, the War of Jenkins's Ear inspired imperial dreams about Cuba and the riches to be gained once the English took possession of the island. In Clarke's letters, in the pages of the *New York Weekly Journal* and the *Boston Gazette,* and in the king's declaration of war, Cuba is depicted as a land of promise and opportunity. The Duke of Newcastle remembered colonists "with a vast spirit who in their imagination have swallowed up all Cuba."[61] Imagining a rewarding imperial venture in Cuba caused concern among colonists that their Spanish enemy was planning to do the same to them. This terrible reflection of England's own imperial ambitions manifested the perversion of English freedom and authority in a "colonial mirror."[62] For Horsmanden the Cuban campaign was at the center of his thinking about the conspiracy. His chronicle represented this reflection of imperial aims in its pairing of two groups, the white militia-men known fittingly as the "Cuba Men" and a quasi-military branch of conspirators. According to the chronicle, the entire conspiracy was tied to the recent departure of the "Cuba Men" leaving the city defenseless, a situation the conspirators supposedly aimed to exploit. Prosecutors were stunned by the boldness of a plot that appeared to copy at every level the political and military hierarchies of English civilization. Even more shock-ing was special intelligence, gathered by the court, that these racially mixed hierarchies, with Hughson as self-appointed king, would be the new gov-ernment for a colony freed from English rule. Faced with the mirror image of the fledgling plan to settle in Cuba, prosecutors ridiculed the conspir-ators' dream of governing as a "fool's paradise."

Like Cuba and the recently departed volunteers, this invisible govern-ment of conspirators also provided opportunities to gain wealth by over-throwing the ruling authorities. The court thought it had uncovered a secret branch of conspirators, a group of privileged slaves "above the common rank of Negroes," who were planning a special mission. According to Jus-tice Horsmanden, "this band of ruffians consisted of no less than twelve," possessed a horrifying ferocity, and were led by Hughson's four top slave lieutenants. Thinking it had uncovered the conspiracy within the con-spiracy, the court was aghast. The lieutenants, Quack, Othello, Jack, and Adam, would lead the secret branch into the homes of white families and slaughter them one house at a time. The first target was supposed to be the Murray house, where the slaves planned to "butcher that whole fam-ily in their beds, then to set the house on fire, after they had plundered it, and were to carry the spoils to Hughson."[63] The slaves and Irish inden-tured servants, it was said repeatedly in dismay, would build their "motley government" with the stolen wealth of their former masters.

Called "cannibals," "band of ruffians," and "bloody villains," the sus-pected slave leaders were previously known for their intelligence and their "great influence amongst the inferior sort of Negroes."[64] Members of the court knew many of them personally, since they were the "head or chief slaves in town" (Othello's owner was the chief justice of the Supreme Court). In assessing blame for the problem of an intelligent, persuasive class of slaves, Justice Horsmanden reserves partial judgment for their "kind and indulgent masters," who had contributed to the conspiracy by not enforc-ing strict discipline, which produced a dangerous "excess" of liberty. This lament is something more than that which follows many conspiracy scares in the colonies. The war effort in the West Indies inspired dreams of new-found white freedoms in Cuba, whether it was the farmer's freehold property or the merchant's open market, but military action also produced nightmares of insurrections on behalf of black freedoms. The fiction of a benign Northern slave system could not hold up under the stress of a war that replaced the myth of a docile house slave with real histories of West Indian slave rebels.

Horsmanden's chronicle depicted this awareness by arming the slave leaders with dangerous liberty that was about to be unleashed against the city. According to the racist underpinnings of slavery, this spectacle was horrifying because the slave was no longer submissive and willing to accept bondage. Even more specifically for New York, there was the sense that the racial categories supporting the entire colonial system were in catastrophic disarray. Thus these privileged slaves, schooled by the white elite, terrified colonists precisely because they blurred the boundaries between white and black. They represented their masters' status, conducted themselves in a civilized manner, interacted with white leaders with intelligence and customary deference, and served as a necessary buffer between races in a divided society. When war and conspiracy hysteria engulfed the city, this middle ground, on which stood the privileged slave who mimicked the values of English civilization, disappeared. Not unlike the conversion of the "praying Indian" into a "savage" during King Philip's War, the War of Jenkins's Ear had transformed New York's once loyal slave into a fierce, foreign soldier.

The different style of warfare in the West Indies contributed to their suspicion. Returning ships carried newspapers, private correspondence, and a repertory of half-truths that reported a new development—thousands of slave troops fighting for the English and Spanish. For over a year the colonial newspapers reported the exploits of these troops, a distinctly "American" colonial military practice that challenged a racist belief in a docile, inferior slave unqualified for combat. More important, slave troops appeared to prove a conspiratorial logic: if there were still colonists reluctant to believe in the capacity or desire of New York's slaves to take up arms, then slave troops in the West Indies made it more difficult to maintain that belief.[65]

Jamaica supplied over 1,500 slaves to the war effort, and there, as elsewhere in the colonies, the prospect of armed slaves raised a familiar debate about the potentially dire consequences of black veterans returning to their masters with knowledge of warfare. For this reason, many slave troops were restricted to burying corpses, digging trenches, pulling artillery, bringing water to white soldiers, and constructing earthworks. Their role changed dramatically when tropical diseases decimated English troops. The expedition to Cartagena in the early 1740s, as Peter Voelz points out, was "the first real awakening to this problem"—that the climate was an even more terrible enemy than the Spanish.[66] Historians speculate that as many as two-thirds of the English troops died while attacking Cartagena, and while commanders learned that the tropical climate would pose a formidable problem to warfare in the West Indies, they also realized that slaves, more resistant to local fevers, could play major offensive roles. Soon these "pioneers"—the name for slave troops—were fighting in greater numbers alongside English troops, working as scouts, and engaging in night missions against fortified Spanish positions.

Perhaps the rapid fall of the white soldier to disease and the rise of the slave "pioneer" as an offensive soldier contributed to the quagmire of racial identification in 1741. Or perhaps it was the leveling tendency of the war, which allowed the slave to play a more pivotal role than digging trenches, or the mere sight of a slave armed with machete and firearm. Whatever the principal cause, the slave became the touchstone for the growing separation of the white Englishman from the white colonist. The "emerging Americanism," which Harkness suggests the war brought about, was exemplified by the British perception of the colonists. Admiral Vernon described many as "slothful," General Wentworth suspected a legion of Irish papists, and a host of others thought the colonial troops were incompetent and cowardly. Yet Harkness, one of the first historians to speak about the conflict as an "American" war, makes a comment that signifies the splitting of the colonial subject that the presence of the slave was helping to bring about: "They were poor soldiers, Irish papists, and fit only for cutting fascines with the Negroes."[67] The metonymic chain redefines the colonial soldier through association with treasonous Irishmen and inferior slaves, which embodies a violent perversion of the soldier as England incarnate. War in the West Indies had deepened the division between two types of Englishmen. If the colonial soldier was only equipped to labor alongside the slave, then he was not fit for liberty, the sacred object of the war.

Whereas the mainland frontier had long provided crucibles of identity

construction for the English colonist, often embodying the glorious extension of liberty, it now appeared that warfare in the West Indies jeopardized
his English heritage. If the sacred concept of English liberty was at stake in
the War of Jenkins's Ear, then its extraordinary horrors appeared to rob the
English soldier of his birthright. Tobias Smollett was a surgeon's assistant
on the ill-fated Cartagena expedition, and he describes the Englishman's
reversal of fortunes by locating the sudden loss of liberty on a hospital ship
rather than a victorious man-of-war. Faced with the unimaginable terror
of dying troops trapped and suffocating beneath the decks, Smollett explicitly invokes the popular metaphor of a slave ship carrying its human
cargo through the Middle Passage:

> They were pent up between decks in small vessels, where they had not room
> to sit upright; they wallowed in filth, myriads of maggots were hatched in
> the putrefaction of their sores, which had no other dressing than that of being
> washed by themselves with their own allowance of brandy; and nothing was
> heard but groans, lamentations, and the language of despair, invoking death
> to deliver them from their miseries. What served to encourage this despon-
> dence was the prospect of those poor wretches who had strength and oppor-
> tunity to look around them; for there they beheld the naked bodies of their
> fellow-soldiers and comrades floating up and down the harbour, affording
> prey to the carrion crows and sharks, which tore them in pieces without inter-
> ruption, and contributing by their stench to the mortality that prevailed.[68]

The hospital ship collapses all distinctions; all are "fellow-soldiers" subjected to atrocities that were only associated with the Middle Passage. This
new war and its mysterious diseases had metaphorically enslaved the per-
sonifications of English liberty. There was no "English" language for it.
Instead, bearing witness to the slaughter taking place in the British colonies,
Smollett depicted the macabre scene with a distinctly colonial "American"
rhetoric in which the English soldier takes on the appearance of a captured
slave. The severed, mutilated, filthy bodies of Englishmen, in Smollett's horrible scene, made the perils of this new war the enemy of English liberty.
    Whether Smollett's horrific hospital ship or Hughson's colonizing army
of vengeful slaves, there is a crisis of racial and national identification that
both the conspiracy scare and the War of Jenkins's Ear bring about. These
two stunning scenes, in which the racial order is turned upside down by

New York's conspirators or when heroic white soldiers turn black, suggest an unsettling fear that the cause of English colonialism in the West Indies had corrupted English values. The excess of Smollett's scene is remarkable for its discourse of mimicry, particularly in the way the hospital ship resists the language of English freedoms. In the process, Smollett redefines the colonial subject; he no longer embodies the very language of liberty he is fighting for.[69] The War of Jenkins's Ear, with its pursuit of profit and open trade routes as well as its black and white troops fighting side by side, threatened to sink English civilization into a quagmire of racial confusion.

WAR AND CONSPIRACY: STATE OF EMERGENCY

In addition to the geopolitical struggle for trade and open markets, long-standing religious differences heightened imperial conflict in the eighteenth century. Conflicts between Protestants and Roman Catholics had caused centuries of civil war in Europe, and Protestant settlers in British North America persecuted Catholics for a wide range of alleged offenses, such as devil worship, possessing firearms, and plotting against English authority. During times of war, the English fear of Roman Catholics was a mixture of both religious bigotry and political distrust of a population that refused to swear allegiance to the Church of England. In New York, the War of Jenkins's Ear generated the old fear of a papal conspiracy. Colonists suspected that the Catholic powers of Spain and France were recruiting Roman Catholics who would conspire against English rule. Prosecutors in 1741 had waited for proof of papal involvement in the conspiracy, and they believed they found it in the person of John Ury. For months, newspapers circulated warnings of disguised priests, traveling as dancing masters and schoolteachers, who were plotting uprisings in North American cities. On June 24, prosecutors, acting on intelligence that "there had been of late Popish priests lurking about the town," arrested Ury, a teacher of Latin and Greek who was suspected of being a Roman Catholic priest.[70] Working on a hunch of Catholic involvement, prosecutors had broadened the scope of the conspiracy so they could potentially connect Hughson and his slave forces with their Spanish accomplices. After the arrest of the suspected priest, such a strategy took the conspiracy trials in an unanticipated direction and they quickly came to a halt.[71]

It should come as no surprise that Burton, after hearing a rumor that

Ury had publicly impugned her testimony, returned to court and identified him as the plot's principal architect. He had been at Hughson's, always whispering with the other conspirators, she said, and he performed ceremonies with strange oaths, offered to hear confessions and to forgive sins, and he kept holy robes and built an altar in his room. In order to sentence him to death, Ferenc Szasz writes, "The magistrates resurrected an old law of William III's time which provided severe penalties for being a priest in New York."[72] By the end of June, prosecutors believed the infiltration of Catholic saboteurs was at the root of the crisis, the only context in which to connect Hughson, the "black guard," the Spanish sailors, and Ury. "Could these be dreams," Horsmanden finally asks, "or is it more rational to conclude, from what has happened amongst us, that they were founded on realities?"[73] Some colonists rejected the justice's appeal to reason and wondered, as Horsmanden suggested, if in fact the conspiracy had been a bad dream; they seemed to have grown weary of the trials and suspicious of Burton. After implicating Ury, she responded to her critics by accusing them, claiming, as Horsmanden remembers, "that there were some people *in ruffles* (a phrase as was understood to mean persons of better fashion than ordinary) that were concerned."[74] Her new accusations against colonists of "known credit, fortunes and reputations" immediately ended the trials.[75] The jails emptied, slaves returned to their masters, and the court came under heavy criticism. Davis observes that "[i]n the end, critics pilloried the prosecutors' means, methods, and motives. What the prosecutors offered as confessions were among the most criticized elements, as critics challenged accuracy and authenticity."[76]

Horsmanden published *Journal of the Proceedings in the Detection of the Conspiracy* because of the court's need to provide a definitive justification of its verdicts. The scandalous conclusion to the trials tarnished the court's reputation; Horsmanden's decision to publish the history in chronicle form, with its conventional indeterminate ending, was the best strategy for claiming the court's final triumph. There is no ending—neither Burton's accusations against colonists "in ruffles" nor Ury's execution—and Horsmanden selects a fitting image that highlights the international dimensions of the conspiracy. The ships that transported banished slaves to the West Indies had returned with "many particulars of intelligence concerning the conspiracy," he warns; "this city and people were not yet out of danger from this hellish confederacy." Representing the final erasure of colonial borders caused by slaves and Roman Catholics joining forces, the ships carry news that depicts both the dangerous loss of order and national solidarity: he cites "several pretended prophecies of negroes that Charles-Town in South Carolina, and the city of New York, were to be burnt down on the twenty-fifth of March next." The southern border of South Carolina now cuts through Manhattan. Horsmanden next introduces an official directive from Governor Clarke, a letter of warning delivered to every town and public official in New York. In it Clarke states that "from the many undoubted informations I have received . . . the insolence of the negroes is as great, if not greater than ever. . . . I doubt there are too many yet remaining among us who were of the late conspiracy, and though we have felled the tree, I fear it is not entirely rooted up." Finally, Horsmanden illustrates Clarke's suspicions of another conspiracy by listing a string of recent fires, allegedly started by slaves and Spanish agents, throughout North America. The example of a local slave named Tom provides Horsmanden with a useful fiction. Inspired by the "villainous confederacy of last year," Tom allegedly set fire to a house. His subsequent execution, Horsmanden remarks, confirms Clarke's "apprehensions . . . concerning the danger which still threatened us from the conspirators remaining amongst us."[77]

Although Horsmanden's documentary account began with a chronological sequence of days and trial documents, it ends with enemies still lurking outside the text's borders. It is not just the insurrection story and its cast of plotting slaves that undermines his attempt at judicial realism— so, too, does the court's conviction that the conspiracy was part of the larger war with Spain. Although the trials took place during a period of patriotic fervor for the War of Jenkins's Ear, the publication of Horsmanden's history in 1744 occurs long after this enthusiasm had waned. Horsmanden tries to recapture this feeling of emergency, since it had dominated interpretations of the fires and galvanized the master class against their own slaves. Thus the main subject of the narrative is no longer a merciful and impartial legal system but a threatened white public. No longer interested in documenting the progress of the trials, since the trials have ended, the narrator surfaces as a way to prolong the state of emergency that paralyzed the public during the trials.[78]

In this context, the uncertain conclusion takes on serious implications for race relations after 1741. The inconclusive ending makes textual disorder commensurate with dangerous conspirators hiding within the city, a potent symbol of a colony still under duress. What had begun with the chronicler's promise to give the reader a "most natural view of the whole" has now become decidedly unnatural and unreal. Depicting the city's slaves as a continuing internal security threat, connected to both Spain and South Carolina's troublesome slave population, the conclusion creates a danger that can only be combated by public obedience to English authority. This strategy was not only central to the state's rhetoric of terror during the trials but also to Horsmanden's chronicle.

To silence critics once and for all, Horsmanden must find a way to craft uncertainty and maintain the colony's sense of disorder. He sustains an image of a city under siege in the final pages by stressing two metaphors of colonial fragmentation. First, Horsmanden encodes the public's terror in the city's decimated architecture. The uncontested fact in the trials is the sequence of the buildings burned: first, Fort George; second, the governor's mansion; third, the houses of the political and social leaders; finally, the enduring threat to the Anglican church. Each violated structure represents a column of English authority—the military, the law, free trade and commerce, and religion—and the metaphor comes to represent what many have come to accept as the real. Representative of English culture and government, the buildings convey a sense of national loyalty that challenges skeptics. Recognizing that the chronicle also exists within this metaphoric realm, Horsmanden makes his history equivalent with the decimated symbols of English authority. Until Fort George and the governor's house are rebuilt, he suggests, the ashes signify the "daily evidence and moments of [the plot], still before our eyes."[79] Spiteful of dissent and having lingering doubts about the star witness, Horsmanden deploys a decimated English city in denouncing those readers who suspect a miscarriage of justice. Ultimately, the truth of the chronicle is located in the colony's patriotic ruins.

There is an alternative conclusion, however, one that we haven't been led to expect from the sequential unfolding of the evidence; this one articulates a cynical vision of colonists and slaves locked in eternal combat. The second metaphor used to articulate the state of emergency is a ledger that lists all the slaves implicated in the conspiracy. Presented in lists of neat columns—each one, from right to left, giving the names of the slaves, their masters, and a mark designating whether the accused was committed, arraigned, convicted, confessed, burned, hanged, transported, or discharged—the accounting gives a distinct impression of the state's power, its ability to enforce order out of chaos. Although not as dramatic as the "naked terror" in 1712 of the executed slave's head on a pike or mutilated bodies displayed on gibbets in 1741, the ledger exerts its own force as metaphor of terror. There were 156 slaves and free blacks committed, 18 executed by hanging, 13 burned at the stake, and 70 deported to West Indian slave markets and plantations. If the spectacles of torture in 1712 and 1741 were primarily directed toward the local slave population, the ledger also attempts to secure the allegiance of white colonists. Nevertheless, this ritualistic purging of the scapegoat has only secured the colony temporarily, since Horsmanden guarantees that the threat of an international conspiracy still remains. The ledger creates a fleeting symbolic space, where English authority seemingly protects the city from foreign threats, but the list both supports and undermines the border between security and insecurity. As a demonstration of colonial authority and the clean logic of its justice and accountability, the ledger supports Horsmanden's guarantee of a future insurrection. His guarantee, delivered first in the preface, joins the final ledger in framing the history. The last passage of the preface claims the history will "awaken us from that supine security, which again too generally prevails, and put us upon our guard, lest the enemy should be yet within our doors."[80] In the aftermath of the trials, Horsmanden tells white colonists to maintain a constant and collective state of emergency.

In short, the ledger resolves the mass of incomplete, contradictory, and false accusations into a unified statement of guilt. What I find intriguing here is not the list of the executed (Horsmanden represents these crucial rituals in the text) but those slaves banished from the colony. Since the executions relied on a logic of contagion, the function of the banishment ritual was to protect that logic. If accused conspirators were allowed to remain, they would challenge the legitimacy of colonial authority, so the court, unable to execute seventy more alleged conspirators, devises an equivalent legal fiction to disarm the threat. The special law of Negro evidence—the key legal instrument of terror in the trials—produces an existence perhaps as terrifying as execution: the law causes the civil deaths of those slaves and free African-Americans who were lucky enough to survive the lottery of executions by severing their connections to their homes, loved ones, and even the half-freedoms of New York. Cast out into the West Indian plantations and slave markets, the banished take their place in a pantheon of fugitive slaves who haunt the colonists' self-fashioning of natural liberty over the next decades leading up to the American Revolution. The chronicle ends fittingly with the symbolic ledger, a sign of the reciprocity between terror and narrative. The problem of interpretation still remains, as it does in all cultures of terror, but none of the guilty will emerge to contest Horsmanden's narrative and his representation of a city finally purged of its slave enemies. The chronicle does the symbolic work of cleansing fugitive threats to the English colonial city, but such action does not lead to enlightenment or resolve long-standing social problems. The banished represent the permanent danger embodied by those slaves who remain in New York City. This has tragic consequences after 1741 because white panic deepened racial polarization with every rumor of unrest. The convergence of the conspiracy scare and the War of Jenkins's Ear irrevocably changed the city, for its white and black survivors as well as its detached onlookers. Obviously, in the wake of the conspiracy scare, the state would subject slaves to even more restrictions on mobility and personal conduct.

Yet white colonists, despite their racial privileges, also felt the effects of imperial authority reach into their own private lives and social gatherings. For example, in 1744, the year Horsmanden published *Journal of the Proceedings in the Detection of the Conspiracy,* the Maryland writer and physician Alexander Hamilton stayed in New York City for a time while traveling through the North American colonies and composing his "Itinerarium," a diary of observations about colonial life. He found that the conspiracy had even ruined the English cup of tea:

> It is a very rich place. . . . they have very bad water in the city, most of it being hard and brackish. Ever since the Negro conspiracy, certain people have been appointed to sell water in the streets, which they carry on a sledge in great casks and bring it from the best springs about the city, for it was when the Negroes went for tea water that they held their cabals and consultations, and therefore they have a law now that no negroes shall be seen upon the streets without a lantern after dark.[81]

This gentleman traveler's anecdote about his inconvenience sheds light on how terror can shape even the mundane events of everyday life in an eighteenth-century colony. Apparently slaves had freely gone on errands into the wilderness for tea water before the conspiracy, but in the wake of the trials the state denied them this liberty because of rumors that these trips had concealed their planning of the insurrection. In addition to this restriction, the city decided to enforce an ordinance—it had been on the books since the 1730s—that made it a crime for slaves to be out at night without a lantern. Such piecemeal legislation represented white power reconstituting itself against a slave population that was more of an international threat than it had been before the first fires in the spring of 1741. Perhaps there is no suitable historical vantage point from which to speculate if the resurgence of imperial power after the trials made New York's colonists feel more isolated and "American" rather than safely "English." What one can say is that the feelings of white panic were channeled into new laws, new customs, and new commerce. Hamilton notes how such tension gave one company the business of carting barreled water into the city; New Yorkers, still believing in their narrow deliverance, were willing to live with the brackish taste and slavery's coercive values.

chapter 2

Unreasonable Discontent: The Politics of Charles Brockden Brown and the *Monthly Magazine*

Charles Brockden Brown wrote all his major novels from 1797 to 1801, a remarkable time of creative outpouring that coincides with a period of political extremism and war crisis that ended Federalist control of U.S. politics. French attacks on American shipping in 1797 destroyed maritime commerce, and relations between the two countries rapidly deteriorated until a diplomatic rift known as the XYZ affair instigated an undeclared war between the two countries.[1] The surge of patriotic feeling was an immediate boon for Federalists. National unity centered on President Adams, suddenly a popular figure for the first time in his political career, and Federalists exploited the crisis atmosphere by attacking dissenters and strengthening their authority. Pointing to the threat of an invasion by revolutionary France, Federalists constructed a legislative agenda defined by unprecedented martial preparations. They created a new military program, including a navy and a permanent army; passed new taxes to pay for the apparatus; and wrote legal measures, such as the Alien and Sedition Laws, that would guard against domestic subversion. The agenda sailed through Congress. In the congressional elections of 1798, with Americans looking anxiously at what Federalists depicted as vulnerable borders and rebellious slaves, the Federalist war program contributed to major electoral gains throughout the country.[2]

Prepared for a French invasion in the summer of 1798, the public's war fever weakened in early 1799 when the French threat had failed to materialize. Instead of leading the public to a more moderate position, or at least giving voice to it, Federalists intensified their war rhetoric, stayed fully committed to their military program, and extended their power into the West Indies. According to Stanley Elkins and Eric McKitrick, Federalists had realized that the military program of 1798 was "their main hope of reinforcing a moral authority that was slowly ebbing away."[3] As it turned out, the Federalists' decision to join their imperial interests in the West Indies with their domestic struggles contributed to their rapid demise at the end of the eighteenth century. Federalists believed that the United States was fighting a two-front war against both France and domestic radicals; pulling back from the new military measures would mean losing a new-found advantage over their Republican opponents, as well as the legislative weapons for defeating, in their eyes, covert enemies. Federalists designed the Alien and Sedition Acts and revised the Naturalization Act so that they could undercut the political influence of German and Irish immigrants, who were key Republican loyalists in 1799. As the public's enthusiasm for war began to wane, Federalists refused to walk away from what had become an imperialist agenda that now characterized their patriotic authority. Attempting to rekindle the spirit for war, Federalist war measures and propaganda appropriated the logic of the old British empire: on the Caribbean frontier, imperial foes were plotting invasion with slave rebels in the West Indies; both enemies, Catholics and slaves, would invade a weakened United States and spark a massive insurrection in the South, a fateful situation that only Federalists could defend against.

Charles Brockden Brown wrote a series of novels that collectively told a story of a vulnerable nation torn apart by internal distrust and foreign conspiracy. Locating the question of national identity in hostile border zones, each novel relied on images of violent, deadly collisions between new American citizens, subversive Irish immigrants, rebellious African-Americans, and French agents. During this period, formulations of national identity often included a threatening double that lurked in the shadows, and in Brown's novels it is the duplicity and violence of mysterious foreigners that devastate the American community. In *Edgar Huntly* (1799) the protagonist's pursuit of a "savage" Irishman suggests the climate of suspicion that produced the Alien and Sedition Laws, which turned Irish immigrants into the enemies of national security. The climate of suspicion and insecurity forms Brown's re-creation of the 1793 yellow fever epidemic in *Arthur Mervyn* (1799, 1800). At the height of the epidemic, the picaresque hero, Arthur, fights to save the national capital, decimated by death, from villainous African-Americans who pillage the property of dying whites. The subversive speech and vocal power of the foreigner Carwin in *Wieland* (1798) reproduces fears of contagious rhetoric that results in Wieland's murdering his family, an allegory of nation torn apart by seditious violence. Another outside enemy, a French mercenary, drives the plot (and the plotting) of *Ormond* (1799). Having infiltrated the United States, Ormond attempts to seduce and ruin Constantia Dudley, an exemplary republican maid whose father's death has orphaned her in the world. When Constantia escapes from Ormond by fleeing to her birthplace, New Jersey, the Frenchman tracks her there and breaks into the family home so that he can murder her. Virtue triumphs, however, when she narrowly defeats him by stabbing the foreign intruder through the heart. Taken collectively, Brown's novels depict a troublesome decade in the emergence of U.S. imperial culture.

Brown's narrative style was a perfect match for a decade in which, as Larzer Ziff remarks, "the literary had not yet separated from political culture."[4] It is precisely Brown's willingness to probe his culture of conspiracy and political extremism that impresses many of his contemporary readers. Naturally, critics have long been in the habit of applying a political litmus test to Brown's literary career so that they can place his novels on the Federalist or Republican side of the cultural divide. Prevailing wisdom once had it that Brown wrote his best novels while still a youthful republican idealist, and that his political conversion to an aggressive federalist politics after 1801, as well as his entry into a world of international trade, effectively robbed the once promising novelist of his prodigious talent. Robert Levine cautions Brown's critics about the difficulty of pinning Brown down politically, since the "aggressively dialogic" and ironic voices that distinguish his novels are designed to evoke the period. And Jared Gardner challenges critics to reject this artificial divide and to bridge it by linking Brown's literary and political writing. In his own insightful reading of *Edgar Huntley*, Gardner connects the novel to Brown's short, if infamous, career as a Federalist pamphleteer. The result is that we "see the continuity of Brown's career," as he consistently draws on racial politics and tropes of race to imagine the United States.[5] Examining the complicated roles literary discourse played in the political and social clashes of the late 1790s, critics, such as Bill Christopherson, Jared Gardner, Teresa

Goddu, Robert Levine, Shirley Samuels, and Steven Watts, have revived Brown's once stagnant reputation. They have converted his body of fiction into an essential touchstone for understanding an American identity under duress.[6]

Critics have been less interested in Brown's other major work of the period, the *Monthly Magazine,* one of America's first high-culture periodicals. Like his novels, the periodical was also shaped by themes of danger, conspiracy, and paranoia. The *Monthly Magazine* presented an array of national narratives, including poems, short fiction, and essays, as well as Brown's reviews of Fourth of July orations, National Fast Day addresses, and George Washington eulogies. Driven by war aims and patriotic jeremiads against disunion, these texts were essential ingredients in an imperial environment that rivals the hysterical rhetoric of today's political leaders and news anchors. In this chapter, I open up the *Monthly Magazine* and demonstrate how its collection of national narratives and other texts refer to an endangered union and consistently urge readers to support Federalist authority: the National Fast Day oration fostered support for political consensus, the George Washington eulogy substituted John Adams and the Federalists as the true heirs of Washington's legacy, and the Fourth of July address celebrated an American liberty that required the expulsion of the subversive threat within. This chapter's first three sections explain how these ritualistic texts, and Brown's reviews of them, construct an American national identity tied to foreign spaces and characterized by imperial warfare and expansionism.

The final section, "Fugitive Bodies," examines how the racial component intrinsic to both Federalist politics and U.S. imperial culture shaped the *Monthly Magazine.* In their efforts to dominate U.S. politics, Federalists authored slave conspiracy narratives and spread rumors of a revolt in the Southern states to pick up crucial support for their military program. Similar to the effects of British military action against the Spanish empire in 1741, U.S. imperial aims in the West Indies in the late 1790s transformed slaves and free African-Americans, from the U.S. government's point of view, into national security threats. Critics consistently overlook how race defines the political transformation of the United States during the 1790s, even though race remains critical to undoing the knot of conspiratorial imagery, ritual, and politics that marked the literary and political depictions of U.S. imperial culture. In this context, it is not surprising that the racially coded outsiders at the core of both Brown's novels and the period's war hysteria reappear in the *Monthly Magazine* in the form of a contagious, threatening African-American population.[7] Using a sequence of Brown's reviews and original contributions, excerpted scientific tracts, and essays on slavery, my conclusion opens the focus to examine the irony of the period's notorious political factionalism: it was over the figure of the slave rebel—race war personified—that white Federalists and Republicans could unite behind the logic of imperial aggression against foreign enemies and find a common expression of white America.

As novelist, Brown featured ironic and dialogic voices that called attention to the decade's unsettling anxieties about foreign enemies lurking within national borders; as proprietor and editor of the *Monthly Magazine,* Brown does not display the same relish for the ambiguity and inclusiveness of national discourse. Instead, the periodical serves as a vehicle for the dominant and didactic voice of Federalist orthodoxy. I offer no excuses for this stark depiction of Federalist politics or the support given it by the *Monthly Magazine*—it is not the Federalism of 1787, when higher ideals gave shape to an ideology, but rather as it hit its extremist, imperial pitch in 1799. Over the course of the decade, Federalists used military forces to quell domestic disturbances, to sever connections with revolutionary France and reestablish diplomatic ties with England, to gain control of both houses of Congress and pass legislation that restricted free speech and demonized immigrants, to build a larger military apparatus and involve the country in an undeclared war with France, and to rally the public against the French enemy by exacerbating white racial anxieties. Indeed, the spectacle of military power had become essential to the imperial power that Federalists had cloaked in patriotic imagery. As Richard Kohn remarks, the military had "quite clearly emerged as a symbol of a powerful, ordered, stable, nationalist, patriotic institution unfettered by dissent or uncertainty."[8] With its consistent presentation of narratives that informed citizens about the virtues of obeying the Federalist government in wartime, the *Monthly Magazine* was complicit with both a specific brand of Federalist patriotism and a wartime agenda that many Americans had grown weary enough of by the turn of the century to elect Thomas Jefferson president. As a result, Brown's *Monthly Magazine* looks less like a stodgy journal disinterested in social and political issues, as it is often said to be, while it begins to resemble its author, who responded to national crisis by pioneering an adventurous, unruly, and passionate American Gothic, and for a brief, promising moment, wrote as if the future of the American Revolution depended on his vision and efforts.

FASTING FOR UNITY

Until Thomas Jefferson's electoral victory over President John Adams in 1801, the Federalist party had dominated U.S. politics. The first advocates for a new Constitution in 1787, Federalists argued for the creation of a strong central government anchored by both a national bank and a constitution that expanded national powers while reducing state autonomy. As the Federalist party evolved over the course of the 1790s, its leaders made no secret of their disdain for what they viewed as dangerous democratic visions; they feared the example of the French Revolution and were quick to label political opposition as being under the influence of Jacobinic democracy. Nevertheless, a wide range of popular opposition challenged Federalist authority during the postrevolutionary period. A cross section of the American populace, including urban workers, artisans, free African-Americans, slaves, and farmers, dissatisfied with a federal government perceived as hostile to their interests, agitated for more expansive personal liberties. Much of this opposition was gradually, and loosely, organized under the auspices of the Democratic-Republican societies.[9] The anti-Federalism of 1787 provided political opponents to the Federalist agenda with a dissenting tradition. The essentials of this tradition were a belief in localized power, a strict interpretation of the Constitution that curtailed national authority, and a diverse and vibrant public sphere. As Saul Cornell has argued, the Democratic-Republican societies saw the public sphere as an alternative to the Federalists' centralization: "[the public sphere] could unite Americans without centralizing authority and rally the people against the Federalist agenda. The broad dissemination of information and the knowledge of their rights would, in the end, lead the people to reject the Federalist conspiracy against their liberties."[10] After 1795 the idealism of a free and diverse public sphere inspiring a public awakening was offset by a Federalist party that viewed this space as crucial to defeating alternative views they saw as subversive.

This battle did not just take place in the press. In Philadelphia during the late 1790s, Federalist leaders encouraged young men to form militia groups so that they could help to enforce the new borders symbolized by the Alien and Sedition Acts. They hung out in the taverns of Brown's hometown of Philadelphia, roamed the streets, assaulted immigrants and African-Americans, and harassed and abused newspaper editors who criticized the Federalist party. Obviously, running a periodical during this period was a highly politicized, even dangerous affair, a fact Brown addresses in the *Monthly Magazine*'s first volume. Writing under the pseudonym Candidus, Brown addresses the difficulty of selling a high-brow periodical to an American audience divided by political opinion: "If, perchance, you should, on any one subject, be profound or eloquent, yet your efforts to please will be frustrated by some unlucky difference of opinion between you and your reader."[11] After reading this statement of neutrality, many critics, taking Candidus at his word, declare the *Monthly Magazine* to be free of politics. One representative opinion claims that Brown, while producing his journal, takes a "prudent approach" to politics, stepping carefully in the minefield of sedition and un-American heresy, and successfully avoids divisive issues. Brown's Candidus misleads critics by offering the reader an editor's time-honored cliché that delivers unbiased professionalism, free from political conflict, as an appeal to a diverse group of American readers whom Candidus invites to the "banquet."

On the contrary, every issue of the *Monthly Magazine* supports a Federalist agenda. One way that the journal contradicts its purported position of neutrality is by giving positive reviews of political speeches and tracts, such as the National Fast Day orations, that were designed to rally support for the Federalist cause.[12] Federalists reintroduced a National Fast Day in 1799 to help mobilize public support and solidarity for the ongoing conflict with France; it also served as a persuasive counterpart to an expensive war program already under construction in the legislature. In the official proclamation, President Adams depicted a nation on the brink of disunion and defined national allegiance as support for U.S. government; Adams urged citizens to obey their duty in these "circumstances of great urgency and seasons of imminent danger." "Public religious solemnities," Adams reasoned, "are happily calculated to avert the evils which we ought to deprecate."[13]

Orators across the nation delivered National Fast Day speeches, many of which exploited the fear of "imminent danger" as a way to build a consensus and to remap the national domain. A day of prayer sponsored and defined by the U.S. government associated the threat of French invasion with the political "evils" allegedly posed by the Federalists' opponents, a diverse group that included Thomas Jefferson and Irish revolutionaries, Southern slaves and the editors of the *Philadelphia Aurora*. President Adams spelled out the duty of each citizen in this time of crisis:

> Earnest and particular supplications should be made to Him who is able to defend or to destroy; as, moreover, the most precious interests of the people of the US are still in jeopardy, by the hostile designs and insidious arts of a foreign nation, as well as by the dissemination among them of those principles subversive of the foundations of all religious, moral, and social obligations, that have produced incalculable mischief and misery in other countries.[14]

Adams draws the chaotic boundaries between domestic and foreign spaces, juxtaposing two types of rhetoric that reveal how American imperial power rejects its idealized position of isolation and quickly closes the distance between the domestic United States and foreign threats. The only patriotic choice for the citizen is to act as a subject of empire rather than as a citizen of the republic. For example, the suggestive nouns "designs" and "arts," freighted by their adjectives "hostile" and "insidious," encode a rhetoric of paranoia. Such rhetoric was shorthand for covert operations undertaken by France and disaffected slaves within the United States. In a move that would become generic to the rhetoric of U.S. imperialism but that also harkens back to the British empire's strategies of colonial rule, Adams depicts a national geography already made insecure by a dangerously contagious subversiveness.

The president prays that God will "withhold us from unreasonable discontent—from disunion, faction, sedition and insurrection." In the process, Adams gives the people a solution to the crisis of a splitting union: submit to the authority of God. This second type, a complementary rhetoric of security, depends on a foreign geography engulfed in "misery." With this image, white Americans can thank God who has given "countless favors" to them and made them "eminently happy, when compared with the lot of others." Citizens can show their gratitude by resisting nonconformist opinions and remaining loyal to their covenant with the Federalist government, the leaders of God's chosen republic. Thus, for those patriots sympathizing with the Federalist cause, a powerful state, even the permanent army, acquired positive connotations. It symbolized a strong union free of dissent, an America unified under an expansive Federalist power, precisely what orators prayed for on National Fast Day.

Brown reported on the public ritual of the fasting day oration for the *Monthly Magazine*. Like the oratory composed for the occasion, his conclusions affirmed the journal's support of Federalist politics. One typical review applauds the "impressive" ability of the orator to exhibit "the accursed things" that threaten the nation. This sentiment, writes Brown, will increase "support of public measures . . . which indicates that he is a very firm friend to the government and administration of his country." Many of Brown's reviews look favorably on poets and orators who prove themselves friends of the administration. In his reviews of the Fast Day speeches, Brown establishes a dialogue with the orator, joining him in fabricating union out of "great urgency" and affirming its unifying impulse. For example, in a review of Reverend Linn's "Day of General Fast" oration, Brown emphasizes a section titled "Want of Union among Our Citizens," which suggests his anxiety about political disagreement—which he imagines as foreign extremism—threatening the United States. Brown approved of Linn's "impressive" ability to exhibit "the accursed things, or the national sins, which have been the procuring cause of national punishments." While this is the familiar language of the American jeremiad, it also an imperialist vocabulary aimed at both real and imaginary enemies. To expunge the "sins" of the "accursed" radical from the nation, one must firmly support the "health" of civil society, which means supporting the government's actions against any opposition. For Brown this solution is "calculated to do good" and earns the orator Brown's enthusiastic support: "with a laudable zeal, [Linn] calls for approbation and support of public measures, with a fervor of discussion, which indicates that he is a very firm friend to the government and administration of his country."[15]

Following the Linn review in the same issue is a response to a speech delivered by Reverend John Kirkland, the future president of Harvard and an outspoken critic of what he saw as Jacobinic radicalism. After Brown gives the reader a sense of Linn's ability to blend religious and secular devotion, he only needs brief commentary to praise similar sentiments in Kirkland's address: "[The speech] maintains with equal zeal, the importance of Christianity, to the welfare of civil society; and is not less decided and warm in inculcating the duty of supporting the government of the U.S."[16] Brown's reviews of National Fast orations and the texts themselves are two of many examples in the *Monthly Magazine* of his loyalty to the Federalist cause. Brown saw himself as playing an important, even patriotic, role in the public sphere. In his position as reviewer and arbitrator of political opinion, Brown urges his reader to support "public measures." None of Brown's reviews of the Fast Day orations reveal traces of political ambivalence or his alleged Democratic sympathies.[17]

In literary discourse of the 1790s, an excess of emotion and sentiment, contesting voices, and violence and death were qualities that could, simultaneously, reflect the era's imperial politics and call forth an inclusive democratic society. Family was the model for social and political affiliations in sentimental fictions and familial relationships evoked a national union in which all its members were common links in a "sympathetic chain." Teaching lessons about the interdependence of all individuals, no matter their race, gender, or social class, these sentimental fictions could offer a democratic vision in which fellow feeling would heal the wounds of the nation-state. Sympathy was fundamental to the evolving national character, Elizabeth Barnes argues, but she also suggests that it had the "dangerous capacity to undermine the democratic principles it ostensibly means to reinforce" because a rhetoric of sentiment could reinforce likeness rather than difference, homogeneity rather than diversity.[18] In his novels, Brown takes advantage of this irony, distilling it into fabulous scenarios of mystery and conflict. For example, in *Edgar Huntley*, the "sympathetic chain" that Edgar wants to extend to Clithero terrifies the Irish fugitive; their midnight wanderings display how the revolutionary virtues of benevolence and sympathy could also mask an irrational need to police the alien.

U.S. imperial discourse was not separated from sentimental literary culture, and both produced political effects in its audience. Federalists employed patriotic spectacles and texts that featured the sentimental rhetoric and imagery of united, if weakened, Americans; these spectacles and texts enabled Federalists to cast their authoritarianism as a family model of national identity, united in the Federalist house of imperial authority. The political imperatives of such a model are clear. Employing the rhetoric of a broken family, an unstable union, the National Fast Day proclamation was an ideological vehicle designed to be an adjunct to Federalist militarism.

For an American to be, as Brown said, a "very firm friend" to the federal government, he must join hands with others in the president's national circle of prayer and imagine the union in serious jeopardy, with "agents of disunion, faction, sedition, and insurrection" at the nation's door.[19]

Thus, the death of George Washington in 1799 was a serendipitous event for the Federalist government, since it enabled them to marshal his substantial political capital for unifying Americans behind a patriotic cause. Even more effective than the day of national supplication, the public ritual of eulogizing George Washington's death helped to persuade Americans to accept the increasing centralization of federal authority, as well as the expansion of it into new spaces of U.S. imperial culture.[20] The political content of the Washington icon had a dual function, giving Federalists the opportunity to celebrate their revolutionary legacy as well as their efforts to build a military power in his image and to defeat what they defined as radicalism in the years afterward. Unlike the novelist exploring the democratic potential of sympathy, the George Washington eulogist had a different disciplinary agenda, one reinforcing the strength of Federalist government. Circumscribing the limits of opposition and appropriating Washington's revolutionary legacy to their contested authority, the eulogy was an important text, and local Federalist authorities strictly managed its authorship and public recital. The 440 addresses and eulogies, delivered in over two hundred towns in only three months, provided Federalists with a powerful icon of national security, a symbolic bulwark against all enemies.[21] Yet the eulogy also enabled Federalists to reconstruct a national genealogy that positioned the administration, after Washington's passing, as his legitimate heir. Their propaganda effort dominated the public sphere. Federalists bet on Washington's appeal as a true American hero, someone who stood for the best patriotic virtues, and the eulogy was designed to transfer that elusive authority to the Adams administration. Their tributes dressed Washington in his military splendor, a just and brave general who could crush domestic insurgents of the late 1790s as easily as he defeated British forces at Valley Forge or the Whisky Rebels in Pennsylvania.

Not only did the *Monthly Magazine* become an important outlet for the Washington myth, but Brown lent his own creativity to the cause. Claiming that a larger war against France was looming, Brown composed a lamentation on Washington's death.[22] The lament concludes with a call for a gifted orator who can transform Washington into a stabilizing force for the nation:

Pagentry and dirges, though suitable, are transitory and imperfect testimonies of our homage, and to genius must be committed the office of imparting to the world at large, and to posterity, faithful pictures of the sentiments which the memory of WASHINGTON excited in the hearts of his contemporaries, and of those who have witnessed his achievements and partaken of his benefits.[23]

Unfortunately, Brown could not predict the future or he might not have put out a call for a peerless orator. As the solitary reviewer for the journal, Brown was overwhelmed by fifty George Washington eulogies he was committed to appraise. Yet despite his approval for their political sympathies, the lack of rhetorical "genius" in the group of orations frustrated Brown. In "Hints for a Funeral Oration," signed under the pseudonym Monendus, Brown undertakes, one imagines, a cathartic response to being besieged by hackneyed rhetoric. He composed rhetorical guidelines for an orator wishing to deliver an awe-inspiring score of Washington, a eulogy that collects the people beneath Washington's patriotic legacy.

The first lesson Brown gives for the aspiring orator is to abandon reason and analysis and to "embellish" so the legend of Washington stimulates "passion" in the reader. With this rhetorical flourish, an orator will promote national security by defining a "universal system [that] regards all things as one plan . . . so you must recognize in our subordinate world, but one creating, modeling, and governing principle; one angel must rule in your storm, and that angel must be Washington."[24] Brown blends the secular and the sacred, substituting General Washington for God, and perhaps thinking of his own fictional, spellbinding characters, he urges the orator to put the audience under a spell so they "almost believe that he was immortal." Once the audience believes Washington to be the "governing" deity of the republic, Brown challenges the orator to accomplish one last political aim and convince those persons who oppose Federalist authority of the true nature of this "subordinate world": "You must hang not only the success of the war, but the safety of our present political system, upon his single life. Without him, nothing could have happened that has happened; and, with his departure, the energies that kept us together as one nation, have taken their flight."[25] Brown's directives indicate his awareness of the function of political rhetoric, an expertise that will make him a successful Federalist pamphleteer after he gives up writing novels in the early 1800s.

The construction of Washington as a military savior in a world unsettled, once again, by armed conflict in the West Indies, insurrection scares, and political subversion was part of an intertextual effort to justify Federalist militarism. Brown's final directive resembles Adams's effort in the National Fast Day proclamation to create an atmosphere of "great urgency" and "imminent danger," a collective anxiety designed to compel self-subordination and to bring Americans within the protection of a unified "political system" governed by Federalists. This rhetoric of security rose in pitch in response to growing internal resistance to Federalist authority. Widespread opposition to government restraints on liberty increased during the 1790s as laborers, farmers, immigrants, and antislavery agitators, many hindered by voting restrictions, formed across the country to voice their anger with a new government unwilling to grant democratic liberties. The broad dissemination of the Washington myth, via elegies, eulogies, engravings, or other ideological vehicles such as Brown's *Monendus*, was an attempt, through the imagery of a strong national father, to reinforce Federalist hegemony. If the Revolution and loss of King George had caused a major shift in the familial metaphor and converted General Washington into the new father, then Washington's death marked a significant transformation.[26] The outpourings of eulogies inaugurated the posthumous reign of a new king who embodied the principles of Roman military might and an emerging U.S. imperial power rather than republicanism. While the political function of the Washington myth helped to unify colonists against the British empire during the Revolution, Federalists revised it to strengthen their flagging authority and to defeat opposition to their rule.

Dedicated to inventing a powerful Washington myth, eulogists succeeded, in part, because the roots of this achievement were in a collective act of mythmaking that took place during the Revolution. Looking back at the canonization of Washington, Adams demystifies the role that rhetoric played in governing the newly independent colonies:

> The great character [George Washington] was a character of convention. . . . [N]orthern, middle, and southern statesman and northern, middle, and southern officers of the army expressly agreed . . . to cover and dissemble all faults and errors, to represent every defeat as a victory and every retreat as an advancement, to make that Character popular and fashionable with all parties . . . as the central stone in the geometrical arch. There you have the revelation of the whole mystery.[27]

This heroic "central stone" assured the solidity of "union," the ur-principle of American imperialism that brought together warring political factions. Supporting the same Federalist ideology, Brown's mythical Washington—the "one creating, modeling, and governing principle"—performs the same conservative function as Adams's foundation stone. Adapted to protect what Brown calls the "universal system," the Washington eulogy was a key vehicle for strengthening the stone's place in the union that social discontent seemed ready to dislodge.

A national hero facilitates allegiance to a faceless state since, as Michael Walzer observes, "the state is invisible; it must be personified before it can be seen, symbolized before it can be loved, imagined before it can be conceived . . . thus the image provides a starting point for political thinking."[28] To illustrate the danger assailing the American state after Washington's death—the anxiety of facelessness—Brown's Monendus urges the orator to "paint the universal affliction" caused by his death: "you must describe men and maids, whites and blacks, grey-beards and striplings, as joining in one universal out-cry of sorrow, for the death of their friend, parent, guide, champion, protecting angel, and tutelary divinity."[29] If the genre were different, perhaps the novel, this sentimental model of political affiliation might suggest a democratic vision for America; despite the signs of Brown's playfulness, however, the political tract depicts the national family under duress and requires a vertical structure of power with Washington at its apex: it is didactic rather than ironic. His authority alone will keep the heterogeneous chain intact, and from his place of supreme authority, Washington, the "protecting angel," comes to embody the protection of Federalist militarism. In Washington, Federalists had discovered a governing symbol of a stable patriotic government and its new army.

Yet Brown advises the eulogist to be subtle, to temper the presentation of union with an almost imperceptible sense of anxiety to create an unmistakable impression of America's dangerous predicament after the loss of the protector. Brown does not confine this rhetoric of insecurity to the eulogy, since the graphic layout of the March 1800 issue of the *Monthly Magazine* demonstrates a state of emergency with its front-page statement. Instead of a scientific or literary essay that might indicate the journal's willingness to maintain a safe distance from political strife, the "original communication" is excerpted from a documentary report titled "Statements of Destruction Produced by the French Revolution." What follows is a numerical table, contrived with an actuary's morbid precision, accounting for the age and sex of those murdered by radicals in France, the citizens driven into exile, towns and farms decimated by the unleashing of dangerous freedoms, and the overall "destruction of life and property." Published three months after Washington's death, this sensationalized ledger documents the bloody facts of disorder and shapes, one might even say restricts, the reader's reaction to the numerous reviews of George Washington eulogies that appear in its final pages. There is a seamless movement from the depiction of disorder to the moment of crisis, to the promotion of a single protector. The eulogies provide a single answer to the question inspired by the documentary account of chaos in France: stay true to the national covenant, stand behind the Federalist successors to Washington.

Adams's revelation that Washington was a "character of convention" created to inspire confidence in an independent nation is an apt reminder of the political substance of nationalist rhetoric and symbols. The *Monthly Magazine* responded to what Federalists defined as the threat of radicalism with a steady flow of texts supporting a conservative appeal for governmental control. Besides juxtaposing the evil of unbridled liberty with the good of Washington's legacy, which served to increase a citizen's allegiance to the federalist government, Brown wrote laudatory reviews of eulogies that adhered to his one "governing principle." The orthodox Calvinist Jedediah Morse, alarmed by what he saw as the spread of democratic principles, composed a eulogy that aimed to protect civil and religious "order" in the United States. Brown pauses over the tomb in his review to paraphrase Reverend Morse's hopeful diagnosis: "over his tomb the spell of party is dissolved; the conflicts of opposing politicians are suspended, and the American people, with one heart, and with all ardour of filial affection and gratitude, crowd around, to do honour to his ashes."[30] The paraphrase suggests Brown's wish for unity, a longing that might not reach as far back as the Revolution but is certainly nostalgic for a time preceding the scares of foreign terrorism and intense factionalism between Federalists and Republicans. Stern has argued that the operation of sentiment in novels of this period could enact both a "collective mourning over the violence of the Revolution and the preemption of liberty in the wake of the post-revolutionary settlement."[31] As the Washington eulogy shows, Federalists also harnessed sympathy for the sake of building an imperial power that could defeat foreign antagonists on either side of changing national borders;

their version of the Washington myth provided a patriotic alternative to a more dangerous democratic vision, dangerous because it worked through the trope of difference and, thus, also the logic of contagion. In contrast, Morse invents his own homogeneous band of Americans, a sympathetic chain of citizens, who surround Washington's tomb and mourn with "one heart"—except a strict hierarchy gives form to this structure of this sentiment and works to resist democratic expressions as well as to silence dissident voices.

What distinguishes Morse's text, however, is an unusual appendix, a 1753 letter written by Morse that accuses the Bavarian Illuminati—a mythical international band of conspirators supposedly under direction of the French Empire—of orchestrating what Morse depicts as the spread of extremism and anti-Federalism in the United States.[32] And who better to inform the American people of the spread of this terrorist organization into the United States than Morse, the author of *Geography Made Easy,* the "father of American Geography"? His anxieties demonstrate a key consequence of American imperialism: extending U.S. imperial power into the West Indies both to fight against France and to control the region's lucrative markets inevitably blurs national boundaries and shapes domestic culture according to practices antithetical with republicanism. Documenting a French-led conspiracy to conquer the North American colonies, Morse's 1753 letter demonstrates, as I discussed in the introduction, how the remnants of empire persist into the "republican period," competing with it, but more often displacing its values with the imperial power of Federalist militarism. Morse's letter teaches the reader that Americans, if they are truly to honor Washington, must serve the Federalist government, like their colonial forefathers served the British empire, and combat opposition to their rule. Instead of calling attention to how Morse's Federalist propaganda seemingly forgets the Revolution or questioning the way he attempts to subsume reason with inflammatory rhetoric, Brown paints a dignified portrait of Morse. The esteemed patriot, Brown remarks, has "lately embarked in the business of detecting conspiracies, publishing intercepted dispatches, and exposing French villainy." Morse did not want to miss an opportunity, Brown assures the reader, to add "another exertion to the very zealous and laudable service which he has already . . . rendered his countrymen."[33] Brown's editorial judgment, his advocacy of Morse's cause, stitches the eulogy seamlessly to an appendix that instructs the reader on how to enter the circle of "filial affection" and guard the domestic space against French "villainy." By 1800 no reader needed a translation for this appeal to Federalist law and order.

CELEBRATING THE THREAT TO UNION ON INDEPENDENCE DAY

Washington's death altered the third most popular patriotic genre in the imperial culture of the late 1790s, the Fourth of July address. Working to forge cohesion and conformity, Fourth of July addresses, Fast Day orations, and George Washington eulogies all complemented each other: the first two forms emphasized union, the eulogy, anxiety about disunion. Each one offered a strong national father (the ruling angel according to Brown's guidelines) who protected the nation from subversive forces already past the gates and living among the people. Because of Washington's death, however, the Fourth of July address and the George Washington eulogy had a unique relation to each other. In a strictly formal sense, the evocation of Washington was often interwoven with homage to the American Revolution presented in the Fourth of July address. The Fourth of July address began in 1778 by celebrating "the Revolution as the beginning of a new age in human history," a theme, Bercovitch writes, that "continues unabated in the long procession of orations that followed through the Federalist period."[34] Dominating the public sphere, the "long procession" allowed Federalists to enforce their claim—like they did with the Washington eulogies and the National Fast orations—as rightful heirs to revolutionary authority. Under their control, the public ritual of independence was a "vehicle of socialization" through which Federalists could engineer consensus both in public and in print.[35] Determined to taint democracy with foreign influence, these Federalist Jeremiahs, as Bercovitch calls the Independence Day orators, "saw their duty at once: they had to keep the Revolution on course by exorcising the demons of rebellion."[36]

Speaking as Monendus, Brown believed the eulogy should promote a renewed commitment to Washington's Federalist hierarchy as the path to order and unity. Nevertheless, Brown instructs the aspiring orator to locate a subversive foe just outside the family's precincts; the ritual of the Fourth of July address transformed Brown's "hint" of national insecurity into its most persuasive appeal. In one typical review, Brown affirms the orator's decision to castigate "the Gallic faction" in the United States, particularly their "community of opinions" that threaten to "subvert our virtuous and venerable institutions, and overwhelm all religion, law, and liberty."[37] Brown then plays the role of cultural critic, criticizing a rhetorical genre that had been dulled by familiar repetition, while finding that the anxiety of political unrest has given the Independence Day orator fresh inspirational material. A speaker could evoke the "horror of the scene," by which Brown means the imminent French invasion, "without fear of satiety."[38] Packed into this phrase is an aggressive impulse endlessly repeated in Federalist orations, which discovers the meaning of America in the collective act of all empires, feeding off an enemy's presence.

Brown participates in the Independence Day ritual, appropriately enough, with the July 1799 edition of the *Monthly Magazine*. More than any other issue, this one is essentially a primer in early American imperialism, particularly in how patriotism conceals its violence and coercion. The introductory "Original Communication" describes "The Festival of Independence," where the author, an anonymous "L" (most likely Brown), is impressed by the orderliness of the loyal citizens and the all-important patriotic toasts delivered by men known for their "sagacity and soundness of politics." Of course, at this particular festival, political "soundness" meant contempt for both domestic political opposition to the U.S. government and a cunning France. To further strengthen the parameters of opinion, the author notes the speakers' equally clear-sighted vision: "[The speeches] all turn upon the present condition of the country in relation to France, and breathe the utmost animosity towards the speculative creeds, as well as the practical deductions of the Parisian philosophes and politicians."[39] Independence Day celebrations and addresses were opportunities for towns and orators to prove their national loyalty and commitment to certain revolutionary ideals; at a time when Republican dissent had managed to partially obstruct the Federalist government's war aims against France and internal "enemies," the introduction to this issue stages a homogeneous celebration of Americans uniformly opposed to France and French-inspired democracy. As if there could be any doubt about the harmonized political mood dominating the celebration, the observer takes final note of the popular songs sung that afternoon: all expressed "sentiments of hatred to the French."[40]

More than a random article, "The Festival of Independence" serves as an interpretive frame for Brown's reviews of the Fourth of July orations by drawing boundaries between U.S. citizens loyal to Federalist authority and those excluded from the mainstream celebration of nationhood. An orator did not have to stray far from these limits for Brown to censure him for inculcating an irresponsible patriotism that could only lead to disobedience to the government. The *Monthly Magazine* provides a window to the public sphere at the end of the eighteenth century, when Fourth of July orators voiced oppositional political visions. Except in the pages of the journal, the anti-Federalist ideal of a public sphere standing for a model of democratic union was nonexistent. For example, Matthew Davis, the Aaron Burr loyalist who collaborated with poet and Republican journalist Philip Freneau on the journal *Time Piece and Literary Companion,* counteracted the Federalist narrative of independent people closely guarded by force and frustrated Brown. Davis delivered his Fourth of July address in New York City before mechanics, tradesmen, and merchants, many having democratic sympathies. He asks the men to remember their fathers instead of Washington; to recollect how "the little band of heroes, unprovided with the conveniences, and scarcely supplied with the necessaries of war, braved the summer's scorching heat, and winter's freezing cold, and vanquished armies numerous, organized, and disciplined."[41] The common soldier had won the war *despite* incompetent military leaders, government officials, and avaricious merchants, all of whom profited from the conflict, leaving the soldiers without food, proper clothing, and arms. By telling the story of a democratic "band of heroes," Davis informs the audience that they are the true heirs to the revolutionary legacy.

Davis's address is the single exception to the block of Fourth of July orations in the *Monthly Magazine,* reviewed by Brown, all of which advocate a strict Federalist agenda. However, one should not mistake Brown's decision to include an oration diverting from the Federalist cause as a sign of his impartiality; Brown is Bercovitch's Federalist Jeremiah exorcising dissent. Through juxtaposition Brown simply reinforces the political atmosphere represented in the festival. He treats Davis rudely, the fate of a democratic straw man, castigating him for teaching children the "bitter spirit of national enmity," and doubting the "justness and propriety [of] recounting to our children the cruelties and barbarity of that nation [Britain] during our revolutionary war."[42] Confronted with the consistent "national enmity" directed against France in the *Monthly Magazine,* Brown's judgment only makes sense in the context of an imperialist politics characterized by the 1794 Anglo-American alliance (the Jay Treaty) and the Federalist war program. "Enmity" toward Britain lacked, in Brown's words, "justness and propriety," but a "zealous" diatribe against France, as his reviews demonstrate, meant the orator was a "friend" of the Federalist government. Just as the description of the festival celebrates a solid union by marginalizing "speculative creeds," Brown's review helps to forge consensus by censuring Davis's language of popular democracy as expressing decidedly un-American principles.

Brown's decision to introduce the July 1799 issue with the festival description stresses the conservative position of the *Monthly Magazine*. On closer examination, the unquestioned allegiance displayed in the toasts, orations, and songs also informs the representation of social space in the festival. As a mechanism of consensus, the festival text in the issue makes the Independence Day feast—the antithesis to the Fast Day emphasis on deprivation and mourning—the focus of the celebration. Stern has argued that public festival, in the sentimental fiction of Susanna Rowson, enacts a space of communion, an "egalitarian space" free of mediation and coercion. On the "grim underside," however, is the "figurative grave" of the "legally unacknowledged others."[43] This insight sheds light on how far the Independence Day feast deviates from the egalitarian ideal and conceals an authoritarian impulse. The writer for the *Monthly Magazine* works hard to make the preparations for the celebration appear like any "political function."[44] One prominent individual is chosen to invite the guests from a list given to him by a committee of "select men." The list guarantees a uniform environment where Federalist politics are represented as the norm: "Some distinctions are of course made in the framing of this list, as to the education, property, and especially the political opinions of the guests." A class of "select men" stand opposed to subversive politics; by turning their list into a symbolic tool that confirms national allegiance, the seemingly objective account judges and literally marginalizes opposition.

Near the conclusion he reintroduces feast imagery to illustrate the price of political nonconformity: "[T]he minor party assembled and feasted by themselves. No menaces, or other proofs of opposition, were given." While the ritualistic feast allegorizes a nation celebrating its sovereignty, it also helps to define mainstream opinion. Lacking the appropriate "political opinions," the "minor party" is thrust to the edge and excluded from the main table, the classical figure of civic fraternity. The reappearance of the feast imagery attests to a wish for national unity deriving from and managed by members of a privileged political class. For those citizens invited to the "banquet," the "disciples of all the professions, the students of all the sciences, the lovers of literature and poetry," the observer bestows civic agency denied those absent from the main table. He associates agency emanating from below, from the interests of mechanics and tradesmen, whom Davis addresses as America's "little band of heroes," with dissension.[45]

The account of the Independence Day festival depicts a segregated social space in which dissent is excluded and the imperialist values of Federalists prevail. Social historians have long observed the symbolic importance of Independence Day celebrations to a laboring class who invoked a revolutionary legacy defined by an egalitarian rather than a hierarchical world view. By situating the Fourth of July address in its historical context, one comes to understand the political choices Brown was making as editor and writer for the *Monthly Magazine*. The Fourth of July address changed its shape according to shifts in national opinion, but the form derived from orations that celebrated the Boston Massacre as the moment of liberation from tyranny. The ritualized conflict between unarmed individuals and the monarchy did not strengthen Federalist ideology in the late eighteenth century, particularly because their opponents pointed to aggressive laws and military expansion as sure signs of the Federalist desire for imperial power.

By subtracting armed resistance to an unjust empire and substituting a new enemy, France for England, the Federalists designed a symbolic patriotic substitute for the Boston Massacre. In order to evade the implications of empire and armed resistances associated with the Boston Massacre, the new Fourth of July address celebrated the secure guiding hand of government by calling attention to the centralized power of the Constitution rather than the list of grievances against the British empire contained in the Declaration. Just as Federalist officials managed the George Washington eulogy and legislators designed the Sedition Acts to restrict the opposition of Republican newspapers and silence dissent, Federalists ensured conformity by controlling the selection of Independence Day orators. Holding to the same pattern as the selection of the George Washington eulogists, an ideology of independence was institutionalized.[46] Orators were elected from the local elite and, at the very least, possessed an ambition to rise to that station. Take, for example, the case of eighteen-year-old Daniel

Webster, who delivered a Fourth of July address to his junior class at Dartmouth, a brief review of which Brown includes in the journal. The standard historicization of Webster begins with his famous antiwar speech, the "Rockingham Memorial," delivered to Federalists in 1812, but his career as an orator of American empire began with war hysteria of the late eighteenth century. On Independence Day, Webster ignores a Federalist tradition that emphasizes the "principles of civil liberty" enclosed in the Constitution and Declaration of Independence. Instead, he turns to the necessity of war in upholding Federalist rule. Webster reflects on the military battles that have led "to its present grandeur the empire of Columbia." The Federalist government had made it possible to imagine the expansion of U.S. power across the globe, a power that Webster, in true imperial fashion, views as freedom. Celebrating the rising political and commercial empire, with its "commerce . . . extended from pole to pole" and a new navy to "bear the thunder of freedom around the ball," Webster asks his classmates on July Fourth to remember the names of every American "warrior."[47] Not only does young Webster reveal the public enthusiasm for imperial adventures, but he also highlights how commerce and military power—rather than colonies—will conceal aims of global domination with the rhetoric of American exceptionalism and the old English imperial aim of spreading freedom throughout the world.

The lost warrior Webster laments is Washington, which typifies how orators wove together the two public rituals of death and regeneration. The Christian doctrine of salvation, as Fliegleman reminds us, asserted that all children seek their divine father and find their salvation as members of a new family. Establishing an elastic notion of family, the doctrine "provided the kernel of a revolutionary insight: the title of father was transferable."[48] Webster uses Washington's tomb to mark the shift to a new adoptive father, President John Adams. In the tomb, Washington "sleeps in dull, cold marble," but Adams exemplifies the general's steadfast authority: "the inflexible *Adams* still survives . . . and with a steady hand, draws the disguising veil from the intrigues of foreign enemies and the plots of domestic foes." A citizen who refuses to support Federalist measures against what Webster presents as a double threat—foreign and domestic enemies—betrays the new imperial family. To turn away from Adams is to "disgrace our lineage" and to fail in "the duties incumbent upon us." Webster's conclusion is littered with exclamation points and bold letters as he rallies his fellow students behind the administration's war aims. As children of the new Federalist administration, they must form a united front against French invasion. This meant repossessing the energy of American independence: "Where the courage, where the heroism which animated the patriots of 1776?"[49] In turn, a united front against foreign aggression translated into the desire to send the new navy into new imperial spaces on a mission of freedom.

Federalist legislators found an equal match for their ardor for war in many Fourth of July orators, who also invoked the new military and its potential imperial might as the true safeguard against conspiracies of domestic and foreign foes. Even in speeches by Reverend Elijah Parish and Amos Stoddard, where no inflammatory, demonizing rhetoric works to mobilize support for the Federalist party or their war, the orator stresses the importance of a citizen's duty to support the Federalist administration. Take, for example, Parish, who had much in common with Jedediah Morse: they collaborated on two geographical texts, shared the same religious background, and, like most New England clergymen, promoted themselves as staunch Federalists and true revolutionary Americans. In addition to geographical elements, Parish also learned from Morse about the Illuminati cells working covertly in the United States. "Their secret papers have been discovered," Parish warned his audience on July 4, 1799, which proves that "seventeen are in the US."[50] Since subversives are difficult to detect (but not so difficult that Parish knows exactly seventeen remain at large), Parish relies on a logic of contagion that effectively defines domestic disobedience as a foreign malady:

> Approach not the raging, dying monster. His contagion is the sting of death. . . . watch those ungrateful fouls, who murmur about taxation and oppression, the burdens of government and religion. They have fellowship with our enemies—they are traitors to God and Christianity.[51]

The issue of new taxes to pay for the Federalist military program had by summer begun to increase public dissatisfaction with the war effort. Parish paints those citizens who "murmur" about this abuse with the brush of treason. Translating the act of dissent into a disloyal act, Parish effectively exorcises protest against imperial authority and assimilates its representatives into an alien and Godless "fellowship."

The *Monthly Magazine,* as one outlet for federalism, exhibits how literary and intellectual culture plays an important role in the formation of American imperialism, not only marking the limits of an antidemocratic politics but also justifying imperial expansion into foreign territories as well as into the everyday lives of ordinary people. Brown's festival description illustrates the labor involved in selecting a speaker who possessed enough social status and who could deliver with a little pep. "The choice [of an orator] usually falls upon an advocate, whose occupation gains him respect," one, the author writes, "who has occupied some post in the government or a seat in legislature; who is endowed with talents of haranguing."[52] An orator who possessed the talent to "harangue" could more effectively demonize the opposition as subversives and stake a conservative Federalist claim to the revolutionary impulse. After the festival, the author promises the editor he will "furnish you with copies of all the speeches that I can procure." The actual copies Brown reviews for the magazine follow "The Festival of Independence," and from within that frame, each review written by Brown restricts alternative visions of the Revolution.

FUGITIVE BODIES

Thomas Jefferson described the victory of his Republicans in 1800 as a "Second American Revolution"; likewise, historians conventionally view this development as the inevitable extension of republican principles, a view constructed with Jefferson's narrow victory looming large in the rearview mirror. It is doubtful, without the fact of the Federalist party's collapse, that historians would be able to tell the standard story of an evolving theoretical republicanism in the postrevolutionary years, a creed based in civic harmony and self-determination; its central characters are political elites who temper the Federalists' forgivable excesses, redefine the "public good" for the American lexicon, and begin the expansion of personal liberties. The question of race never comes up, even though a master class helped fashion the famous civic harmony and the issues of slavery and racial justice consistently intervened in national politics throughout the period. Intrinsic to the story of the "Second American Revolution" was another revolution occurring over the course of the 1790s: race emerged as a central trope in public discourse when rival factions realized its usefulness in laying claim to America's revolutionary legacy and yoking it to the aims of empire.[53] Race was even more than a trope, however, since the practices of racial domination lay at the root of U.S. imperialism and often erased the divisions between the nation's two warring parties.

At a time when African-Americans like Absalom Jones and Richard Allen worked to abolish the Fugitive Slave Law, and in the process promoted a vision of a truly democratic nation, Federalists rendered legitimate democratic disagreement as a *racialized* threat of insurrection. They exploited a growing national concern that disaffected slaves would attack the nation, a ploy designed to make republican slaveholders loyal to Federalist authority. A key subject of President Adams's congressional address in 1799 was a request for an increase of military forces to protect the United States from French-inspired slave insurrections.[54] On a campaign trip to South Carolina, Adams's secretary of state, Timothy Pickering, stunned his audience with a claim that he possessed evidence that the feared slave leader Toussaint-Louverture, in conspiracy with France, would land outside Charleston with an army of his rebels. Such Federalist conspiracy tales give credence to Michael Rogin's claim that "racial and political demonology define the peculiarities of the historic American empire."[55] Former secretary of war Henry Knox supported Pickering's claim that France had secretly recruited ten thousand slaves to raise an insurrection. The rumors carried by Pickering and Knox soon found their way into print in the language of a horrific nursery verse: "Take care, take care, you sleepy Southern Fools, your Negroes will probably be your masters this day twelve month."[56] So provocative was Pickering's speech and the rumors of insurrection, that Southern Republicans defected en masse to the Federalist cause. Having exploited the public's fears of a slave uprising, Federalists won supporters throughout the United States, justified the increase in army troops in the South, and heightened the feeling that only Federalist authority could protect America.

These cases, in which Federalists exploited racial anxiety as an electioneering strategy, were a well-worn tactic and not very subtle. Less obvious are the ways in which the political problem of slavery was a training ground for the Federalist administration's attack on civil liberties at the end of the decade. Before 1793 black and white antislavery activists constituted, I argue, a democratic movement, but it ceased to be viable when Paris and Saint-Domingue erupted in violence that same year.[57] Part of the standard explanation for the movement's demise is that the spectacles of violence frightened many white supporters, driving them away from the cause, but the role the U.S. government played was also critical. The passage of the 1793 Fugitive Slave Law was designed to bolster Article IV of the Constitution, a clause giving masters the legal power to recover their escaped slaves. Centralizing white power to an even greater degree against African-Americans, the 1793 law made it even more difficult for escaped slaves to find refuge in Northern states and brought the power of the federal government against the movement, effectively criminalizing sympathetic whites' cross-racial affiliation with African-American abolitionists. In addition to the Fugitive Slave Law, local and state laws, passed throughout the decade, were aimed at policing the movement of free African-Americans and slaves, especially the twelve thousand Saint-Dominguan slaves brought into the United States by their fleeing masters and suspected of being "infected with the malady of insurrection."[58]

Repositioned in this context, the imperial turn of U.S. culture at the end of the century is something more than an anomalous bump on the path toward true republicanism and democracy. Imperial power, specifically the passage of the Alien and Sedition Acts, was based on the government's efforts to both control a slave population it saw as foreign "malady" and to neutralize the divisiveness of slavery issues in Congress. Possessing the arbitrary federal power to seize and banish a suspect, the Fugitive Slave Law of 1793 was a precedent for the later Alien Act. The Federalists' willingness to use the government to destroy opposition—which James Roger Sharp calls the third stage of the decade's political evolution—was only a new phase if we fail to reconcile the government's repeated attempts since the Revolution to dominate free African-Americans and slaves. The view this opens on the rise and fall of the Federalists takes us back to 1793, when their political authority became even more tightly wound with the notion of a white Republic made vulnerable by the threat of slave enemies.[59] In such a scenario, excessive imperial force was the solution that, in a few short years, would cross racial borders and be directed against white citizens.

The racial component of U.S. imperial culture entered literary discourse in a number of ways, many of which appear in the *Monthly Magazine,* but the racial element diffused across a variety of narratives. No single generic form contained it. Race played an essential role in many political pamphlets, including *An Address to the Government on Cession of Louisiana to the French,* written by Brown in 1803. He draws from his experience as a novelist to invent a wild tale of an impending slave insurrection that awaits the final order from France. Published after the discovery in 1800 of a slave conspiracy in Virginia called Gabriel's Rebellion, the pamphlet further convinced many Americans of the truth of a historical fear—the French were going to use a proxy army of slaves to threaten the United States. The tract is a consummate example of Federalist propaganda, a fictional letter written by an imaginary French official, who claims that America, torn by factionalism and discontent, is ripe for the picking.[60] While Brown writes no such tracts for the *Monthly Magazine,* that journal did present a range of narratives that contemplated race, slavery, and the precarious future of the United States. So why does Brown, whose stated editorial desire was to steer clear of divisive subjects, present these potentially combustible texts in the *Monthly Magazine*? And how does the larger context of Federalist politics deepen our understanding of the *Monthly Magazine* as a vehicle of white racial solidarity?

In this context, Brown's inclusion of excerpts from Johann Blumenbach's "Observations on the Conformation and Capacity of Negroes" does not appear controversial. As Linnaeus's successor, Blumenbach's environmental theory established a quantitative system for racial classification with five varieties of mankind (American, Ethiopian, Caucasian, Mongolian, and Malay), although he believed one could not definitively demarcate between the races. Even though he argued against those who claimed the superiority or inferiority of a particular race, he was an avid collector of human skulls and believed the Caucasian skull was the most perfect of his collection. Brown's selections affirm the self-assurance of enlightened "men of feeling"—despite their retreat from the antislavery movement after 1793, they hold to a belief in the biological equivalency of the human species. Blumenbach's first claim notes the diversity among "Negroes": "between one Negro and another, there is as much (if not more) difference in the color and lineaments of the face, as between real Negroes, and other varieties of the human species."[61] His second claim links biology with aptitude: "That the Negroes, in the mental faculties, are not inferior to the rest of the human race." The excerpts that Brown includes are standard representations of the environmental theory of racial classification before it begins to change into nineteenth-century pseudoscience. A reader might have wondered where the *Monthly Magazine* was leading with these speculations on race.

In the next issue, Brown uses the "Original Communication"—placed below the masthead on the front page where it was guaranteed to attract interest—to extend the debate on "Negro capacity." If Blumenbach's scientific "observations" reassured readers of a humanistic conception of a single humanity—at least at the origin of mankind before extreme climates changed the universal color white into darker shades—then the headline of this particular issue, "Thoughts on the Probable Termination of Negro Slavery in the U.S.A." alludes to the possibility of abolition, if not for the important qualifier. "Probable" reassures readers that slavery will disappear without altering the Constitution or violating the rights of white property owners. Signed by H. L., the article recycles the conjectures at the core of the period's liberal response to the slavery crisis by listing reasons for the inevitable disappearance of the slave population. First, both nonimportation—a euphemism meaning the approaching end of the international slave trade—and harsh labor conditions will "decrease stock"; second, the slave population will decrease by manumission; finally, the slave population will decline because the Southwest is supposedly an infertile desert and because westward expansion will bring migrants with opinions "incompatible with slavery."[62]

Underlying this desire to believe in the disappearance of slavery is a unique blending of religion and reason that, according to H. L., is responsible for creating a national "current of opinion [that] sits strongly against Negro servitude." The Constitution is the expression of this secular religion, and H. L. positions the Constitution as the superior, if intentionally ambiguous, force: "above all, the fundamental rules of our government have a real or apparent hostility with every species of slavery." For H. L., the Constitution's ambiguity affirms the crux of the problem and allows for only a conservative response. The ambiguity demands stewardship in the body of national legislators who can manage the available options; one should trust the representative government to interpret the Constitution and define the public good. If this is done and government is allowed to roll unobstructed, H. L. assures the reader with an unmistakable irony to the historian, "slavery will nearly disappear from the US in a less period than Sixty years."[63]

Brown positions the "Original Communication," as he did in the Independence Day issue of July 1799, to frame and influence the reception of the reader. Following the commentary of H. L., Brown reviews an oration that he summarizes as attacking the "gradual encroachment on the rights of persons" caused by two "species" of slavery, imprisonment for debt and African bondage.[64] In response to the orator's plea to change our conduct toward "imprisoned debtors and slaves," Brown applauds legislators who are finding "remedies for these evils" that will preserve equally the "just claims for all."[65] Quite in keeping with his eventual commercial career, which included investments in the global slave economy, Brown ignores the slave and expresses his concern that financial restitution is made to the three white parties in the debate—creditor, debtor, and slave owner. The transition from Blumenbach's scientific argument for monogenesis to H. L.'s and Brown's political pleas to trust in government constitutes the boundaries for a liberal, moral response to slavery in 1799. The periodical's moral stance has a political price. It allows the reader to profess fraternity with, and sympathy for, the suffering slave, but only to reinforce the logic of white equality and the racial borders of U.S. imperialism.

It is not surprising that white Americans, anxious about the potential of a French-led slave insurrection, would place the "race problem" on the back burner. This had been the case since 1793, the last year that the question of emancipation had been discussed in public. In less than ten years a biracial antislavery movement—which had inspired innumerable orations on themes of universal freedom, converted Benjamin Franklin, and produced visions of a multiracial America—was dead. Instead of arguing for racial justice, as they had done before 1793, white supporters after 1793 undercut the interests of African-Americans by insisting that they subordinate their democratic demands to the larger interests of the white nation. Serving as a new context for these putative humanitarian views, the *Monthly Magazine* emits a clear signal about the necessity of this new demand and adapts Blumenbach's conclusions, once voiced by white protestors against slavery, to the purpose of sweeping political discourse clean of racial issues. If imperial expansion confuses racial identity and national affiliation, then cleansing race from national discourse attempts to reclaim stable racial and national identities. The language needed to express this cleansing at the turn of the century is tainted—as all language of cleansing must be— by a disregard for the humanity of African-Americans that the writer either cannot or simply does not care to hide. After Blumenbach argues for the biological and mental equality of blacks, H. L. calmly relates to the reader that thousands of slaves will gradually disappear over the course of sixty years. Does he offer a colonization fantasy or propose a lukewarm manumission law? He does neither, assuring the reader that either a severe, debilitating climate will kill the remaining slaves off or they will simply work themselves to death. The juxtaposition of a statement of black humanity and a calculated genocide is alarming. An explanation eludes any republican context, since calculation about racial domination and (finally) homogeneous white power are structures of American imperialism reaching back to the New York Conspiracy trials in 1741 and earlier. Brown contributes to this chilling calm by reassuring the reader that the legislature, acting according to a political vision that passed the hostile measures of 1798, that cynically inflamed racial tensions for political gain, that drove Irish, French, and German immigrants from the country, that encouraged militias to attack nonconformists, will provide "just claims for all."

For the *Monthly Magazine* to lobby for trust in the government's ability to convert the "fundamental rules" into freedom and civil rights for African-Americans is, to put it mildly, disingenuous when one considers the legal attacks leveled against black America during the 1790s. The fact that delegates at the Constitutional Convention sanctioned slavery in the United States is well-known, but this national agreement needed continuous repair. The boundaries between black and white, slave and freeman, required constant policing, and in order to understand the nature of race relations in the 1790s, one must follow a trail of evidence linking the domination of slaves and free African-Americans with an aggressive constitutional government. The 1790 Naturalization Act, an early example of racial segregation, restricted citizenship rights to whites, and that same year legislators—alarmed by an "overzealous" petition by abolitionists to eliminate the slave trade—agreed not to discuss slavery issues. The 1793 Fugitive Slave Law reinforced this agreement. During this period, most states extended political agency to free African-Americans, but the vision of upheaval in Paris and Saint-Domingue made slavery the proverbial third rail of American politics, and few politicians dared to touch it. While they feared exacerbating factionalism by challenging the unofficial gag order on slavery issues, they also did not want to be responsible for opening up a larger debate about civil liberties. When we interject race into the story of American republicanism, we arrive at a development left out of our grand narrative. Even though factionalism afflicted political discourse in the 1790s, Federalists and Republicans were in agreement more often than not on slavery issues, and both groups built a legislative wall of silence around the slavery dilemma.

Since racial domination is considered an essential component of U.S. imperial culture, I would like to suggest that Federalist and Republican rivals defined the nature of American imperialism over the course of the decade as they jointly opposed the democratic visions of African-Americans. In other words, forms of racial domination—such as local and federal slave codes, local policing, slave raiders, and segregation—were as fundamental to the cultural elaboration of imperial power as the rise of Federalist militarism and expansion into the West Indies. At least, African-American activists interpreted legislation like the Fugitive Slave Law as the symbolic epicenter of imperialist authority. More than a treaty between free and slave states, the law protected the property of slaveholding interests, eliminated the North as the slave's potential refuge, and allowed white kidnappers— more real to free African-Americans than the Bavarian Illuminati were to white Americans—to terrorize black freemen living in the North. The unscrupulous kidnapper is the caricature in historical memory of a nation debased by slavery, but the kidnapper is to American imperialism as Thomas Jefferson is to American republicanism. The kidnapper embodied longstanding imperial practices, incorporated into the Constitution and consistently upheld by Congress. As I discussed in the introduction, the fate of Absalom Jones's petition to abolish the Fugitive Slave Law, written on behalf of four runaway slaves, is a remarkable illustration of how imperial power, working through Republican machinery, maintained racial division. Failing to reconcile the imperial remnants of racial domination distorts historical perception of this vexed period of U.S. culture. For example, more than Jones, African-American activists consistently approached Congress with appeals to abolish the 1793 Fugitive Slave Law, often employing the language of democracy in ways that anticipated abolitionism. Like committed democrats who, as Dana Nelson reminds us, understand such change as protracted, risky, and chaotic, they returned with another petition in 1800. Egerton speculates that they may have been emboldened by Gabriel's attempted slave uprising that same year, but it is equally plausible that the anti-Federalist petition movement flooding Congress also had an effect. Unlike those petitions against new taxes and military programs, Jones and the other activists were defeated. Yet historians leave Jones and other antislavery activists out of traditional accounts of democratic or "populist impulse" in the early republic, even though their efforts to repeal the Fugitive Slave Law can, at the same time, be interpreted (and then forgotten) as the "unanticipated first fruits of nationhood."[66] What is also left out of the narrative of American republicanism is how a legislature—essentially divided on all major social, political, and economic aims—unified in their effort to maintain the fugitive status of African-Americans because their resistance could literally bring down the Constitution and destroy political order. Referring back to the 1790 congressional decision to suppress racial issues, Harrison Gray Otis, a Federalist who had pledged famously to keep all the "wild Irish" out of the United States, justified an 85–1 vote to suppress the petition. Congress should not, Otis explained, "legislate upon subjects from which the General Government is precluded by the Constitution, and have a tendency to create disquiet."[67]

The act of manumission provides an additional example of how trust in congressional "remedies" actually undercut efforts by African-Americans to find protection under the law. During the 1780s, Pennsylvania had passed gradual abolition acts in 1780 and 1788 that prohibited their owners from taking slaves out of the state and granted emancipation within six months. When waves of French planters and their slaves landed in Philadelphia after fleeing uprisings in the Caribbean, they landed in an unfriendly refuge, but with the help of Philadelphia lawyers they created a legal loophole that enabled them to keep their investments. After manumitting their slaves, their masters immediately signed them to indentures and, as a result, reclaimed their labor until they were twenty-eight years old. An indentures market emerged in the capital. As Gary Nash writes, "Among 659 slaves released between 1787 and 1810, only 45 received their freedom outright. Many French planter refugees, particularly those in need of cash, recouped their investment in chattel property by quickly selling the indentures of manumitted bondsmen and bondswomen."[68] Because a majority of slave refugees were young children, the master class effectively retained many of them until the early 1820s. The practice of lengthy indentures, Nash continues, "assured French slave owners of commanding the labor of ex-slaves for much of their physically productive years, while obviating the need to support such servants after their physical resources dwindled."[69] Brown's advice in the *Monthly Magazine* to believe in the ameliorating "rules of our government" is unsettling, particularly when one considers how his brief law career coincided with the rise of the indentures market in Philadelphia.

This new development certainly demonstrated to him that the institutions of slavery were essential to advancing U.S. geopolitical aims and would not soon be abolished.

The bipartisan suppression of racial justice was a hegemonic operation of U.S. imperial culture that included the April 1800 issue of the *Monthly Magazine*, which excerpted a lengthy address on "Negro Leprosy" delivered by Benjamin Rush, a physician and former revolutionary leader widely known as enlightened on the race question. Rush theorizes that black skin was a disease that inevitably created personal and social strife, and he speculates on how science could cure such a malady.[70] Referring his listeners to a picture of Henry Moss hanging in Peale's museum, Rush says that leprosy occasionally manifests itself as black and white spots, and the leper always gives off a "disagreeable smell," which reminds Rush of a "mortified limb." This odor, Rush believes, "continues with a slight modification in the African to this day." Rush's surgical experience is one source for his racial theory. He claims a "morbid insensibility in the Negroes" that prevents blacks from feeling the same kind of sensations as whites. "I have amputated the legs of many Negroes," Rush declares, "who have held the upper part of the limb themselves." Rush finishes his discourse by describing common symptoms that link blacks with lepers: venereal diseases, "a big lip and a flat nose," and a "wooly head."[71]

As a disease, blackness resembles the yellow fever; while a particular symptom might not be infectious or even visible, the disease is, nevertheless, always present. Rush's diagnosis of an infectious blackness initiates what Foucault describes as the diffusion of disciplinary mechanisms throughout a society to help prevent a deadly mixing of bodies.[72] The taxonomy of the black leper is a "political dream" that allows for the strict regulation of social and political spaces. At century's end in the United States, where miscegenation and segregation laws served to maintain imperial culture, the dream of the black leper helped Rush to illustrate the necessary prevention of white-black interaction. A white woman would acquire "not only a dark color, but several features of a Negro, by marrying and living with a black man."[73] As a result of these "reasons" and "facts," Rush can respond to slavery with the self-confidence and sympathy of an enlightened citizen. In her reading of Rush's theory of "Negro Leprosy," Nelson remarks that "Rush envisions his search for a medical cure as a corrective to the tyranny of 'whites,' both ignorant and learned."[74] When the cure for blackness is discovered, all false white claims of superiority—"founded in ignorance," since African-Americans are supposedly diseased—will be replaced by a stabilizing belief in the common descent of the human race. The political consequences of Rush's theory are enormous for the future of the United States. If the man of science can find a cure for blackness and defeat the dangerous "state of leprosy," then the cure will erase an equation of blackness with inferiority, thus removing one of the central justifications for slavery.[75] His effusiveness on the disease of blackness veils, as Nelson aptly puts it, an underlying "scientific discourse on whiteness," which does political work. Rush "[deploys] race as a 'white' strategy for managing social anxieties about instability, chaos, and fragmentation"; thus, blackness works as a "receptacle for social instability in the early Republic, and makes whiteness correlatively available as a recuperative (and supra-class) social order."[76] Brown's decision to excerpt Rush's address on "Negro Leprosy" in the *Monthly Magazine* does not seem so curious when one considers how what I'll call Rush's "white strategy" complements nationalist politics and its imperialist aims in 1800. Rush internalizes the contagion metaphors current in political discourse; maintaining social and political stability meant preserving the purity of the white population, since racial mixture complicated all questions of civil rights and national loyalty. Rush draws a clinical line that undermined the efforts of African-American abolitionists to petition federal and state governments for legal remedies. Racial difference obstructed the functioning of what Rush elsewhere envisioned as a smooth Republican machine; it failed to eliminate the institutions of slavery. Whether accidentally or by design, Rush's clinical fantasy has the effect of restoring theoretical harmony by fortifying white racial solidarity and "union."[77] Given the period's vitriolic political rhetoric, which cultivated feelings of racial anxiety and imperialist enthusiasm for war, we can anticipate Rush's fantasies of racial difference that call forth a nation unified in whiteness.

The theories on race and slavery excerpted in the *Monthly Magazine* leave the reader with no alternative interpretation, no opposition, no ambivalence. The journal's position persuaded a reader to acquiesce to a society stabilized by a constitution with a short but explicit tradition of suppressing the civil rights of African-Americans in the interests of a stable white republic. Even more tragic than Brown's journal, however, were leaders who learned how to make political capital out of racial tensions; by century's end, theories of racial contagion and racial difference provided in part the justification for a new imperialism, which included a military apparatus that could protect vulnerable racial boundaries inside as well as outside the United States. As I discuss in the next chapter, any depiction of the period's nationalism or factionalism remains incomplete, and presents a partial depiction of Brown's involvement, if we fail to consider the emergence of this imperial force in American culture. However, as long as war, slavery, and commercial expansion defined the growth of the United States, the threat of insurrection and retribution would continue to undermine national harmony. Those fugitive histories become the subject of Brown's novel *Arthur Mervyn,* a story of America's recovery from a fever that resembles the political unconscious of a nation divided by race.

chapter 3

Imperial Geographies and
Arthur Mervyn

As the American Revolution drew to a close, John Adams reflected on the future of a national economy forced to thrive without the benefit of a protective English empire, its merchants, consumers, and favorable mercantile policies. Political independence would be bittersweet unless the United States could develop a trade policy that could rebuild a North American economy destroyed by warfare. Lacking a continental infrastructure that could make profitable connections between the eastern seaboard and the western frontier, the United States focused its efforts on developing the previous British imperial relationship with the Caribbean slave economies. "The commerce of the West Indian islands is a part of the American system of commerce," Adams wrote. "They can neither do without us, nor we without them."[1] This insight, that commercial expansion into West Indian markets would strengthen U.S. power, was a cornerstone of nationalist ideology in postrevolutionary America.

Perceiving the importance of the commercial relationship between the United States and the West Indies, Adams also draws our attention to a general dynamic that was to circumscribe U.S. imperialism at the end of the eighteenth century. According to William Weeks, this fundamental dynamic is founded on the "principle of political and economic union and what it promised: safety from attack and the prospect of boundless expansion."[2] As we saw in the first two chapters, political and economic expansion into West Indian territories, resulting from armed conflicts like the War of Jenkins's Ear and the Federalists' undeclared war against France, effectively undermined public feelings of union and collective security. Whether directed by England or the United States, imperial expansion into the Caribbean frontier inspired fantasies of freedoms *beyond* these borders, as well as fears of a sudden slave invasion or insurrection *inside* them. Racial antipathy and exclusion were central to this particular imperial dynamic in the United States, which stressed the need for military action to protect the union and to keep the public safe. At the end of the eighteenth century, Federalists exploited what they believed to be a two-front war against France and internal enemies. They joined their rhetoric of insecurity with a new military apparatus that could patrol the murky border and defend the nation from an alien invasion.

The promise of military protection and expansion characterized the transition from British to American imperialism during the revolutionary and postrevolutionary periods. Political and commercial leaders in the United States yoked their future to the international slave economy, particularly the raw materials and market incentives of the West Indies. After England and France went to war in 1793, this development became even more significant, as the Western Hemisphere's most lucrative markets fell into the lap of U.S. merchants and investors. Reluctant to sacrifice profits from their rich plantations in the East and West Indies, England and France designed a trade policy that enabled them to wage an economic war. The re-export trade, as the policy was called, redirected all exports to the United States, where her neutral ships would then safely carry English and French goods to the European continent. The profits gained through the "neutral trade" created unparalleled prosperity in the United States during the 1790s and helped to pull the nation out of an economic depression.[3]

Of course, the theoretical premise of U.S. imperialism—that it would live up to its promise to protect commerce and to guarantee expansion—is only half the story. More compelling are the moments when this promise collides with forces that resist its inexorable push. For example, expansion into the West Indies exacerbated racial anxiety in the United States and created real and imagined security threats, such as slave rebels infiltrating the country along routes already pioneered by enterprising merchants. This had a profound effect on U.S. political development, since a culture of terror worked, as I will discuss, alongside republican mechanisms. Thus, if Federalists had not joined the terrifying scenario of insurrectionary slaves to French subversion within national borders, it is doubtful, in my eyes, if

Congress would have been willing to give Federalists all they asked for in 1798; it would have been more difficult to do the imperial work of locating, and then linking, internal and foreign enemies; without the specter of a slave invasion force, the Federalist electioneering strategy would not have been as effective in persuading Southern Republicans to switch their allegiances and support Federalist war measures; and, finally, lacking the fiction of an insurrectionary force of slaves, Federalists would have been hard-pressed to sustain the public's war fever and extend it into 1799–1800. Exploiting the public's appetite for war is always a gamble; there is a measure of justice that it backfired on the Federalists. Without the racial component, perhaps Federalism would have remained a moderate conservative politics rather than accelerating toward its imperial pitch in 1798–1799. All the same, their racist rhetoric played a key role in the victory of Jefferson and the Republicans, a triumph already conditioned by forms of racial domination that undermined inclusive notions of republicanism.[4]

As I discussed in the last chapter, Charles Brockden Brown presented an array of politically charged texts in the *Monthly Magazine;* in this chapter, I turn to Brown's fictional practice. If Brown's *Edgar Huntley* articulates, in one sense, the perils of expansion as a bloody conflict between Native Americans and encroaching whites in the West, then the geography of *Arthur Mervyn* shifts our attention to the Caribbean frontier. Brown's double vision in both novels, narrating a nation caught between the vices of East and West, is not surprising: he composed *Edgar Huntley* and *Arthur Mervyn* simultaneously, while the United States was trying to establish an imperial presence in the West Indies.[5] The novel enacts a crisis of national identity in which engagement with and dependence on West Indian markets inflicts a deadly pestilence on the citizens living in Philadelphia, the nation's capital in 1793. One of the worst disasters to ever hit an American city, the epidemic killed approximately 5,000 Philadelphians that summer, drove 17,000 into the countryside and neighboring states, caused national and local leaders to flee, and abandoned the poor without food or medical care.[6] The yellow fever was not simply a public health crisis: it decimated commerce, heightened class and racial conflict, and toppled city government. The inexplicable disease generated theories for its presence in Philadelphia. As Philip Gould has observed, many Philadelphians interpreted the epidemic as divine retribution for national sins, particularly the "ills of commercial society."[7] No matter what the particular discourse, talk of the yellow fever gravitated toward the Caribbean frontier, where a legion of "contagionists" located the origin of the epidemic. While the West Indian trade fueled an economic resurgence, there was concern among contagionists that contact with that region was a deadly corruption. Furthermore, a massive slave insurrection and imperial conflict in Saint-Domingue between England, France, and Toussaint-Louverture's slave forces increased public anxiety about contact with a region infected by disorder. The unstable sugar islands—subject to slave insurrections, imperial mercantilism, piracy, and European politics—meant that a nation bent on profiting from Caribbean resources would inevitably suffer from the same imperial tremors.[8]

Some American patriots had long held that an imperial relationship with the West Indies would generate wealth and foster collective security, yet going to war over Caribbean markets in the late 1790s fostered political and social instability in the United States. This chapter argues that the metaphor of contagion that Brown locates at the heart of *Arthur Mervyn* calls the achievements of this "American system of commerce" into question.[9] The opening section examines the cultural consequences of expanding U.S. military and economic power into the West Indies. National dependence on the global slave economy no longer promised wealth but the terrifying possibility that permeable borders might allow "dirty money" gained through slavery to pass through into the United States as secretly as the yellow fever. The next section traces the movement of this currency as it flows between the West Indies and the United States. Focusing on the key metaphor of contagion, this analysis will identify two entwined strands of meaning and demonstrate how the fortunes of empire in the Caribbean slave economies gets figured in the novel as racial unrest in Philadelphia. Bill Christopherson remarks, "*Arthur Mervyn* is certainly one of the first books in our literary canon to register the drama of black presence as perceived by whites and to hint, however obliquely, at the nightmare of black insurrection."[10] By positioning the contagion metaphor within a context of war and imperial expansion, I build on Christopherson's insight to demonstrate how Brown's novel collides with, rather than obliquely hinting at, a black presence that assumes forms of resistance.

One specific form this presence takes is the fever; section three of this chapter, "A Federalist Fever," locates the fever's movement in a hidden imperial economy that crosses national borders and connects the fluid wealth of slave plantations to the fortunes of the novel's most important businessmen. This section argues that Philadelphia cannot be reborn as a healthy city until Arthur returns the money, tainted by empire, to its rightful owner, now transplanted in the South. Consequently, the final section, "Bush Hill and the Rebirth of Whiteness," reevaluates the conclusion to *Arthur Mervyn*, often read as utopian because of the passing of the fever and the hero's aspirations to run the city hospital. The novel's ending fails to reconcile this appeal to America's patriotic ideals with Brown's earlier, feverish meditations on the connections between racial volatility and the U.S. presence in the West Indies. I conclude by putting Brown's depiction of the pestilence in dialogue with other accounts of the fever, particularly a 1794 report written by Absalom Jones and Richard Allen, two black leaders of the Free African Society. This contest of memories—and of two fevers, white and black—resists the novel's final vision of a white republic. It is this final irony of *Arthur Mervyn*, however, that makes it a prime location from which to examine connections between race, empire, and American identity at the end of the Federalist era.

HOUSES OF SPECULATION

The grand theme of dispossession in *Arthur Mervyn* is a result of a suddenly unstable economy that violates the pastoral security of Arthur and robs him of his republican legacy: a civic identity rooted in the family farm. His father, after marrying the former servant, casts Arthur out of the house:

> I had no independent provision; but I was the only child of my father, and had reasonably hoped to succeed to his patrimony. On this hope I had built a thousand agreeable visions. . . . I had no wish beyond the trade of agriculture, and beyond the opulence which an hundred acres would give.[11]

Voicing a Jeffersonian ideal of the yeoman as the quintessential American, as well as a legal fact that possession of property constituted personhood in the United States, Arthur speaks a clever language of excess. He measures his "opulence" not in a currency of bank notes but in relation to the "thousand agreeable visions" once, but no longer, made possible by his republican inheritance.

Leaving the farm, Arthur travels to Philadelphia, a city plagued by greed and disease, and he becomes an apprentice to Welbeck, the novel's villain, who teaches Arthur about new forms of opulence that originate outside national borders. In the first part of the story, Arthur periodically returns to the country, a journey that depicts the hero's struggle for virtue and independence, and after one farmer gives him refuge, Arthur promises to marry his daughter. Some critics believe that Arthur's decision to marry Eliza indicates Brown's original vision for the novel, a tale of contrast between pastoral charms and city vices, especially since once Arthur returns to the city in part two, he ultimately abandons Eliza and vows to marry Achsa Fielding, an older Jewish woman of considerable property.[12] While we cannot ignore Arthur's willingness to trade his rural roots for the city's promise, his transformation does not indicate a fall from the pastoral into the den of urban corruption. What is remarkable about Brown's handling of such a classical distinction is his ambiguous depiction of it. His genius lies in perceiving the effects of an international economy that connects the West Indies and Philadelphia, even crossing the Schuylkill River—running alongside the old Mervyn farm—and into the country. Rather than representing a departure from pastoral virtue, his decision to abandon Eliza and return to the city is the hero's realization that he has acted foolishly nostalgic for a republican legacy that his own father has already sold out from under him.

Brown's talent for undermining such divisions, and making them appear ironic, is part of the enjoyment of reading *Arthur Mervyn*. So, too, is Brown's refusal to present a hero whose character is only skin-deep. Is Arthur truly the innocent country youth he claims to be, misled by the villain, Welbeck, but having seen the light, faithfully following Doctor Stevens's path to enlightenment? Which surrogate father has he finally decided to emulate—the virtuous Stevens, a benefactor who inspires Arthur to dedicate his future to medicine and to the city's public health? Or is Arthur's innocence and pledge nothing more than proof that he is Welbeck's star pupil and only wishes to elude the law? When the novel ends, the contest between these father figures is left undecided, and the reader can only base a judgment on the hero's virtuous self-representation and sentimental rhetoric. This situation is certain to make apprehensive those readers familiar with Brown's proclivity for deception.

The reason for the plot's ambiguity and chaotic social relations is the result of a lesson Arthur learned about American commerce on his first journey into the city: the city's economy is corrupt, and the citizens who

IMPERIAL GEOGRAPHIES 81

profit from it use their republican character to disguise their cunning. Homeless in the city, Arthur meets Wallace, who offers him safe lodging in the home of his employer, the Thetford family. Entering the central room, Arthur gazes at "decorations of opulence" and feels "beguiled by some spell." Wallace takes advantage of Arthur's disorientation and, as a prank, leads him into a chamber in the main bedroom and locks him in for the night. It is Arthur's figurative blindness, however, that allows him to perceive the criminality beneath the glare of the family fortune. When Thetford and his wife speak outside the door, Arthur can hear "the most secret transactions of their lives," including a venture to defraud a wealthy investor (eventually, Arthur will discover that this "nabob" is Welbeck). The plot to defraud the "nabob" is based in the West Indian markets, an illicit exchange that characterizes the family. From the closet, trapped within the "perilous precincts of private property," Arthur learns the corrupt nature of the Thetford family and its investments. Whenever domestic virtue becomes a subject of scrutiny in *Arthur Mervyn*, critic Eliza Hinds reminds us that commerce is usually at the root of the problem: "[the] emphasis on the economic locates virtue in the realm of money—especially where the money comes from."[13] Families and their houses in Philadelphia, such as the Thetfords', stand as allegorical structures for an imperial economy tied to fantasies of wealth to be gained in the Caribbean.

The illicit order of the Thetford house only begins to manifest the novel's anxiety about the effects of an imperial economy on republican virtues; when Arthur's flight from the Thetfords ends at Welbeck's magnificent estate, one encounters the novel's key allegory for U.S. imperial expansion into the West Indies. Analogous to the commercial boom that transformed the United States during the 1790s, Welbeck's house is literally produced through a global economy, specifically the U.S.–Caribbean exchange. Gazing at the structure through a "knot-hole" in the fence, Arthur sees a "house of the loftiest and most stately order. It seemed like a recent erection, had all the gloss of novelty, and exhibited to my unpracticed eyes, the magnificence of palaces."[14] Welbeck does not own the mansion—he leases it with money stolen from a planter in the West Indies named Vincentio Lodi. Looking for a safe refuge in the United States, Lodi sells his plantation, but before he can transport his family, a slave assassinates him. Lodi's son takes possession of the assets, launders it, manages to maintain the stability of the patrimonial line, but then he suddenly falls ill and dies upon arriving in the United

States. Welbeck takes possession of the property, which had assumed different shapes. First, a plantation and slaves were transformed into Portuguese gold, then converted into banknotes, then invested in Welbeck's mansion. Such shape-shifting capital, however, fails to erase the slave's assassination of the elder Lodi. The symbol of an insurrectionary slave, one willing to die as a martyr to freedom, has taken root in the nation's capital.

Importantly, neither Welbeck nor his leased abode is "native" to the United States. The mansion is a foreign castle, a "recent erection" in the capital city, while Welbeck resembles the structure's impermanent "gloss of novelty"—his position in Philadelphia is as artificial and deceptive as the mansion's facade. With the Lodi money in hand, Welbeck enters the United States and is reborn as a man of position. Reminiscing about his "sudden appearance on the stage," Welbeck, a master forger, describes his fraudulent exterior self:

> There was no difficulty in persuading the world that Welbeck was a personage of opulence and rank. My birth and previous adventures it was proper to conceal. . . . My sudden appearance on the stage, my stately reserve, my splendid habitation and my circumspect deportment were sufficient to intitle [sic] me to homage.[15]

What lay behind Welbeck's facade? One clue lay in the past, in the West Indies, where a destitute Welbeck was "on the brink of suicide."[16] With the Lodi pocketbook and its $20,000 in banknotes now in his possession, Welbeck feels the "larger portion of my anguish . . . now removed," and the wealth from the plantation transforms him into a person of "opulence and rank." His new identity makes him a desirable figure in the city, a wealthy newcomer who can fund a trading venture. His "splendid habitation," the new American mansion that conceals the West Indian planter's stolen patrimony, persuades one group of investors. Arthur looks on in wonder as his patron works the room, his eyes glittering like gold, "operat[ing] like magic" on the crowd.[17]

A FEDERALIST FEVER

Depicting the transfer of West Indian wealth to the United States as a debilitating disease, *Arthur Mervyn* resembles political discourse at the height of the war crisis with France, which depicted the Caribbean as infected with disorder and violence. Prophesizing an invasion of slave rebels from Saint-Domingue, Federalist hawks employed a metaphor of contagion in order to justify the war and the expenses of building a new military establishment.[18] How do we reconcile this cynical view of the West Indies with a commercial policy that professed the benefits of U.S. expansion into the region? This fundamental contradiction was actually a catalyst for increasing the American presence in Caribbean markets. Driven by military and commercial aims, the United States sent its forces into the Caribbean, and then, following close behind under their protection, merchant vessels would methodically open specific ports for trade. The Federalist administration went so far as to order the new U.S. Navy to intervene in the civil war in Saint-Domingue. The United States favored Toussaint-Louverture because his forces could protect U.S. merchant vessels; the United States provided his slave forces with food, weapons, and military training, while the navy shelled ports controlled by Rigaud, Toussaint-Louverture's rival.[19]

U.S. involvement in the West Indies was particularly troublesome for those Americans who believed the decade's yellow fever outbreaks were tied to expansion and warfare in the Caribbean. In this sense, attacking the foreign source of the epidemic was conflated with underlying concerns about the harmful effects of U.S. imperial power. In *A Sketch of the Rise and Progress of the Yellow Fever,* published in 1799, the same year as the first part of *Arthur Mervyn,* William Currie argued that historically the West Indies was the common origin of the disease, but unless accompanied by war, yellow fever rarely reached epidemic proportions. As proof, Currie claimed that the rebellion in Saint-Domingue in 1793, as well as armed conflict between England and France, ended a decade that displayed no traces of disease in the sugar islands. It was not a coincidence for Currie, and other members of the "foreign contagion" school, that this new war between the United States and France coincided with a yellow fever outbreak in American cities that threatened national health and prosperity. According to advocates of "foreign contagion," military action put more naval and merchant vessels in the West Indies, increasing the odds of the disease's importation into the United States. Currie believed the disease followed in the path of the war's major battles, as well as in the wake of merchant vessels arriving in American ports. "With those islands [Guadaloupe and Saint-Domingue] the American commerce has been carried to

a greater extent than with any others; and as the American vessels necessarily have had frequent communication with the [naval] fleets in the ports
of those islands, they could not avoid being infected." Two other advocates of "foreign contagion," Thomas Condie and Richard Folwell, also
subscribed to the theory that war in the West Indies created the necessary
conditions for an outbreak, particularly since increased trade with the West
Indies imported infected commodities into the United States.[20]

In the U.S. context, imperial actions created a national climate in which
the dominant metaphors of disease and race blurred the borders between
international and domestic arenas. Contagion was an elastic metaphor
throughout the 1790s because of its utility in articulating the spread of a
variety of social, political, and economic threats. Competing uses of the
contagion metaphor—pointing to either a French-led invasion, subversive
political activity, or the importation of yellow fever—were easily conflated
in public consciousness. For example, taking yellow fever as both historical subject and dominant metaphor, Brown's *Arthur Mervyn* communicates a cultural anxiety that close ties with the West Indies would produce
disease not simply reducible to yellow fever.[21] Instead of profit and national
health, engagement with the West Indies might create the potential for
both the region's racial violence and its infected assets to cross the border
into the United States as secretly and violently as the yellow fever.

Recall, in *Arthur Mervyn,* the terrible chain reaction caused by Vincentio
Lodi's decision to liquidate his Guadeloupe plantation and transfer it to
the United States: Lodi's slave assassinates him and his slave kills himself,
while his son lands in America, promptly dying of fever and making it
possible for Welbeck to obtain the fortune. I want to call attention to the
first link in this deadly chain, the conflict between master and slave:

> It appeared that the elder Lodi had flattered one of his slaves with the pros-
> pect of his freedom, but had, nevertheless, included this slave in the sale
> that he made of his estate. Actuated by revenge, the slave assassinated Lodi
> in the open street and resigned himself, without a struggle, to the punish-
> ment which the law had provided for such an occasion.[22]

Discovering that Lodi has included him in the bill of sale, the slave resists
his own reification as an asset and takes revenge. On one level, the scene,
pitting the desperate slave against his owner, stages the anxiety at the core

of a slave society, but another level emerges when one measures the slave's action against the narrator's reportage. The assassination resists the slave's reification and makes his humanity visible. No longer reduced to a figure in Lodi's ledger, the slave commits a crime that restores his physical body to the transaction, a visibility that the master class must overpower. The narrator, however, cannot admit either that the slave's punishment is execution or that the master class's legal system will also be "actuated by revenge." While the plot requires that the narrator report on the event, the narrator's circumlocution betrays ambivalence about probing the assassination's effects on social and political order. Not interested in inciting an insurrection, the narrator surmises, the slave targeted only his master and quietly accepted his execution, or "the punishment which the law had provided for such an occasion." The narrator's circumlocution evokes a national anxiety about linking future prosperity to a region characterized by imperial warfare and insurrection.

Since this anxiety was replayed over and over in political discourse of the late 1790s, one can easily forget that *Arthur Mervyn* is a historical novel about the yellow fever epidemic of 1793. One of the first American historical novels, *Arthur Mervyn* manifests what would become standard about the genre: the novel loudly announces its desire to represent a faithful depiction of the past, while keeping quiet about another wish, to make a statement about how this past continues to haunt the present.[23] Brown's metaphor of contagion blurs the boundaries between past and present precisely because its logic was used to comprehend both the horrible yellow fever outbreaks every summer from 1793 to 1800 and mounting fears of racial violence and political unrest. (In 1798 alone, yellow fever outbreaks occurred in Portsmouth, Boston, New London, New York, Philadelphia, Chester, Wilmington, and Charleston.) In *Arthur Mervyn,* the slaves who prey on sick and dying Philadelphians during the fever embody the threat, a threat heightened by Federalist propaganda in the last years of the decade, that Caribbean slaves would join with foreign agitators and attack America.

The novel's depiction of the public's racial anxiety in 1793 begins to take shape when Arthur returns to Philadelphia at the height of the yellow fever to rescue Wallace. Here the metaphors of contagion and race meet under hazardous circumstances. Upon his arrival, Arthur discovers an apocalyptic city where dying white citizens are at the mercy of African-Americans. In his search for Wallace, Arthur enters a house and finds a dead body.

Surveying the "traces of pillage" that indicate a home invasion, Arthur fears some "casual or mercenary attendant, had not only contributed to hasten the death of the patient, but had rifled his property and fled."[24] The identity of the attendant exists only as a manifestation of Arthur's foreboding: "In the present state of my thoughts, I was prone to suspect the worst." And the worst, during the yellow fever of 1793, was an African-American figure who terrorized the city while seemingly immune to the fever. Looking to slaves in the Caribbean who were thought to use the pestilence as a weapon of insurrection, white Philadelphians anticipated a similar type of militancy as the city weakened and African-Americans maintained their strength. They were accused of robbing unprotected houses, neglecting infected masters, extorting white patients, burying the still breathing, and, as the above example shows, pillaging their master's possessions (*Arthur Mervyn* dramatizes all of these accusations).

Arthur's first glance at the crime scene reveals evidence of a thief and murderer, but no detail indicates whether the figure is black or white. But as Arthur tries to ease his panic with thoughts that the disorder did not result from a crime, a mirror reflects the presence of the "mercenary":

> A moment scarcely elapsed, when some appearance in the mirror, which hung over the table, called my attention. It was a human figure. Nothing could be briefer than the glance I fixed upon this apparition, yet there was room enough for the vague conception to suggest itself, that the dying man had started from his bed and was approaching me. This belief was, at the same instant, confuted, by the survey of his form and garb. One eye, a scar upon his cheek, a tawny skin, a form grotesquely misproportioned, brawney as Hercules, and habited in livery, composed, as it were, the parts of one view.[25]

The mirror, which in the end allows Arthur a fragmented picture, reflects the nightmare of racial violence, the "train of horrors," afflicting the city during the fever. What was at first simply a "vague suggestion" of a "human figure" gradually takes the shape of the dead man's ghost. Arthur gazes at the whole scene through a filter made hazy by his presupposition of a criminal presence: "To perceive, to fear, and to confront this apparition were blended into one sentiment." As a result, his panic gives the ambiguous apparition the form of a dark-skinned villain. Death does not just "hover" like a vapor in that moment when it becomes embodied; Arthur's panic has dressed the figure with the exaggerated strength, physical marks, and "livery" of the vengeful slave. His presupposition has come alive.

Part of the racial sickness Brown depicts in *Arthur Mervyn* reveals not only the particular animosity directed toward African-Americans during the yellow fever of 1793 but also how imperial power shaped race relations *inside* as well as *outside* national borders.[26] The reflection Arthur sees in the mirror is an invention of Federalist propaganda, a black villain preying on a vulnerable nation. During the war fever of 1798, the logic of contagion articulated the spread of racial violence from Caribbean and Southern borders into Northern cities. As Saint-Domingue collapsed in flames during the summer of 1798, an eighteen-month string of fires, stretching from New England to Georgia, convinced city dwellers that their slaves had carried the battle to the United States. That same summer, thousands of French planters and their slaves fled to the United States to seek refuge just as another yellow fever epidemic ravaged Philadelphia and other cities. The fever helped to focus public scrutiny on free African-Americans and slaves, and rumors circulated that the former were covert agents and guilty of supplying weapons to a secret army of enemies in the United States. The state of Pennsylvania reacted by arbitrarily expelling many free African-Americans.[27]

How is Brown's representation of Arthur's conflict with the black "Hercules" positioned within the imperial context of racial domination prevalent in the last years of the eighteenth century? First, the use of the mirror gives a reflection one cannot trust—changing, in only an instant, from nondescript human figure to a dead man, then to a black mercenary. Rather than a stable signifier of racial disorder, the ambiguous black figure in the mirror evokes suspicions of a foreign threat, in the figure of the slave, who also can appear covertly as a trusted servant. Second, the narrator claims that fear has warped Arthur's perception of the anonymous African-American, which suggests Brown's own understanding of the role race played in upholding the racial hierarchies of U.S. imperial culture. Paranoia was one important effect, and the author dramatizes its force by making the onrushing shadow, which Arthur perceives as issuing forth from the dead man's ghost, more than an abstraction. It literally attacks him, delivering "a blow upon [my] temple." In a dreamlike state, still groggy from the blow, Arthur discovers his hands and feet bound and "two grim and gigantic figures . . . stooped to lift [me] from the earth. Their purpose methought was to cast me into this abyss." On one level, the scene depicts a fear of

African-Americans particular to the 1793 setting. The pestilence imprisoned those left in the city, closed the houses, and the dread of being overpowered by the disease appears to Arthur in the symbolic form of his dark assailants. They embody Arthur's earlier reflection on the "horrors that pursue mankind"; his own fantasy of liberation ultimately dispels the nightmare of racial violence—central to the working of U.S. imperial power in any period— derived from his fear. "My terrors were unspeakable," Arthur declares, "and I struggled with such force, that my bonds snapt and I found myself at liberty. At this moment my senses returned and I opened my eyes."[28]

The captivity scenario, sensational and sentimental, displaces history and transforms it into a mythic American narrative in which the white hero is a victim of savage violence.[29] The scenario initiates the movement between temporal levels—1793 and 1799—and reveals the relationship between racial anxiety and amnesia in the white American unifying against a foreign enemy. While Brown intends to deliver a realist account of the epidemic, racial anxiety produces Arthur's opaque view of reality. Whether the mirror, his fear, or a loss of consciousness causes such misrecognition, the endangered white hero and his black assailant depict the ambiguity inherent in the period's paranoid narratives about imminent invasion and insurrection.[30] The analogy that Brown draws between Arthur's bondage and captivity was a narrative strategy also featured in *Edgar Huntley*. In that novel, Edgar rescues a young girl held captive by Native antagonists, and from this experience the hero learns how to kill in defending his community from racial incursions. It is not unusual for a captivity narrative to demarcate national and cultural borders. Christopher Castiglia argues that the "metaphoric usefulness of captivity" to an author lies in the genre's capacity to evoke an era's political and racial anxieties. And for this reason, I would add, the captivity narrative is an inferior form for representing history. An ideology of white supremacy conditions the narrative's interpretation of events; the resulting narrative effectively "stabilize[d] the borders of cultures and nations by insisting that the narratives document essentially differentiated racial identities."[31] Thus, the captivity narrative's essential racial fictions called forth a white nation held "hostage" by the forces of evil—a phrase Castiglia uses in his reading of Patty Hearst's captivity—and, in *Edgar Huntley*, the white hero's rescue of the young girl and his massacre of her Native captors help to restore a defensible racial border of the United States.

Likewise, the captivity scenario in *Arthur Mervyn,* which illustrates a white man shackled by his black assailants and held hostage in a diseased city, tells a larger story about national crisis. Just as his "gigantic persecutors" have pushed him to a precipice overlooking a "bottomless gulf," Arthur frees himself from the shackles, but not before observing an accomplice waiting "with hammer and nails in his hand, as ready to replace and fasten the lid of the coffin, as soon as its burthen should be received."[32] The tale of African-Americans burying white victims alive was often told during the yellow fever of 1793. Yet Arthur's nightmare of black assailants evokes the larger obsession dominating U.S. imperial culture after 1793: invasion from Saint-Domingue's slave rebels, aided by France, while American slaves and free African-Americans stood waiting nearby. One additional detail suggests that panic has warped Arthur's perception of events: when the "mist and confusion" vanished, one of the men helps Arthur to his feet— an inexplicable act considering the testimony of the assault—and one is left to wonder if the black men, Arthur's "gigantic persecutors," were friends or enemies.

As metaphor, captivity served a special purpose in an American historical novel like *Arthur Mervyn,* since the generic tendency is to move backward and forward in time and trace historical fragments as they reappear in the present. Having promised to give the reader a realistic picture of the massive upheaval caused by the epidemic, Brown must have found the captivity scenario to be especially useful because it reproduced the loss of perception, ambiguity, and racial antagonism that characterized the crisis. Captivity established a bridge between literary and political discourse because it effectively converted the logic of empire into a scenario of contagion by which a nation battles against both incoming enemies and slaves within its borders. This dynamic was fundamental to Federalist propaganda after 1798; having depicted a vulnerable America held hostage by French and alien subversion, their narrative helped to justify a militaristic response to the crisis. Thus, the captivity scenario in *Arthur Mervyn* has a dual purpose in its bridging of past and present: while Arthur's bondage articulates the racial tension exacerbated by the 1793 fever, his captivity is also an emblem for how national hysteria after 1798 could make one forget and distort historical memory, particularly recollections of a risky U.S. experiment in the West Indies that disrupted national stability.[33]

Still dazed by the assault, Arthur meets a Quaker neighbor, who pleads with him to stay in the house; rest will allow Arthur to avoid contracting the disease, as well as to provide guard against the mercenaries' return. Arthur makes this curious decision after the Quaker tells him about the character and true identity of the dead man, Maravegli, a young man dedicated to virtue and knowledge, and who, at the height of the fever, became the self-appointed protector of a family of "helpless females." The Quaker informs Arthur that

> The house has no one to defend it. It was purchased and furnished by the last possessor, but the whole family, including mistress, children and servants, were cut off in a single week. Perhaps no one in America can claim the property. Meanwhile plunderers are numerous and active. An house thus totally deserted, and replenished with valuable furniture, will, I fear, become their prey. Tonight, nothing can be done rendering it secure, but staying in it. Art thou willing to remain here till the morrow?[34]

After listening to the Quaker's plea, Arthur "embraced" the proposal. In this bizarre twist of the captivity scenario, the entire family is dead, leaving the house, and all its valuables, as the key character. Unlike Maravegli, who tried, and failed, to protect the vulnerable maidens from disease, Arthur chooses to defend the house from becoming "prey" to the black mercenaries. Of course, a citizen standing guard outside an upper-class home during the 1793 yellow fever epidemic is a historically accurate depiction, even if it is a duty unfit for the novel's hero. Nevertheless, this event faithfully represents a realistic scene from 1793 while, at the same time, evoking the ambiguous political climate after 1798. The impending collision between the lone hero and the black mercenaries, who have already assaulted him, suggests a national space made insecure by war and racial tension.

Robert Levine suggests that republican maidens in distress or under assault in Brown's novels are a key political allegory for a vulnerable nation.[35] This scene is unusual, however, because the epidemic has already wiped out the Maravegli women, which has no effect on Arthur's decision to guard their property from attack. While this duty may not appear especially heroic, Arthur's selfless behavior looks more patriotic when positioned within the context of imperialism in the late 1790s. Widely perceived as a conflict over trade routes and commercial freedom, the undeclared war against the French

empire located America's future health and prosperity in the lucrative West
Indian markets. Success was measured by the percentage drop in insurance
rates for Atlantic ventures and by the security of American property. Such
a climate helps to explain Arthur's decision to risk his life while defending
the valuables of the home front from foreign attack. At state and federal
levels, new imperial spaces were mapped within local and national borders, while legal measures stabilized *white* social spaces from racial incursions. For example, during the 1790s, black refugees from the South and
the Caribbean hoped to find peace in the "city of refuge"—which led to
a tripling of the African-American population in ten years—while white
Philadelphians experienced apprehension that "took the form of conspiracy."[36] In 1799, with Federalists warning of a military invasion, Pennsylvania used the same strategy to control social space as at the height of the
yellow fever epidemic of 1793. That summer the state instituted quaran-
tine acts to prevent the spread or importation of the disease from the
Caribbean; in 1799, terrified by the stream of former slaves and free African-
Americans coming into the city, political leaders made a similar attempt
to halt the flood of these "dangerous" immigrants into the city. Consequently, President Adams authorized Pennsylvania to "erect a barrier on
its borders against incoming blacks."[37]

   Arthur's motive to secure the property of the "only descendant of an
illustrious house of Venice" against racial violence resembles the white panic
after the barrier's erection. Mired in pestilence, Arthur is not concerned
about the health threat posed by African-Americans but by their insurrectionary, anti-imperial force. A persuasive rumor of 1799 told how hundreds of slaves, "well armed, trained to war," were about to land in New
Jersey and march to Philadelphia.[38] Captivity elaborated this culture of
conspiracy: the twinned captivity scenarios in *Arthur Mervyn* capture the
social tension embodied in the state's actions taken to stabilize racial boundaries and political order. Collapsed national and racial boundaries, the spread
of alien subversion, and fears of impending conflict in American cities—
a breakdown of social and political order caused, in part, by U.S. imperial expansion into the West Indies—finds expression in the story of captivity. While Arthur snaps his chains and escapes death, the uncertain fate
of the Venetian Maragvegli house, once the beacon of capitalism and a
healthy national economy, stands as a warning to a diseased white America of its imminent collapse.

HIDDEN ECONOMY

Slaves and free African-Americans who escaped to the North were a political danger to the new United States. In the view of congressional representatives from the slave states, their Northern refuge undercut the civil rights of slaveholders. Consequently, the Fugitive Slave Law passed by Congress in 1793 was a compromise that protected the rights of the slaveholder even as it erected another constitutional barrier against freedom-seeking African-Americans. Congressional debate on the law demonstrated how slavery, imperialism, commerce, and nationhood were bound up together in political discourse. One solution was to make the federal government a recipient of proceeds gained from reselling captured slaves back to the South, a solution rejected by those unwilling to accept federal participation in slave trafficking. Just as the presence of the word "slave" in the preamble would have brought the nation's political contradictions to the surface, federal involvement in selling fugitive slaves would undercut the patriotic claim that its people were only the unfortunate republican heirs of a slave system instituted by the British empire. Such congressional accounting, in one sense, was symbolic. It could not, however, conceal how the United States also maintained a dependence on the global slave economy, especially since the combined force of the U.S. Navy and American merchants sought control of Caribbean slave markets at the end of the eighteenth century.[39]

By refusing proceeds gained through the selling of fugitive slaves, the United States attempted to separate its republican principles from an imperial economic foundation that contradicted them. This preoccupation to sort clean from dirty money, while fixed on the fugitive slave in 1793, broadened in the years after to include increased U.S. activity in the West Indian markets. The family fortunes in *Arthur Meryvn* are all connected to the global slave economy; the moment the pestilence enters the city, the infectious origin of this affluence is revealed. Only recently have critics begun to consider the effects of the global slave economy on *Arthur Mervyn*. In her study of the "shadowy world of slavery" in Brown's novel, Goddu remarks that the "specter of slavery lurks in every economic transaction. Money from slave societies ubiquitously circulates to America, revealing America's international and domestic economies' dependence on slavery."[40] Goddu's frank admission of how slavery was always bound up with issues of nationhood is unusual, particularly since critics continue to dismiss the significance of the global slave economy in Brown's career.[41] Yet the life-line between the United States and the West Indies, what President Adams called the "American system of commerce," is the force that bends the narrative arc in *Arthur Mervyn*.

Before the yellow fever strikes Philadelphia in *Arthur Mervyn*, a family like the Thetfords, who profited from fraudulent investments in the West Indies, presented a "plausible exterior" and a "general integrity" to the world. During the outbreak, however, the source of their income is revealed. The Thetfords exploit a "boom" caused by a paucity of resources in the quarantined city, a decision that exposes the family to yellow fever and death. Doctor Stevens, the moral exemplar of the novel, condemns a home that loves profit more than countrymen. "This man's coffers," laments Stevens, "were supplied by the despair of honest men and the stratagems of rogues."[42] Stevens articulates a larger concern about the corrupt source of wealth in a free republic, since in the "coffers" of the Thetford house, like in the United States itself, are fortunes of empire. An important plot twist in *Arthur Mervyn*, one that will lead to Welbeck's death and Arthur's rebirth as an honest American youth, is linked to this corrupt fortune, buried, unbeknownst to Welbeck, in the basement of his house. This second fortune—once again the liquidated assets of a West Indian slave plantation—is also translated into banknotes, transferred to Philadelphia, entangled with death and disease, and separated from its planter-owners. What the novel proposes is that if Arthur can join this missing fortune with the Maurice family, now stranded in Baltimore, then he can clear his name and recuperate himself as a viable republican. This is no easy task, particularly because of the money's infectious origin:

> The Lady thought it eligible to sell her husband's property in Jamaica, the Island becoming hourly more exposed to the chances of war and revolution, and transfer it to the United States, where she purposes henceforth to reside.[43]

The Maurice and Lodi estates, which constitute the two largest household economies in the novel, share the same disease. The confused grammar of the passage—the "it" of the last clause ambiguously refers to either revolution or property—reveals the unstable origin. The transfer is told in the language of a pestilence choosing its victims arbitrarily, implying that the fortune, "exposed to the chances of war and revolution," upon its burial in America, has infected Philadelphia with corruption and murder.

Similar to the Lodi transfer, the violence attaching itself to the exchange leads to the courier's death. After arriving in the city with Maurice's wealth hidden in a money belt, the courier, Watson, looks to settle an old score with Welbeck, enters a duel with him, and is killed. With the money belt still hidden from his sight, Welbeck buries the corpse. As long as the fortune of empire lies festering in the basement, exposing the republican capital to disease and violence, Philadelphia cannot remain healthy, but how does one remove the infected money without risking contact with disease? Doctor Stevens, upon learning the money's location, can't figure it out:

> It was just to restore these bills to their true owner; but how could this be done without hazardous processes and tedious disclosures? To whom ought these disclosures be made? By what authority or agency could these half-decayed limbs be dug up, and the lost treasure be taken from amidst the horrible corruption in which it was immersed?[44]

Looking on the same building earlier in the narrative, Arthur described the palatial facade, which makes the mansion seem like a foreign transplant. Now Stevens turns his attention to the house's basement. The money found there is marked by crime (Welbeck's murder), speculation, empire and revolution (the money derives from the Maurices' desire to flee Jamaica), and the profits gained from slave labor. The result is a hybrid home whose structure is rooted not in republican farms but in the imperial network of the slave trade. Confused and afraid, Stevens backs away from solving an American conundrum: he refuses to separate the "lost treasure" from its source, the "horrible corruption" of empire, slavery, and homicide that brought it into the republic's capital city. Contact risks entangling oneself "in a maze of perils and suspicions, of concealments and evasions, from which he could not hope to escape with his reputation inviolate. The proper method was through the agency of the law."[45]

Doctor Stevens's alarm is a warning that anybody who comes into contact with the money risks infection. It corrupts individuals, such as the courier Watson, who loses his life as well as his character as a result of carrying the Maurice fortune into the United States.

Deriving from the Caribbean, "mysterious and unseen," the money belt

strapped to Watson infiltrates the city like the yellow fever. Once the infected capital has attached itself to his body, he can't shake it, like the
Philadelphians in 1793 who hung garlic ropes around their necks, soaked
their clothes in vinegar, and smoked cigars, hoping that these odors would
cleanse the air of disease. Employing secrecy and cunning all in the name
of security inevitably casts a shadow over this man chosen for his "probity
and disinterestedness."[46] Watson does not become a stronger, more finan-
cially secure individual as a result of his complicity in the commercial
exchange; on the contrary, he loses his autonomy, forfeits his good name,
and is shot dead. Failing to deliver, and buried with the fortune, Watson
carries the infection, an association that groups him together with Arthur's
black assailants. With a slave owner's estate strapped to his white body,
Watson is pursued like a runaway slave.

The Fugitive Slave Law was a major effort aimed at dividing the contradictory relationship between constitutional liberty and chattel slavery;
while a missing white man, suspected of robbery, might not initially bring
to mind this law, it did address the growing problem of unfettered or lost
property. Both the economic fugitive and the fugitive slave undermined
the property relations that defined constitutional liberty in the United
States; for some Americans both figures were victims of an economic system that robbed them of their freedoms. My association of Watson with
a fugitive slave is hardly an anachronistic critical imposition. This part-
nership was apparent in public discourse in the late eighteenth century,
even in Brown's *Monthly Magazine,* where he included and reviewed a tract
that advocated easing two types of bondage: the institutions of slavery,
including the Fugitive Slave Law, and harsh laws that imprisoned the
debtor. Brown's review actively supports the writer who castigates a reckless business culture that conscripts a white individual's liberty as severely
as the system of slavery subjugates the slave.

In its pursuit of Watson, the novel borrows from this context by turning
the courier, an honest friend, into a criminal who easily crosses international borders. His associates draw up and publish an advertisement for
the lost money, complete with "a description of the person and the dress
of the fugitive."[47] His transformation into a fugitive is a sign of America's
rapid fragmentation after exposure to fortunes tainted by their relationship to the global slave economy. As suspicion of Watson demonstrates,
participating in and profiting from these markets undercuts the notion of

a virtuous national economy. Not surprisingly, it is the novel's villain, Welbeck, who eventually learns that a small fortune is buried with the corpse in his basement; unlike the virtuous Doctor Stevens, he bypasses the law and digs up Watson's body. Philip Gould traces Welbeck's criminal behavior back to his childhood in Liverpool, one of the global slave trade's most vital ports, and to his slave trader father. Welbeck is the major figure of corruption in the novel, and as Gould suggests, he embodies its "own fictive version of the triangular trade."[48] I want to extend Gould's reading by following this figure of the slave trade into the South. When Welbeck flees his hybrid mansion—its facade purchased with Lodi's money, its miasmic foundation yet another West Indian slave plantation—with the money belt now attached to himself, it seems logical that he would run to the Southern slave states with his fugitive capital. His flight is the novel's condemnation of one who traffics in dirty money: the corpse exposes the mansion's imperial and criminal foundation; when his creditors send him back to Philadelphia, his final home—debtor's prison, just like his father's—symbolizes his illicit practice. Unlike the magical atmosphere of his former residence, the prison cell is an atmosphere "loaded with the exhalations of disease."[49] This "new residence of Welbeck," Arthur says, contrasting it with the mansion, contains no "splendor, pictured walls, glossy hangings, [or] gilded sofas." On the eve of his death, before Welbeck meets his "fate" in his new "residence," he confesses a late epiphany to Doctor Stevens and Arthur, and hands over the money belt to his former apprentice. "Receive this, said he. In the use of it, be guided by your honesty and by the same advertisement that furnished me the clue by which to recover it. That being secured, the world and I will part forever."[50]

Accepting the money belt from the dying Welbeck, who in turn received it from the dead Watson, suggests an ominous future for Arthur. He, too, must journey into the South, where young American protagonists confront imperial power and risk losing their freedom. Only by returning the money can he clear his name and prove his story that he was innocent, unaware of Welbeck's corrupt schemes. Doctor Stevens warns Arthur how his complicity in exchange will surely mark him as a criminal: "the suspicions . . . respecting the cause of [Watson's] disappearance" would surely implicate whoever returned to Baltimore with the property. If we listen to the period's uneasy discourse on the separation of "clean" federal money from "dirty" slaveholding money, then Arthur's duty has more to do with nation-building than critics have acknowledged. Welbeck's last wish—to "secure" the infectious money to the Maurice family—comprises the novel's solution, or cure, for a city corrupted by the chaos beyond its borders. The solution, however, puts Arthur in a terrible fix: completing the exchange might remove the infection from the city but will jeopardize his well-being.

Because Arthur's redemption must take place in Baltimore, the journey into the South marks a major shift in *Arthur Mervyn*. In contrast to the setting of Philadelphia, the Southern setting functions as a receptacle for dangerous property misplaced in the North. Until his departure, the geography of the novel was primarily bound by the imperial connections between Philadelphia and the West Indies. Traveling south, Arthur completes the disrupted transfer of the Maurice money that originated in Jamaica, became "lost treasure" in Philadelphia, and now, if Arthur is successful, will be deposited in Baltimore. By removing the money from Philadelphia, which carries with it a history of disease, speculation, and slave labor, Arthur creates the possibility of a harmonious future in an American capital detached from the risks of the global slave economy and positively unlike a Southern slaveocracy ruled by the antirepublican practices of brutality and terror.

Arthur's departure in a stagecoach suggests this fantasy of removal and stands as a microcosm for a nation made vulnerable by imperial expansion into the insurrectionary sugar islands. Not only does Arthur carry the money, but he is joined by a French Creole from Saint-Domingue, a monkey, and two female slaves:

> The Frenchman, after passing the suburbs, took out his violin and amused himself with humming to his own *tweedle-tweedle*. The monkey now and then munched an apple, which was given to him from a basket by the blacks, who gazed with stupid wonder, and an exclamatory *La! La!* upon the passing scenery; or chattered to each other in a sort of open-mouthed, half-articulate, monotonous, and sing-song jargon.[51]

Leaving behind the sick city, the stagecoach communicates a national process of self-definition undermined by the presence of these refugees from Saint-Domingue. Perhaps if Arthur were alone in the stagecoach, the doors and windows womblike in their protection, then his trip would resemble a dream of a self-contained, homogeneous nation separated from the racial and linguistic confusion outside. However, enclosed in this heterogeneous space, Arthur feels anxious, like a foreign traveler in his own country. Unlike his first experience of dispossession on the farm, on this occasion the group's racial difference crowds out and alienates Arthur, the solitary white traveler. He cannot understand the Frenchman's songs or the black women's "jargon." The isolation of Arthur, ironically, gives form to an ideal, if besieged, U.S. citizen.[52]

As the stagecoach leaves Pennsylvania behind and moves into the South, Arthur experiences a crisis of white subjectivity. Like any traveler, he surveys the "country as it successively rose before me." But his gaze on every "shape and substance of the fence, the barn and cottage" includes within its scope a racialized human landscape:

> I sometimes gazed at the faces of my *four* companions, and endeavored to discern the differences and sameness between them. I took an exact account of the features, proportions, looks, and gestures of the monkey, the Congolese, and the Creole-Gaul. I compared them together, and examined them apart. I looked at them in a thousand different points of view, and pursued, untired and unsatiated, those trains of reflections which began at each change of tone, feature, and attitude.[53]

Following the chaotic "jargon," this passage attempts to overcome the confusion by a scheme of racial classification that reflects the author's interest in the racial theorist Johann Blumenbach, whose work Brown had excerpted in the *Monthly Magazine*. Arthur's "exact account" begins with the *four* that includes the monkey within the racial grouping of the others. Yet *four* permits Arthur to inspect their physical features from "a thousand different points of view," while separating himself, the *fifth* traveler, from the study. Discerning the racial affiliations that link this mixed cast suggests Arthur's willingness to distinguish his whiteness from his traveling companions. Most important, Arthur views race in a political rather than purely scientific framework. He constructs his sense of whiteness against the political pressures of imperial conflict; the foreign figures he encounters on the road south, on presumably American soil, evoke the infiltration of imperial conflict into the country.

This notion prepares Arthur for his arrival in Baltimore. Just as the houses of Philadelphia served as a barometer for a contaminated city, the Maurice house in Baltimore symbolizes a setting in which hostile relationships between the family and their slaves is a normal state of affairs rather than an aberration. Unlike Arthur's first impressions of Philadelphia's brilliant houses or the nostalgic memories of the Mervyns' lost "rural retreat," he stares at the Maurice house, "naked and dreary," absent of decoration and pastoral "charms."[54] When Arthur rings the bell, the presence of a discourteous slave signals his arrival in a foreign place:

> A Negro came, of a very unpropitious aspect, and opening the door, looked at me in silence. To my question, was Mrs. Maurice to be seen? he made some answer, in a jargon which I could not understand.[55]

Speaking the same "jargon" as the mixed cast in the omnibus, the slave serves a similar function, defining a heterogeneous landscape that puts Arthur's mission in jeopardy. Appearing to Arthur in "silence," his meaning inscrutable, the slave is the house's gatekeeper who prevents Arthur's entry. During the plague Arthur defended the Maravegli house against a black gang, but in the South Arthur becomes a white intruder in a house defined by miscegenation and supported by slavery.

The fever that afflicts Philadelphia was only temporary, a consequence of the city's illicit relationship with the West Indies; in the slaveholding South, however, the fever is a permanent part of society. Whereas the outbreak in Philadelphia has created a situation that puts the republican maidens of the Maravegli house in jeopardy, the Maurice women are tyrants. They command their slaves, "Bob and Cato, two sturdy blacks," to throw Arthur out of the house. While the Maurice women do not speak in "jargon," neither do they offer Arthur sympathy. They strike Arthur as bigoted and mean-spirited: he sees "nothing but sordidness, stupidity, and illiberal suspicion."[56] Hardly weak or pure, the Maurice women are not appropriate figures of "republican womanhood," but they still serve a key function in the novel's demarcation of national borders. The familial metaphor of nationhood can articulate surprising connotations during moments of national duress. According to Shirley Samuels, acute crisis can potentially conflate the "national and bodily symbolics" and produce a transgressive fiction in which incest or miscegenation comes to evoke a threat posed to the national family by some alien force or contagion.[57] As we saw in the last chapter, the familial metaphor is not reducible to a domestic nation; family could also depict an imperial power, its strict hierarchy and values of conformity and whiteness serving to justify military action and economic expansion. In the Baltimore of *Arthur Mervyn*, slavery has ruined the Maurice family. Their demise is not due to their faulty republicanism; rather, the slaveholding family, like the South itself, is an unreformed product of the prerevolutionary age of empire. Lacking a white male patriarch to oversee its dangerous racial mixture, their economic dependence on the assets from their plantation creates a sickly environment. Lethargy manifests itself in the mother's confinement in the bedroom and in her bitter commands to the family's slaves.

On his journey, Arthur dreamed of restoring a lost patrimony to a great family, but to his surprise, "they had wherewithal to live upon beside their Jamaica property."[58] Disappointed by their affluence and, astonishingly, even unwilling to attempt marrying into such a rich, if acrimonious, family, Arthur has learned the truth about his mission. The Maurices, with their fortune still linked to the British empire, can never be a true American family. Thus, even more important than returning their dirty money is Arthur's insistence on following the spirit of the Fugitive Slave Law and removing the slave capital from Philadelphia so that America can regain its health. Ironically, the villain Welbeck's dying wish prepares the reader for the novel's utopian ending where Arthur works toward a healthy republicanism in the U.S. capital.

BUSH HILL AND THE REBIRTH OF WHITENESS

Arthur's mission to Baltimore transforms Philadelphia: Bush Hill, the public hospital dedicated to the city's future health, replaces the diseased structures of American empire: the homes of Welbeck, Thetford, and Maurice and debtor's prison. If American imperialism was characterized by foreign dangers embedded in the nation—"lost treasure" buried in "horrible corruption"—a new republican impulse has arisen from that same ground. Arthur hopes to scale the heights to the "lofty site and pure-airs" of Bush Hill, sitting above Philadelphia like Winthrop's golden city on the hill, and restore the promise of America. With Welbeck dead, Arthur apprentices himself to Doctor Stevens and dreams of becoming Bush Hill's superintendent. In contrast to the global slave economy that ruined the houses of Philadelphia and Baltimore, the presence of Bush Hill at the end of *Arthur Mervyn* suggests the emergence of an ideal republican structure.

Brown's preface indicates his desire to resurrect a memory of the yellow fever that can model exemplary republican behavior. His construction of a useful past is a patriotic narrative designed to help citizens survive in times of crisis:

> [It] is every one's duty to profit by all opportunities of inculcating on mankind the lessons of justice and humanity. The influences of hope and fear, the trials of fortitude and constancy, which took this city, in the autumn of 1793, have, perhaps, never been exceeded in any age. It is but just to snatch some of these from oblivion, and to deliver to posterity a brief but faithful sketch of the condition of the metropolis during that calamity. Men only require to be made acquainted with distress for their compassion and their charity to be awakened.[59]

His eagerness to deliver a "faithful sketch" calls attention to the complexity of historical writing, particularly when composed within U.S. imperial culture. In a turn of phrase that forecasts his career as a Federalist pamphleteer, Brown admits that he wants to get his readers "acquainted with distress," and he hopes that distress will produce sympathy and a more perfect union. Yet the African-American threat lay at the root of his sentimentalism, since such a threat was essential to the novel's suspense. This final section considers the interrelationships among literary, political, and historical writing about race in U.S. imperial culture. A series of questions guides my analysis: How does Brown's story of Philadelphia's rebirth depict the role African-Americans played during the 1793 yellow fever epidemic? Why are the historical fragments that Brown "snatches from oblivion" silent on the heroic efforts of the city's African-American population? Why are African-American figures conspicuously absent in Philadelphia after Arthur returns from his errand into the South? How is this absence connected to a national climate of the 1790s that increasingly came to view African-Americans as a national affliction? Considering these questions ultimately puts the novel's final vision of republican rebirth under historical scrutiny and produces three results. We perceive how race undermines the novel's concluding republican impulse, we encounter the limits of Brown's historical memory, and we examine how African-American leaders contested the dominant history of the yellow fever.

One can answer these questions by putting *Arthur Mervyn* in dialogue with other texts that take the yellow fever epidemic of 1793 as their subject. Since many affluent Philadelphians escaped the horrors of the pestilence by finding refuge outside the city, knowledge of events was dependent on written histories and rumors. (Since Brown did not reside in Philadelphia during the pestilence, his knowledge of crisis necessarily came through hearsay or written accounts.) Like many Philadelphians, Brown was familiar with the most influential history, Matthew Carey's *Short Account of the Malignant Fever*. Race figures prominently in Carey's narrative, since his depiction of the horrors brought on by fever inevitably concludes with the image of heroic white republicans restoring the city's health. Carey showers them with praise. The white citizens are a "noble group," possessing "benevolent motives," blessed with "magnanimity" and willing to sacrifice, and they conduct their "praiseworthy office" in a glorious cause for their fellow citizens. While African-Americans performed just as heroically and selflessly, as I will consider later, Carey excludes them from his representation of worthy republicans. Instead, he rebukes the city's African-American population for allegedly preying on whites, particularly the infamous black grave diggers and nurses who "extorted" money from sick whites. "The great demand for nurses afforded an opportunity for imposition," Carey writes, "which was eagerly seized by some of the vilest of the blacks."[60] He omits any mention of exemplary black conduct, except for a grudging remark about the help offered by the two leaders of the Free African Church, Absalom Jones and Richard Allen. As for the sacrifices that African-Americans made in attending the sick and burying the dead, at the risk of their own lives, Carey is silent. Instead, his narrative transforms African-Americans into a feature of the diseased landscape, uncontrolled and predatory. For example, with a tale similar to the one Brown includes in *Arthur Mervyn*, Carey tells of a conspiracy in which a white ringleader, "a hardened villain from a neighboring state, formed a plot with some negroes to plunder houses."[61] (If indeed this incident were true, it would have been unusual, since the city experienced few burglaries during the crisis.) Carey's *Short Account of the Malignant Fever* thus initiates a historical interpretation of the epidemic that renders the tragedy as a white experience. In addition, the narrative produces a silence around the actual roles played by African-Americans that summer, making it more difficult for future readers to see the event clearly. This distortion marks Brown's novel, which also misrepresents the experience of the African-American

community that summer, and establishes the rebirth of a racially homogeneous city as a natural turn of events.

One further account of the epidemic is offered by J. M. Powell in his
Bring Out Your Dead (1949), the seminal history of the epidemic. At first
glance, he reveals a very different picture from the one represented by
Carey or Brown. The essential difference is that Powell depicts African-
Americans as humanitarian agents of healing. The terror caused by the
fever had instigated a massive white flight—policemen, bankers, council-
men, notaries, aldermen, constables, social welfare workers, and merchants.
Private and public institutions closed; as a result of the mass exodus, bodies began to pile up and "no scavengers could be hired, or anyone to do
the dirty jobs at hand."[62] Prominent whites who had relationships with the
African-American community, such as Benjamin Rush, published urgent
appeals to them to come to the city's aid.[63] The dire circumstances forced
Mayor Clarkson to approach the Free African Society, a socioreligious
organization formed by Absalom Jones in 1787 after he refused to sit in the
back pews of a segregated church. Jones and Richard Allen considered the
mayor's appeal by taking a walk through the devastated city. They witnessed scores of dazed citizens, starving and orphaned children, and dying
whites and made a decision that the Free African Society would organize
a relief effort.[64] They moved quickly, organizing African-American volunteers to carry the dead (a job Jones and Allen performed themselves), to
dispose of soiled beds and to purchase new ones, as well as to drive trans-
ports to Bush Hill and to nurse the sick. Jones and Allen even took up
food distribution, since the flight of the Guardians of the Poor—a body
of citizens who collected a poor box and distributed relief to the indi-
gent—left many Philadelphians on the verge of starvation.[65]

Their heroism did not improve, as Jones and Allen had hoped, the lives
of African-Americans in the years after the epidemic. Perhaps it was the
white community's indifference that channeled their efforts to save the city
into political dissent. One can see in the collective effort to repeal the
Fugitive Slave Law—the focal point of African-American political opposition during the 1790s—the traces of that early catalyst, the yellow fever.[66]
As a moment of cultural self-definition, the yellow fever led to a neglected
document of African-American activism and another account of the epidemic: Absalom Jones and Richard Allen's *A Narrative of the Proceedings of
the Black People* (1794). Dismayed by Carey's charges of black criminality

and infamy, and aware how the racist images he put into circulation undermined their efforts to achieve freedom in America, Jones and Allen wrote
a history of the yellow fever from the African-American point of view. Writing one year after their labors during the fever, they invert the racial typology of Carey's account; they counter his caricatures of African-Americans
who prey on a weakened city with realistic stories of humanitarian action.
Responding to Carey's accusation that "blacks alone [have] taken advantage of the distressed situation of the people," Jones and Allen depict
African-Americans who buried hundreds of poor whites without asking
the destitute families for a penny. Carey represented mainstream opinion,
indeed, he helped shape it, and Jones and Allen use the narrative to address
the larger community that suspects them of wrongdoing. Sometimes this
means interrupting their narrative with some careful bookkeeping, as Jones
and Allen do at one point in order to document the amount of money the
Free African Society paid for beds. Instead of profiting from the yellow
fever, as their critics claimed, Jones and Allen illustrate a net loss of £171.[67]

Each new edition of Carey's *Short Account of the Malignant Fever* brought
in more profits for the publisher, Carey himself, particularly because of an
updated appendix of the names of the dead and advertisements for the
missing.[68] Jones and Allen reverse the charge of extortion leveled by Carey
and claim that he took advantage of a grief-stricken public: "We believe
he has made more money by the sale of his 'scraps' than a dozen of the
greatest extortioners among the black nurses."[69] In addition to Carey, Jones
and Allen accuse political leaders of exploiting African-Americans with
a reckless disregard for their safety. Pointing to the appeals for assistance
printed in newspapers, Jones and Allen question the motives of men like
Benjamin Rush, who touted their immunity to the fever and recruited
them with assurances that "people of our color were not liable to take
the infection."[70] The theory of their immunity was sustained during the
first week of the pestilence because relatively few African-Americans died
during that period. The rapid increase of African-American deaths due to
fever, however, demonstrated a devastating contradiction. Jones and Allen
write:

> When the people of our color had the sickness and died, were imposed
> upon and told it was not with the prevailing sickness, until it had become
> too notorious to be denied, then we were told some few died but not many.

Thus were our services extorted at the peril of our lives, yet you accuse us of extorting a little money from you.[71]

The moral force of this passage is unmistakable. In repudiating the theory of immunity, Jones and Allen describe a system of labor common to plantation societies. Whites command labor at the "peril" of black lives, even when their deaths refuted the theory of their immunity. Carey witnessed these deaths, but he still wrote that "the number of them that were seized with it [fever], was not great."[72] And yet beyond the need to compel black labor at any cost, which in fact kept the city running during the epidemic, white Philadelphians possessed the power to narrate the first stages of the crisis. In control of the discourse, their dominance of print enabled whites to manipulate the cause and number of African-American deaths. One of the more compelling moments in Michael Warner's *Letters of the Republic* is when he speculates on how Olaudah Equiano might have encountered print discourse in the eighteenth century. For Equiano, Warner writes, "Printing constituted and distinguished a specifically white community; in this sense it was more than a neutral medium that whites simply managed to monopolize."[73] Jones and Allen experience a similar encounter with the print medium, as authors like Carey denied the loss of black life, tacitly supported a theory of immunity, and reserved praise for a few white Philadelphians who remained in the city to fight the fever. Jones and Allen attempt to counter these distortions with depictions of African-American humanity, but, careful to avoid any backlash, they do not mention the exodus made by affluent whites. Instead, they tell of the courage of black workers who gave their lives in the service of the city. Surrounded by the plague's horrors, they lost their families due to a strong sense of duty, "many of them having some of their dearest connections sick at the time, and suffering for want, while their husband, wife, father, mother, etc. have been engaged in the service of white people."[74]

Like *Arthur Mervyn*, historical narratives that told only tales of black antagonism helped to repair a white nation's borders violated by imperial conflict, fever, and racial anxiety. Jones and Allen realize that they intervened too late—the cycle of silences had already begun—but they still appeal for sympathy, noting that while the Free African Society worked to save Philadelphia, three editions of Carey's history had already "gone forth in the world." In a discourse dominated by whites, their ironic use of the contagion metaphor focuses attention on the effects of crisis on white racial solidarity. The rumors of black depredation during the fever have produced white racism; Jones and Allen announce their intention to write a counterhistory of reform: "We have many unprovoked enemies, who begrudge us the liberty we enjoy, and our [sic] glad to hear of any complaint against our color, be it just or unjust."[75] The authors hope that a growing racist storm would weaken if Americans could "hear" true examples of loyal African-Americans during the epidemic.

In *Arthur Mervyn,* a majority of the depictions of racial hysteria center on the hospital, Bush Hill. When a youth named Wallace relates his near-death experience there, he gives Arthur a "disastrous picture": "I was confounded and shocked by the magnitude of this evil. The cause of it was obvious. The wretches whom money could purchase, were of course, licentious and unprincipled; superintended and controlled they might be useful instruments, but that superintendence could not be bought."[76] The "wretches" responsible for "this evil" were not perceived as white citizens. Carey's description of Bush Hill as "a human slaughterhouse" reflects a wider belief of city dwellers (and readers of Carey's narrative outside Philadelphia) who associated the hospital with criminal African-American nurses, hearse drivers, and grave diggers. Furthermore, Carey's foundational account of "profligate, abandoned set of nurses and attendants," who left "the dying and the dead . . . indiscriminately mingled together" causes Jones and Allen grave concern. They take issue with Carey's implication that African-Americans were responsible for immorality and violence. Jones and Allen claim that only two African-Americans worked as nurses at Bush Hill during the early stage of the pestilence, and the new hospital administration, dedicated to reform, retained their services.

The recuperation of Arthur at the end of the novel is linked to an early wish to act benevolently, like his exemplar Doctor Stevens, by reforming the hospital. He desires to enter the fray, to manage the "wretches" and make "useful instruments" out of the laborers. His dream is to "offer myself as superintendent of the hospital":

> What qualities were requisite in the governor of such an institution? He must have zeal, diligence, and perseverance. He must act from lofty and pure motives. He must be mild and firm, intrepid and compliant. One perfectly qualified for the office it is desirable, but not possible, to find. A

dispassionate and honest zeal in the cause of duty and humanity, may be of eminent utility. Am I not endowed with this zeal? Cannot my feeble efforts obviate some portion of this evil?[77]

Leaving Welbeck's life of crime behind, Arthur now hopes to emulate men like Stevens who strove to cure the city of the pestilential "evil." Out of the ashes of the plague will rise a new republic and a new citizen, but the passage introduces a crucial subtext. "Firm" governance is a necessity, and his "zeal" will tacitly be directed to the racial "mayhem" that putatively defines an experience at Bush Hill at the height of the plague.

If Brown's and Carey's narratives ultimately reinscribe racial stereotypes and hostilities, Powell's *Bring Out Your Dead* offers instead a more positive and feel-good story about democratic renewal and racial inclusiveness. In his version, Powell charts the eventual triumph of republican values as a reconstituted city government rises from the ashes to save the American capital. Unlike Carey's, Powell's narrative is sensitive to racial hostilities. It works hard to offer up its liberal vision of a city's populace, once divided along racial lines, taking its first steps toward embracing a more civic identity. And yet, notwithstanding its liberal sympathies, Powell's story is as steeped in racial fictions as Carey's. In fact, paradoxically, Powell's account is informed and limited by the very racial hierarchies it seeks to reject. This is significant, since many literary historians rely on Powell's history for their understanding of the epidemic's historical context. At first Powell appears to finish the work Jones and Allen started by praising the efforts of African-Americans, while criticizing the racist battery of them. He laments that "the city shunned them as infected, vilified them as predatory," and acknowledges the tragic fact that "[n]o conduct, however heroic, could expiate the original sin of a dark skin."[78]

But when Powell recounts the refashioning of a political system, the efforts undertaken by the Free African Society are inevitably relegated to the background. Despite his condemnation of racist attitudes, Powell is conspicuously hampered by a conventionally narrow conception of political life in Philadelphia. By the end of this historical narrative, it is clear that the heroes of the piece are those whites who occupy the "middle walks of life." His story is not of black resistance, struggle, and sacrifice, but of whites coming to their senses and rediscovering their American values. Nowhere in the "strangely assorted lot" of citizens who formed that new government is there any mention of an African-American figure. Jones, Allen, and the many African-American workers fail to make it to this republican stage. For Powell's narrative, therefore, racial hierarchies are inherent in the act of history writing. One can measure how Jones and Allen aid our historical understanding of this tragic period. By making African-Americans central to the historical event—as victims, survivors, and heroes—Jones and Allen lay bare the myth of white republicanism that has structured the dominant narratives of the pestilence and Philadelphia's recovery. Reading "against the grain" in this style will help critics develop responses to Trouillot's call for a historiography that reveals the "differential exercise of power that makes some narratives possible and silences others."[79] Brown's fiction, Carey's reportage, and Powell's history are all, in their own ways, allegories about the triumph of the (white) republic. Significantly, such myths are only made possible by reenacting the very racial hierarchies inherent within those myths. In other words, Powell's story about the rise of civic identity can only be told if the role of African-Americans is ignored, a problem shared by all scholars who attempt to write narratives of republicanism. As a result, the labor, emergency funds, and organizing efforts of the Free African Society, whose story Powell told so eloquently earlier in the history, has no final place in the story of Philadelphia's rebirth precisely because historians generally did not view African-Americans as political participants in the white republic. Even Jones and Allen disappear from the narrative. In the end, Powell claims white Americans overcame panic and fear because of three great men—Benjamin Rush, Stephen Girard, and Matthew Clarkson—none of whom are the leaders of the Free African Society.[80]

And yet Powell wrote an illuminating work that continues to be an indispensable aid for scholars. The reason I draw attention to the disappearance of race from his narrative is to demonstrate a fundamental problem in American history writing: the story of the republic had to erase the racial origins of the nation itself. By reading Jones and Allen alongside Brown, Carey, and other interpreters of the yellow fever epidemic, we become aware of how white power shapes historical "facts," embeds them in print archives, and continues to distort historical perception long after the event has passed. For instance, the standard source for many contemporary readers of *Arthur Mervyn* is the bicentennial publication edited and introduced by esteemed literary historian Norman Grabo. After a summary of the yellow fever, Grabo tells the reader that he gathered all the "details of that summer" from Carey's 1793 version of *Short Account of the Malignant Fever,* the very edition that angered Jones and Allen both for its silencing of the African-American experience and for its racist distortions. And to compound the error, he refers to a statement made by Carey in a later edition in order to validate, in Grabo's eyes, Brown's keen historical vision: "The novel of *Arthur Mervyn . . .* gives a vivid and terrifying picture, probably not too highly coloured, of the horrors of that period."[81] Instead of scrutinizing the limits of Carey's eyewitness account or challenging the authority of his facts, Grabo takes his word for it. This critical introduction to the novel's context thus perpetuates a cycle of silences initiated by Carey's first history of the epidemic. Since the yellow fever narratives were as much about virtuous republicans as the deadly epidemic, the resistance of Jones and Allen to such an interpretation reminds us that they were writing to accomplish something more than simply correcting the record. Brown and Carey telling a story of a white republic reborn constituted the writer's patriotic duty. Protesting against Carey's vision, Jones and Allen suggest that he has buried an unthinkable reality for whites: African-Americans, scorned by whites, had done more to save the national capital than those prominent citizens who fled to country estates, and had at least equaled the efforts of those who remained in the city. Jones and Allen recognize that the power of history writing begins at the source. The meaning of the fever begins in the silence around the republic's racial hierarchies.

chapter 4

Snug Stored Below: Slavery and James Fenimore Cooper's White America

Founded in 1787 by Absalom Jones and Richard Allen, the Free African Society was rooted in the humanitarian ideals of the Great Awakening and the American Revolution, and its members were committed to confronting racial segregation with a visionary black consciousness. Their mutual aid society became a center for social and political activities in Philadelphia's African-American community, providing literacy and self-improvement training for many of the city's newly freed or fugitive slaves. True to their ideals, and intent on demonstrating their patriotism, the Free African Society answered the call for aid during the yellow fever epidemic of 1793. Even though they organized and paid for the relief effort, nursed the sick, and buried the dead, malicious rumors circulated that accused African-Americans of stealing from the dead and raiding the abandoned homes of the rich. In his initial histories of the crisis, Matthew Carey converted these rumors into fact. Politicized by these events, and hoping that real examples of black heroism and compassion would dispel a prejudiced view of their criminality, Jones and Allen published a counternarrative of the yellow fever epidemic.[1]

A stanza concludes their measured account of the yellow fever, and it is one of the rare moments in which Jones and Allen criticize, if only obliquely, the conduct of the white community:

God and a soldier, all men do adore
In time of war, and not before;

When the war is over, and all things righted
God is forgotten, and the soldier slighted.[2]

Even then, after witnessing Carey's historical account circulate through
the city, Jones and Allen feared that the nation would forget how white
and black Americans, in a joint venture, saved the American capital. Inverting the revolutionary legacy, the poem represents Philadelphia's African-
Americans as the nation's holy warriors who sacrificed their lives for the
country. For Jones and Allen, the epidemic exposed the hypocrisy of a
Northern white public that proudly announced its revolutionary sympathy for the downtrodden while it treated African-Americans with malice
or indifference. To the founders of the Free African Society, this response
signified white Philadelphia's apostasy. The epidemic and suffering now
over, their allies in the white community forget both God and the black
soldier, a sin that calls into question their moral authority as national
leaders. Their history of the yellow fever was a remarkable intervention in
nationalist politics. They could have easily reminded their readers that local
and national leaders had fled the city, effectively abandoning the poor and
the sick; instead, Jones and Allen based their appeal in the nation's revolutionary ideals, and they imply that Philadelphia's African-Americans were
the *real* republicans. Committed to the values of the Revolution, they
stayed and fought a national scourge, embodied civic virtue, and offered
sympathy to the suffering.

   Their vision, while forged in the fever, also owed a portion of its inspiration to their former white allies, worried about social unrest, who abandoned
the antislavery movement in the early 1790s. Lacking its white stewardship, the movement began to acquire a new shape during that pestilential
summer. In addition to their relief efforts, the counternarrative written by
Jones and Allen distinguished an oppositional, anti-imperial voice, rejected
a narrative of white victimization, and substituted a multiracial patriotism
in its place. Throughout the United States, African-Americans activists
petitioned state and federal government for an expansion of political rights.
In Philadelphia, the Free African Society took aim both at local cases of
racial intolerance and at the nation's most visible symbol of division, the
Fugitive Slave Law. Absalom Jones was a leader in the fight to repeal the
1793 law, exemplifying the ideal of American optimism even as a divisive
racial climate persuaded Congress to refuse debate on two petitions in

1797 and 1801. The alternative to Jones's democratic politics was armed resistance. The white establishment saw this alternative clearly in the conspiracy scenarios depicted in Federalist propaganda, as well as in the news of Gabriel's planned slave insurrection in Virginia in 1800.

The rise of the slave rebel may be a more gripping historical tale than that of an activist who gathers signatures so he can petition Congress, yet the effort of Jones and other black activists to repeal the Fugitive Slave Law has an equally compelling plot, one rarely viewed as a part of America's political evolution during the Federalist era. Gary Nash remarks about this absence, "black struggles to expand the sphere of liberty were in fact an important, if largely unrecognized, part of nation-building in the new American republic."[3] The political activism represented by Jones promoted an anti-imperial vision of an inclusive nation that could only be brought about by eliminating the "fugitive" identity of African-Americans in the United States. To win this battle would move the United States away from its imperial legacy and toward racial justice; a victory would strengthen a civic identity already undermined by a constitutional system that protected the civil rights of the white male majority. Equally important to these heroic struggles for racial justice, however, was the deathblow that Federalist militarism delivered to this democratic movement at the century's end. In particular, the imperialist narrative that linked African-Americans with foreign enemies produced a divisive racial climate that silenced the democratic politics embodied by Absalom Jones and the fugitive slaves on whose behalf he petitioned Congress.[4]

Viewed from this perspective, the triumph of Jefferson and the Republicans is tragically ironic, appearing more like a second American Revolution because of its commitment to imperial authority rather than to republican principles. The events of the 1790s caused a shift in imperial discourse, which increasingly came to view the racial divide in the United States as impassable. Brooding about the state of race relations in *Notes on the State of Virginia* (1784), Thomas Jefferson supplied this doctrine with its two main principles. The differences between the two races were "fixed in nature," Jefferson wrote, and to free the slaves without a plan for "expatriation," to let ex-slaves live alongside their former masters, would fill those of African descent with "ten thousand recollections . . . of the injuries they sustained."[5] Contained in Jefferson's statement are two rationales: one for the Naturalization Act of 1790, which limited naturalization of citizens to *white* immigrants, and the other for the creation of a plan to remove free African-Americans from the country. Even more than a belief that the races were fundamentally different, the insurrectionary threat of African-Americans—Jefferson's uncanny awareness that they might act like revolutionary Americans—seemed to necessitate their removal from the United States.

During the war crisis of 1798–1800, Federalists converted the slaveholder's nightmare into a central piece of their imperial rhetoric, and Jefferson's victory did nothing to dispel the white public's fear of a defiant black population. To make matters worse, new technology resuscitated slavery, which many had predicted would soon weaken and disappear from the nation. At the turn of the century, Southern planters and Northern investors purchased slave labor and plantations to take advantage of the cotton gin and a new hybrid cotton seed. Slavery and imperialism had always been connected in U.S. culture; thus, the expansion of slavery also entailed the expansion of the national domain in the first decades of the nineteenth century, an evolution that the abolition of the slave trade in 1808 spurred rather than checked. Slavery's increased profitability gave rise to an internal slave trade far more productive and lucrative than the previous triangulation between Europe, Africa, and North America. A plan for deporting free African-Americans to Africa became even more urgent during these years when it became clear that slavery was a permanent and vital part of the U.S. imperial economy. Growing black resistance to the slave system led political leaders on a search for a mechanism that would both stabilize the Southern slaveocracy and neutralize politically active African-Americans. A group of prominent white citizens provided an answer in 1817, with the inauguration of the American Colonization Society. Taking Jefferson's theory of a fatefully segregated and fractious society to its logical end, they devised a plan to deport free African-Americans to a new African colony. Paradoxically, the U.S. imperial imagination located the solution to building a racially homogeneous America in Africa, at the outermost reach of U.S. expansion.

In their efforts to create this African nation, the American Colonization Society believed they could achieve the revolutionary ideal—articulated in the 1790 Naturalization Act—of white freedom in the United States. The society immediately became the key instrument of racial reform in the United States after 1817, voicing an imperial idea that dominated the social

landscape until the rise of abolitionism in the 1830s.[6] Not simply giving voice
to an American identity based in white racial solidarity, the American Colonization Society also gave the nation an opportunity to resolve its central
political contradiction through the expatriation of African-Americans to
Africa rather than through amendment to the Constitution.[7] The movement rehearsed a looming political debate about the future of slavery and
citizenship in America. In 1819 Congress began to redefine the slave system;
after two years of dissension between Northern and Southern representatives, they ended what had become known as the Missouri controversy
with an ominous compromise. Admitting Maine into the union as a free
state and Missouri as a slave state, legislators completed the agreement by
drawing a geographical line along 36°30', a barrier that forced slavery
south of the line and forecasted the coming of the Civil War.[8] This chapter links the Missouri debates and the colonization movement, two events
pushing toward the same goals of imperial expansion and white power.
Both triggered a range of racial anxieties, from insurrection and miscegenation to black suffrage and a growing free African-American population, and they worked well in tandem. Admitting the escalating dangers
of slavery, the Missouri debates increased support for the American Colonization Society's plan for an African colony, a plan for removal that promised to give shape to an "American" identity restricted to whites only.

When James Fenimore Cooper began writing novels in 1819, the resurgence of slavery and the new colonization movement had already begun to
define the limits of a democratic politics. This chapter draws on a politics
of slavery, racial segregation, and colonization to explain their influence on
The Pioneers, the first novel in Cooper's Leatherstocking saga.[9] Loosely
based on the frontier settlement of Cooperstown, New York, founded by
the author's father, William Cooper, *The Pioneers* is his son's memory of a
postrevolutionary era distinguished by social instability and caused by rapid
progress. Land disputes, class and racial conflict, environmental ruin, and
inept officials—all these define James Fenimore Cooper's historical memory, while, at the same time, they indicate his distaste for the growing influence of Jacksonian democracy in the early 1820s. The novel's figure for a
noble republican authority, Judge Temple, repeatedly comes up against characters who contest his authority. Representing the laws of nature, Natty
Bumppo and Indian John resist the judge's restrictive game laws and encroaching settlement; Richard Jones and Hiram Doolittle are democratic,

working-class characters, ambitious for more control and aggressively looking for opportunities to rise up the social ladder; and Oliver Edwards is a
mysterious white figure who defends Native property rights and challenges
Judge Temple's legal claim on the lands. Relics of the past, Natty and Indian
John highlight a process in which the wilderness is rapidly disappearing
and being replaced by the burgeoning town of Templeton. The question
of ownership of Judge Temple's lands hangs like a storm cloud over this
symbolic setting of young America. Temple discovers that Oliver Edwards
is actually the son of his former business partner, the loyalist Colonel
Effingham, who fled the colony at the outbreak of the Revolution. The son
has returned only to discover that Temple, instead of holding his father's
property in trust, appropriated the title and made himself the region's single largest landowner. Attempting to provide a vision of American progress
that resolves the question of ownership rights, Cooper relies on a conventional fictional strategy: he joins the two heirs, Oliver Edwards and Elizabeth, the judge's daughter, in matrimony. Their union represents the birth
of a new nation unencumbered by past disputes of British empire.

Accelerating into the future, and blurring the temporal boundaries of
the historical novel, *The Pioneers* challenges our conventional notions about
how that literary genre represents the past. Cooper composes *The Pioneers*
in the midst of a critical evolution of American identity, a fact not lost on
critics who attempt to gauge the contemporary pressures on Cooper's historical memory.[10] In his reading of the imperial pressures on the novel,
Eric Cheyfitz claims that legal wrangling over Native American sovereignty
in the early 1820s actually drives the novel's drama of disputed property
and citizenship in the year 1793. He puts *The Pioneers* in dialogue with the
Supreme Court's ruling in *Johnson v. M'Intosh,* an 1823 decision that made
it more difficult for American Indians to maintain possession of their lands.
Reading these two texts together, Cheyfitz demonstrates how they do the
"work of dispossession" by inventing a racially homogeneous nation in
which American Indians possess no property, cannot be assimilated, and
are destined to disappear. The force of dispossession in *The Pioneers* helps
readers to imagine a white nation, unified in its possession of whiteness as
well as in its collective defense of this special right.[11] If the historical novel
played a part in justifying Indian removal, then I want to address how this
political function operates in relation to an intractable African-American
presence in *The Pioneers*.

Unlike the first three chapters of this book, which trace the emergence of an insurrectionary racial threat *external* to the United States and imported from the Caribbean frontier, this chapter examines a nationalist dynamic in which the threat is fully realized as *internal* to an expanding American empire. Despite the magnitude of both the Missouri debates and the colonization movement in nationalist arguments, the prevailing tendency among critics is to extract *The Pioneers* from its historical play in debates on slavery and nationhood. By restoring the issues of slavery and colonization to the novel's context, this chapter considers how *The Pioneers* understands the link between African-American removal and national unity. The logic of this changing dynamic advanced the agenda of the American Colonization Society, particularly after the Missouri debates, when the public increasingly came to view African-Americans as a hazardous presence in the United States. For many whites, Indian removal seemed possible, even inevitable, and suggested a peaceful resolution to a long-standing national crisis. On the other hand, a plan for African-American removal appeared neither feasible nor permanent and was fraught with social and political dangers that could destroy the union. This difference between the two imperialist projects sheds some light on Cooper's representations of racial solidarity in Templeton. Coming into constant conflict with their antagonists, anxious white citizens constantly terrorize slaves and free African-Americans in order to sustain their own grip on American selfhood.[12] Perhaps unexpectedly, a stark realist narrative runs beneath Cooper's romance of America's founding, more often a lament about an endangered union, less a version of his racial antipathy.

A HUNGER FOR (RACIAL) UNITY

While the American Colonization Society was promoting a vision of a racially homogeneous America, the United States was experiencing an imperial revival elaborated in patriotic ritual. Doing his part, President James Monroe revived the processional tradition, last practiced by George Washington after the Revolution, to repair a nation divided by the War of 1812 with England. Traveling three thousand miles across the United States, from Baltimore to Maine, across New York along the lower Great Lakes to the western frontier, Monroe renewed a patriotic attachment to the Revolution.[13] In the opening pages of *The Pioneers,* Cooper reproduces one of

Monroe's visions of an ideal America. Gazing on the landscape from a distance, one encounters an American historical tableau:

> The whole district is hourly exhibiting how much can be done, in even a
> rugged country, and with severe climate, under the dominion of mild laws,
> and where every man feels a direct interest in the prosperity of a common-
> wealth, of which he knows himself to form a part. The expedients of the
> pioneers who first broke ground in the settlement of this country, are suc-
> ceeded by the permanent improvements of the yeoman, who intends to
> leave his remains to moulder under the sod which he tills, or, perhaps, of
> the son, who, born in the land, piously wishes to linger around the grave of
> his father. Only forty years have passed since this whole territory was a
> wilderness.[14]

This opening passage alerts the reader to the novel's historical perspective,
which spans forty years of rapid change. Not only has the American farmer
subdued the wilderness and made it pay, but the passing of fathers and
sons has also begun to create a fundamental ingredient of national loyalty.
Unlike the Native characters in the Leatherstocking tales who are forced
from the graves of their fathers, the American son can choose to linger, to
put down roots. This change is due to the republican machine that runs
smoothly here. It has successfully tamed the inhospitable country; the economy is booming as individual hard work yields prosperity; each citizen is
an important cog of the representative government. This national mythology, as critics have argued, is a demonstration of Cooper's ideal of a model
government founded on an enlightened legal and political order.[15] However, as Cooper slowly lowers his camera eye to focus on the customs of
Templeton, episodes of racial division and unrest severely test this hypoth-
esis of a representative government.

These episodes rehearse the imperial message of the American Colonization Society: only the removal of free African-Americans from the United
States would foster national unity. Because their agenda targeted national
racial sentiment, the arguments for expatriation drew on any trope that
might move a white public to view the presence of free African-Americans
as dangerous. The most useful tropes marked black freemen as a population that could never assimilate into (white) America. Basing their social
theory in Jefferson's racial science, leaders in the colonization movement,

such as former U.S. representative and senator Robert Goodloe Harper, claimed that blackness was an "impassable barrier" to assimilation.[16] An unreformed South Carolina Federalist, the events of 1798–1799 instigated Harper's turn to the right, and his fear of slave insurrection and foreign influence never lessened in the years afterward and shaped the movement's political rhetoric. This particular case of the "impassable barrier" of race also reveals a secondary move, conventional enough in removal discourse. For added effect, Harper solidifies the trope of a racially divided United States by characterizing free African-Americans as potential paupers and criminals who would forever prey on white society. Finally, the "Great Compromiser" Henry Clay, one of the nation's most famous politicians and a vice president of the American Colonization Society, turned to the logic of contagion to explain the danger, and civil death, of free African-Americans: "experience proved that persons turned loose, who were neither freemen nor slaves, constituted a great moral evil, threatening to contaminate all parts of society."[17]

The colonization movement solved the ambiguity of black subjectivity in the United States; its supporters insisted that free African-Americans were a "distinct nation" between slave and freeman that needed to be relocated to their African homeland before they contaminated the American way. Speaking about what they assumed to be the wishes of all African-Americans, Clay and the American Colonization Society argued that only mass expatriation could assure their happiness. Clay presumed, and spoke openly about, the desires of free African-Americans: "And can there be any thing to a reflecting freeman . . . more humiliating, more dark and cheerless, than to see himself, and to trace in imagination his posterity, through all succeeding time, degraded and debased, aliens to the society of which they are members, and cut off from its higher blessings?"[18] The "contemplated colony" would supposedly make free African-Americans happy by granting them basic needs and political rights. Most important, the colony would serve as a receptacle for a dangerous population long ago tagged as alien. A successful removal policy promised to fortify an incontrovertible color line and protect the purity of a white nation.

One witnesses in *The Pioneers* how this leading theory of race in Cooper's American society—inferior, alien, dangerous—is an imperial construction that comes to define the limits of the novel's depiction of an ideal republican community in 1793. A melting pot of multinational individuals,

Templeton is a postrevolutionary settlement in which a collective American identity had to be forged despite a variety of religious, social, and political differences. The allegory for a republic under construction is Judge Temple's house, an unstable structure that is supposed to objectify an evolving and heterogeneous America. Cooper selects two men, Richard Jones and Hiram Doolittle, who confirm this idea. These two amateur architects pioneer a style they call the "composite order," which, like the republican architecture itself, is really a mixed bag of classical, French, and English designs that Jones and Doolittle have picked up from a few textbooks. By pointing to the house's interior as a model republican stage for the diversity of people that congregate there, critics translate this architectural style into a civic ethos but ignore how they exclude and scapegoat African-Americans. In *Sensational Designs,* Jane Tompkins goes as far as to remark that a "peaceful coexistence" is made possible by the "composite order" of the interior; her census of the house's occupants fails to include the slaves, laboring in the cellar and kitchen, the very foundation of social order in Templeton.[19]

Cooper demonstrates the process of nation-building inside Temple's house by staging a community dinner that is disrupted by a racially mixed figure named Oliver Edwards. His racial hybridity instigates a clash between Temple and Jones over seating arrangements. Temple casually puts forth a belief in monogenesis, which bequeaths a social hierarchy with "unenlightened" races at the bottom, and espouses platitudes about educating Edwards in order to gradually assimilate him into the community. Jones, whom one critic dubs a "nightmarish emblem of leveling democracy," explodes when Temple suggests that Edwards will eat in the cellar with the slaves:

> You surely would not make the youth eat with the blacks! He is part Indian, it is true, but the natives hold the negroes in contempt. No, no—he would starve before he would break a crust with the negroes.[20]

As an allusion to the classical trope of civic brotherhood, the dinner table is an ironic representation of an emergent democracy in Templeton. While Temple's paternalism invokes an ideal of social harmony, particularly because the clearly defined hierarchy is stable and fraternal, Jones's democratic ethos anxiously circumscribes, and then protects, the color line. Thus this ethos marks the difference between Temple's abstract benevolence, out of touch with the racial temper in Templeton, and Jones's aggressive attempt to strengthen the community through segregation and racial antipathy.

Reinforcing the divide between mainstream Templeton and the society of slaves living in the basement, Jones's attempt establishes the novel's social geography and is critical to comprehending the type of racial politics to which Cooper draws our attention in *The Pioneers*. Instead of brotherhood, the dinner table organized by Jones produces racism more hostile and divisive than the type usually associated with Temple's paternalism. Jones's anger, so different from the aristocratic composure of Temple, is the response of a new order. This difference enacts both an underlying assumption of U.S. imperialism and a key belief of the colonization movement: antipathy for African-Americans was an indelible mark that would never disappear from the United States. Since the two races could not live peacefully together, free African-Americans—not bigotry—needed to be cleansed from the nation. The trope of the dinner table also circulates in the discourse of colonization. After acknowledging how white Americans "recoil with horror from the idea of an intimate union with the free blacks," Harper claims that aversion for African-Americans exists in all parts of the nation. "There is no State in the Union where a negro or mulatto can ever hope to be a member of Congress, a judge, a militia officer, or even a justice of the peace; to sit down at the same table with the respectable whites, or to mix freely in their society."[21] How degrading would it be for Oliver Edwards to mix with the slaves and eat at the same table with them in the cellar? Reaching the height of his bombast, Jones claims that Edwards, before eating in the cellar with the slaves and surrendering his place at the table, would rather "starve."

Intent on converting his "composite order" to the social interior, Jones makes the main floor more inclusive by assimilating the "part Indian," Oliver Edwards. Exemplifying a process that Ernest Renan famously called "national forgetting," Jones allows Edwards to pass into white society, but only because he is exceptional for his racial ambiguity. Absorbing Edwards also means subjugating the slaves in the cellar. As a way to oppose Temple's antiquated notion and thus find a seat for Oliver at the central table, Jones creates an origin story that legitimates his opposition to the authority of Judge Temple. Jones personalizes his architectural style: his great-grandfather was "either a great merchant, in London, or a great country lawyer, or the youngest son of a Bishop." The self-styled democratic

Everyman undermines the judge's rule and causes him to capitulate to Jones's demand. In his own house, Temple is reduced to a lament about the loss of order in a nation that has strayed from a single genealogical, and racial, origin: in America, Temple muses, "everything is obscure."[22] Yet some aspects of the changing social climate make sense to Temple, such as when Jones explains the new seating arrangements. While Temple's lament about democratic "obscurity" evokes a dangerous disorder, the plight of the domestic slaves and free African-Americans, marginalized by the political conflict between the white citizenry, remains unchanged by democratic reform. Jones's "alteration" of Temple's social hierarchy overlooks the cellar populated by dispossessed slaves. There is not a place at the table for everyone.

A TRIAL IN THE FOREST

The strife surrounding the dinner table depicts a racial divisiveness in an American society that was working against the theoretical harmony of an ideal republic. These scenes challenge a reader of *The Pioneers* to reevaluate the issues of law, property, and citizenship that scholarship posits as the novel's central subjects. Only by ignoring the period's racial politics can critics use *The Pioneers* to discuss the evolution of a theoretical liberalism. In addition to Temple's divided house, a quasi-legal episode in the forest demonstrates the conflict between the discourses of race and constitutional liberty. When a deer runs between Judge Temple and Edwards in the first chapter of *The Pioneers,* both men aim their guns and fire and the buck drops dead to the ground. An informal trial ensues to determine the rightful claimant of the deer. Literary critics examining the intersections between national identity and law have rightly seized on this opening scene. The confrontation between the aristocratic property owner and an itinerant hunter dramatizes an incipient democratic ethos—particularly the frontiersman's claims—located on the national margins. Thus, Cooper makes a claim for frontier democracy as part and parcel of natural law. Later in the novel the citizens of Templeton gather in a tavern to discuss the details of the shooting. An attorney inflames the people by arguing for the right of the most lowly citizen to defend his interests against a powerful authority such as Judge Temple: "This is a country of laws," he yells, "and I should like to see it fairly tried, whether a man who owns, or says he owns, a hundred thousand acres of land, has any more right to shoot a body, than another."[23]

At issue in the case is the principle of revolutionary liberalism: each citizen possesses the civil right to be free from the tyranny of empire. Although recent critics have seen in this passage Cooper's commentary on constitutionalism and citizenship, they focus only on the white disputants and overlook the plight of an African-American witness whose strategic presence complicates efforts to reach a resolution. Only by nullifying the vote of this witness can Temple defeat the hunter and repossess his property rights and political authority. "'There is Aggy,' says the Judge, 'he can't vote being a slave.'"[24] Even the defiant egalitarianism of the prosecuting attorney, who attacks Temple with the principle "that all men are equal in the eye of the law," cannot disengage from the contradiction of slavery. His ideal of a court case "fairly tried" means that "the testimony of the blacks," as he tells another character, "could not be taken, sir, for they are all property of Mr. Jones who owns their time."[25] Recently appointed sheriff of Templeton by his cousin, Judge Temple, Jones acts as the adjudicator, and he views the deer episode as an opportunity to gain additional power and status. Jones owns the "time" of the slaves, meaning he has leased them, and the social status they signify, from Temple. Jones's provisional ownership of Aggy becomes the key to Jones's efforts to use the lawsuit to defeat the frontiersman and challenge the power of his superior, Judge Temple.[26]

It is no accident that Cooper places the slave at the center of the legal controversy. Aggy's presence represents the novel's prescient criticism of how the rhetoric for a plebiscitary democracy facilitates white dominion over the slave in U.S. imperial culture. Temple claims to have killed the deer, and by disproving this claim, Jones can turn the tables, gaining fame and authority at the judge's expense. This political contest between a vulnerable judge and an ambitious sheriff has ugly consequences for Aggy, and from the slave's perspective, the conflict is not primarily about legal discourse but white power. This is a pattern in *The Pioneers:* when a white citizen is in danger of falling into an inferior social and political position occupied by "lowly" slaves and free African-Americans, the end result is a violent confrontation that reestablishes white domination and stages a resistance to crossing the color line. Thus, Jones's realization that the erstwhile Aggy possesses the truth results in a brutal trial scene, a scene that renders Northern civil law little above the arbitrary violence of the Southern plantation.[27]

Unlike the representation of white identity, taking place within a "country of laws," the dilemma of black citizenship is repeatedly pushed outside the law. Without the legal power to bear witness, African-American characters in *The Pioneers*—many of whom live and work in Templeton, virtually unnoticed by readers or critics—are physically abused and terrorized. Temple had anticipated Jones's suspicion, an indication of the ever-present conflict between the two men, and preempted him by purchasing Aggy's silence with a cryptic promise that "there will be a visit from Santaclaus to-night."[28] Temple's promise of a holiday bribe masks the tension of the scene and the approaching conflict, both of which are embodied in a double dilemma. Can Aggy maintain his purchased silence when Jones asserts a legal claim on the testimony of his slave? And, having given his testimony, does Aggy's lack of rights nullify the testimony of an eyewitness by an erasure of the political subject?

Sheriff Jones will uncover the truth about the shooting, and usurp some of Temple's power, by terrorizing Aggy. The scene turns from the humor of local color to a spectacle of imperial power. Aggy busies himself with the pretense of unbuckling the saddle, while his efforts to vanish before his master's arresting gaze intensifies a mood of looming fury. The minstrel-like comedy gradually progresses until an anxious Aggy is finally entangled in Jones's web of questions:

> "Perhaps he [Edwards] is land-hunting—I say, Aggy—may be he is out hunting?"
>
> "Eh! yes, massa Richard," said the black, a little confused; for as Richard did all the flogging, he stood in great terror of his master, in the main—"yes, sir, I b'lieve he be."
>
> "Had he a pack and an ax?"
>
> "No, sir, [he had] only a rifle."
>
> "Rifle!" exclaimed Richard, observing the confusion of the negro which now amounted to terror. "By Jove! he kill'd the deer—I knew that [Temple] couldn't kill a buck on the jump—How was it, Aggy; tell me about it, and I'll roast the duke quicker than he can roast his saddle—How was it, Aggy? the lad shot the buck, and the Judge bought it, ha! and he is taking the youth down to get the pay?"[29]

Unlike the playfulness of the wilderness trial, this dispute evokes the brutality inherent in an interrogation "outside" the law. Cooper's exclamation points, dashes, and imperatives reflect the terror provoked by the interrogation's central question: "How was it, Aggy?" The comedy dissipates in relation to Jones's increasing proximity to the truth. Until, entirely evacuated of humor, Jones makes a violent rush at his slave:

> "Don't lie, you black rascal," cried Richard, stepping on the snow bank to measure the distance from his lash to the negro's back: "speak truth, or I trounce you." While speaking, the stock was slowly rising in Richard's right hand, and the lash drawing through his left, in the scientific manner with which drummers apply the cat, and [Aggy], after turning each side of himself towards his master, and finding both equally unwilling to remain there, fairly gave in. In a very few words he made his master acquainted with the truth, at the same time earnestly conjuring Richard to protect him from the displeasure of the Judge.[30]

Critics routinely ridicule Cooper for his awkward style, but here he skillfully presents a cold-blooded interrogation, each sentence unraveling in the measured movements of Jones's cat-o'-nine-tails. The first command epitomizes the slave's limited options when excluded from the safeguards of the law: "speak truth, or I trounce you." Yet, paradoxically, Jones expresses his sadism by the manner in which he calmly "measures" the reach of his lash, the methodical choice of "measures" connoting the unstable balance between an excessive and yet systematic movement. African-American characters in nineteenth-century fiction may have been, more often than not, "vehicles for white enjoyment," as Hartman suggests, but Cooper's scene appeals to more than a reader's prurient tastes.[31] As the scene moves from minstrel comedy to the final act of the slave's terror, the narrative captures a political dilemma that revealed the persistence of empire in a supposedly republican nation. Not only did the lack of constitutional protections abandon African-Americans to the unrestrained power of men like Jones, but the dilemma also made a mockery of the national ideals of revolutionary liberalism. Believing it could solve this dilemma and make America live up to its version of a revolutionary creed, the American Colonization Society advocated the removal of free African-Americans from the United States.

THE TURKEY SHOOT

Many Americans feared that the language of natural rights—symbolized by the Declaration of Independence—circulating in the Missouri debates would inspire a massive slave insurrection in the South. Like many of his contemporaries, Thomas Jefferson believed that the architects of the Missouri Compromise had sidestepped the real and more important issue by failing to design a plan for deporting free African-Americans who were perceived as agents of insurrection. Jefferson went as far as to call the final compromise line the "knell of the union," and he prophesized a vast slave insurrection where "all the whites south of the Potomac and the Ohio must evacuate their states, and most fortunate those who can do it first."[32]

Trying to forestall this racial apocalypse, the American Colonization Society cultivated relationships with African-American leaders who might lead emigrants to Africa. One who refused their overtures was a preacher named Denmark Vesey. In 1822 two collaborators betrayed his elaborate plan for a slave insurrection in Charleston, South Carolina. The State of South Carolina responded to this plan to burn the city and massacre the fleeing whites with a routine brutality, the type usually carried out against real or imagined slave rebels and their real or imagined conspiracies against white power. In a single month, state officers, newly deputized officials, overseers, and slave masters interrogated free African-Americans and slaves, arrested 131, sold 43, and whipped 48. In the end, South Carolina executed Vesey and 37 of his alleged rebels, a number exceeding those executed during the New York Slave Conspiracy trials. As a mobile freeman, Vesey embodied a national fear that the insurrectionary threat was intrinsic to the nation and that racial violence could strike any region. Fighting the immigration of these dangerous figures, Northern states expelled free African-Americans, passed laws to prevent their settlement, created physical markers of distinction, such as clothing, and armed white militias in case of race riots.[33]

The colonization movement exploited this collective fear of and antipathy for free African-Americans. The backlash against them, which would become even more intense after the insurrection led by Nat Turner in 1831, inspired William Lloyd Garrison to write *Thoughts on African Colonization* (1832), a devastating attack on the colonization movement that helped to catalyze the abolitionist movement.[34] Before working toward the larger goal of eliminating the institution of slavery, Garrison knew that one must first expose the fallacious reasoning of the American Colonization Society and counter its racist rhetoric. His manifesto declared that the colonization movement's primary motive, and its only mode of disputation, was to depict the "naked terrors" of free African-Americans in the United States.[35]

The movement exploited the insecurity of those white Americans who occupied an unstable class position. Their racial antipathy became a tool to fortify their self-identification as free white Americans, the "impassable barrier" between them and a dispossessed class of aliens. This type of self-identification through racial antipathy occurs throughout *The Pioneers* and in every corner of Cooper's Templeton. For example, in one late-night conversation between the former seaman Ben Pump and the house servant Remarkable Pettibone, taking place in Temple's house above the cellar where the slaves are held captive, we witness an exchange that depicts the volatile intersection of race and class. As members of the white laboring class, Pump and Pettibone have worked hard to achieve their positions as head servants in the house and do not share Judge Temple's wealth and sense of freedom. The presence of slaves in the cellar interrupts the peacefulness of a fireside chat when the day's work is done: "The niggers are snug stored below," Ben Pump says, "before a fire that would roast an ox whole."[36] Even as a minor character, Pump plays a major role, since he is the single character who draws attention to the slaves being held beneath the house. Having spent twenty-seven years at sea (and only seven on land), Pump speaks in nautical metaphors, his conversation as "perfectly unintelligible" to readers as it is to Pettibone. Pump knows the oceans like Natty knows the wilderness. He has sailed the hemisphere, learned the "fashions of nations" and the "shape of a country," has fought in naval battles against the French, and can read the stars and trade winds like a book. His experience has made him an expert on global trade and his vernacular consistently erases the geographical boundary between a domestic United States and the international world. Having a dram of rum with "Prettybones" while sitting above the slaves, Pump judges it to be high quality, imported from the West Indies, which only an "old tar" like himself could consider "so close aboard."[37] Thus, landlocked on the western frontier, Pump's lesson about the West Indian trade and his epigrammatic description of slaves "snug stored below" alludes to the global reach of slavery by evoking the crypt of an Atlantic slave ship; having spent his life working in that economy, Pump raises the nation's great contradiction from the basement to the ground floor. Standing in contrast to the idealism of the dinner table, the image of the slave crypt is marked by the raw imagery of the Middle Passage: claustrophobic, hellish, slaves stacked like corpses in a floating graveyard; Pump, sitting above them on watch, reveals a hard truth about how slaves, arriving via the imperial network of slavery, help to produce the nation. While the national house may be under construction on the western frontier, the seaman recognizes that the global slave economy is the structure's true foundation.[38]

Wealthy republican and slaveholder, Judge Temple simply overlooks the presence of the slaves "snug stored below," stoking the powerful fire that fuels the house's domestic economy and keeps its occupants warm, if not safe. Juxtaposing his blindness with the hypersensitivity of Pump and Pettibone, Cooper draws attention to the ambivalent effects of slavery on the formation of national identity. Like the symbolic dinner table, the fireside chat between the two servants produces a notion of democratic order based on the lowly, "alien" position of the slaves whose bondage in the basement is essential to the social order that Pump and Pettibone imagine and discuss. Anxiety and ambivalence, however, define this order. When Temple's daughter Elizabeth was absent from the home, Pettibone took over the duties of managing the house. As they await the arrival of Elizabeth, Pump tries to sweet-talk Pettibone by teasing her about her impending demotion to her new "mistress": "'Mistress!' cried Remarkable, 'don't make one out to be a nigger, Benjamin. She's no mistress of mine, and never will be.'" Fixed on the bottom of the social hierarchy, the slave lacks political agency and what Pettibone perceives as dignified labor. Faced with her own demotion, she reacts to a future "governed" by Elizabeth Temple and projects her fear of falling onto the black scapegoat.[39] At the same time, Pettibone's overreaction suggests her strained relationship to the household economy; her labor, like that of the slaves "snug stored below," is essential to maintaining domestic order.

The connections between empire, race, and class voiced in the fireside chat prepare us to read the eventual dispossession of Natty Bumppo who, like Richard Jones or Remarkable Pettibone, resists his own loss of freedom by attacking a free African-American named Abraham Freeborn.[40] By the end of the novel, as the conventional reading suggests, the laws of Templeton overpower Natty, the paragon of natural liberty in the Leatherstocking tales, who is forced to flee deeper into the frontier. Critics, however,

overlook an unlikely and ironic alliance. The pathos of Natty's decline—
a broken-down old man, he can't shoot straight anymore, game laws restrict
his natural freedom, and Sheriff Jones invades his home—is told through
his tenuous union with a free African-American. Natty's problems begin
in a folk scene called the "Turkey Shoot." As Natty takes aim at a tethered
turkey owned by Abraham Freeborn, Cooper explains that man's strange
metamorphosis:

> The mirth of Brom [Freeborn], which had been again excited . . . vanished.
> His skin became mottled with large brown spots, that fearfully sullied the
> luster of his native ebony, while his enormous lips gradually compressed
> around two rows of ivory, that had hitherto been shining in his visage, like
> pearls set in jet. His nostrils, at all times the most conspicuous features of
> his face, dilated, until they covered the greater part of the diameter of his
> countenance; while his brown and bony hands unconsciously grasped the
> snow-crust near him, the excitement of the moment completely overcom-
> ing his native dread of the cold.[41]

Freeborn is dismembered, cut up, classified, and fetishized, each body part
creating an image of an alien figure that exploits cultural anxiety about
dispossessed African-Americans living in the North. Freeborn is about to
lose both his turkey and his meager income, a possibility that transforms
him into a menacing figure. His excitement represents the white fear of
free African-Americans stimulated by a desire for political and economic
power. His "mirth" disappears, his black skin is "fearfully sullied," his lips
and nostrils grow to absurd proportions, and he reaches about in an "unconscious" spell. Freeborn's base self-interest, instead of goodwill or hearti-
ness, "overcome[s] his native dread of the cold."

Loaded with political purpose, this demeaning caricature depicts a black
freeman deformed both by the power of ownership and his self-possessed
attempt to assimilate into American society. As a point of contrast, consider the different function of a sentimental description of Aggy, the slave
that greets the reader in the beginning of the novel:

> His face, which nature had coloured with a glistening black, was now mot-
> tled with the cold, and his large eyes filled with tears; a tribute to its power,
> that the keen frosts of those regions always extracted from one of his African

origin. Still there was a smiling expression of good humor in his happy
countenance, that was created by the thoughts of home, and a Christmas
fire-side, with its Christmas frolics.[42]

An inordinate mass of adjectives create a nostalgic portrait of Aggy, a con-
tented slave in "good humor," Judge Temple's loyal coachman, who valiantly
maintains a "happy countenance" so far from his native Africa. The winter cold stigmatizes both Aggy and Freeborn as racial outsiders, and the
fantasy of their removal invokes a fantasy of a white nation. Interestingly,
the slave's reaction to his environment distinguishes him from Freeborn.
Unlike Freeborn, whose self-interest enables him to forget his fear of the
cold, Aggy survives in a hostile climate that violates ("extracts") his features; he "still" remains obedient and happy in this foreign world but he
yearns to return to his "African origin." Garrison pointed to this imperial
rhetoric of expatriation as a powerful strategy employed by the American
Colonization Society. They depict free African-Americans, Garrison writes,
as "aliens and foreigners, wanderers from Africa—destitute of the *amor
patrie,* which is the bond of union—seditious—without alliances—irresponsible—unambitious—cherishing no attachments to the soil—feeling
no interest in our national prosperity."[43] As an ideological counterpart to
the alienated African-American in the North, the noble savage serves to
sanitize racial conflict by neutralizing Aggy's disaffection and reminding
Americans that slavery and slaves, in legal "alliances" with their masters
and unburdened by an "irresponsible" freedom, were not the problem.

Cooper's representation of Aggy and Freeborn is one indication of the
historical novel's political function in inscribing contemporary history.[44]
As the poles of African-American representation in *The Pioneers,* Aggy and
Freeborn also organize the discourse of colonization. Cheyfitz has argued
that Cooper has a penchant for allegorizing Native figures for the "purpose
of telling stories about property" and white citizenship. Similarly, Cooper's
allegory of the twinned African-American characters, Aggy and Freeborn,
works to unify American imperialism behind the racist logic of removal
and colonization. Their representation in the novel contributes to a larger
discourse that was attempting to win liberal skeptics in both the North
and South. The message that advocates of colonization delivered was clear:
the proposed African colony will not affect slavery, and it will lessen racial
tension in the United States. Sadly separated from Africa but loyal to his

American master, Cooper's Aggy is not an insurrectionary threat and reinforces the colonizationist message, and Freeborn serves a similar function
on the other pole of representation. But they are potentially dangerous,
Cooper argues.

Unlike Cooper's representation of a powerless slave, the free African-
American embodied the "naked terrors" of a more dangerous population
willing to fight for their rights. The caricature of Freeborn evokes this
putative threat. When Natty's gun misfires, Freeborn seeks to protect his
bird, his interest, from a second shot by attempting to enforce a rule defining the ineffectual "snap" of the flintlock as a legal "fire":

> "A snap—a snap," shouted the negro, springing from his crouching posture,
> like a madman, before his bird. "A snap good as fire—Natty Bumppo gun
> he snap—Natty Bumppo miss a turkey."
>
> "Natty Bumppo hit a nigger," said the indignant old hunter, "if you don't
> get out of the way, Brom. It's contrary to the reason of the thing, boy, that
> a snap should count for a fire, when one is nothing more than a fire-stone
> striking a steel pan, and the other is sudden death; so get out of my way,
> boy, and let me show Billy Kirby how to shoot a Christmas turkey."[45]

Freeborn's claim that old Leatherstocking's rifle issued an impotent "snap"
humiliates Natty in front of the townspeople, curious to witness the powerful skill of the legendary frontiersman. To get a sense of Natty's humiliation, recall a contest in *The Last of the Mohicans* in which the younger
Hawkeye, held captive, decides to show off his skill with "kill-deer" even
though success will prove his identity and risk his life.[46] All this "man
without a cross" possesses is a reputation based in his deadly skill with the
rifle, a skill signifying his whiteness and granting him the freedom to roam
the forest. Confronting the Christmas turkey, the aging Natty is unable to
win a simple holiday contest. Thinking Natty has cheated him, and des-
perately trying to protect his turkey, Freeborn leaps like a "madman" before
it. The ensuing debate over Natty's rifle leaves Freeborn in an unprotected
position. Already defeated by the younger and stronger Billy Kirby, and
now facing a challenge from this black "madman," Natty reacts to his own
loss of agency by attacking Freeborn. Mocking Freeborn's disjointed speech
pattern, repeating the debasing "boy," Natty attempts to authorize a superior claim on language and reason. Confronted with the insubordination

of Freeborn, Natty uses a combination of reason and brute force to claim another shot at the turkey.

Previously, when the "twisty" ways of Temple's authority oppressed Natty, he denounced a society where "might makes right" and that had become "stronger than an old man."[47] Such a statement is a credo for many critics who argue for Natty's freedom outside the law, but how does one reconcile his distaste for the law and his own use of it as he terrorizes Freeborn to secure his own interest? Yet it is not only his expedient appropriation of the "twisty" ways of legal reasoning that dominate Freeborn but also Natty's willingness to reassert justice within "the reach of his rifle" in the same terrible manner Jones brought Aggy within the "reach of his lash."[48] Natty must fight Judge Temple to repossess his lost freedom but he must also maintain his white racial purity. Thus he also must resist any identification with a degraded Freeborn; along with Aggy, these two African-American characters are the only characters who both share Natty's powerlessness and experience his alienation from Templeton.

This overt threat against a free African-American, who desires to protect both his body and investment, replaces the calm legalese of the forest trial and banter of the Bold Dragoon. Unlike the slave Aggy, Freeborn asserts his claim on justice and it must be dealt with in an at least quasi-legal setting. Confronted with Natty's threat to "hit a nigger," and given no legal recourse, Freeborn appeals to the democratic sentiments of the crowd by debasing himself:

> "Gib a nigger fair play," cried the black, who continued resolutely to main-
> tain his post, and making that appeal to the justice of his auditors, which the
> degraded condition of his caste so naturally suggested. "Ebbery body know
> dat snap as good as fire. Leab it to Massa Jone—leab it to young lady."[49]

While Freeborn is firm in his belief that a "snap" equals a "fire," and is ready to argue his point, his individual claim carries no political weight. His call to "gib a nigger fair play" sounds repeatedly throughout the scene. This mantra evokes the peculiar lot of an African-American living in the North; unlike Aggy, whose agency is subject to his master's whim, Freeborn must repeatedly call for "fair play" in a murky area governed by a dangerous Constitution.

The "degraded condition of [Freeborn's] caste" denies him an individual voice. The pun on his name denotes a degenerative freedom and reinforces the real political actors in the novel, since the only way for him to have "fair play" is finally to appeal to the cruel Sheriff Jones. "Bound to preserve the peace of the country," this architect of the house's "composite order" issues a comically inept legal judgment:

> It appears that there was no agreement, either in writing or in words, on the disputed point; therefore, we must reason from analogy, which is, as it were, comparing one thing with another. Now, in duels, where both parties shoot it is generally the rule that a snap is a fire; and if such is the rule, where the party has a right to fire back again, it seems to me unreasonable, to say that a man may stand snapping at a defenseless turkey all day. I therefore am of opinion, that Nathanial Bumppo has lost his chance, and must pay another shilling before he renews his rights.[50]

A duel epitomizes the regulated use of firearms in civilized society and symbolizes social conflict; subject to its bond, Natty cannot freely use his rifle. Jones's judgment can only sound like another instance of the law's "twisty" ways to Natty Bumppo. The satire on legal rhetoric and reasoning depends on Jones as the "unskillful architect," since his use of analogy pairs Natty in a legal duel with a turkey. As a result of his incompetence, Jones stumbles his way to a decision that does not, on the surface, subordinate the rights of Natty to Freeborn since the analogy addresses the turkey's rights instead of the rights of its owner. As a result of the verdict, Natty must pay above the regular rate for another shot at the turkey, and after he hits it, he deposits the prize at the feet of his benefactor, Elizabeth, who, in turn, flips Freeborn a silver dollar. While the paragon of natural liberty regains the power of his rifle, the black freeman is fully compensated, if indirectly, for his claim. Unwilling to reason directly on Freeborn's rights, the entangled resolution articulates the novel's ambivalence about the relationship between the law and free African-Americans.

Natty's final humiliation occurs in the courtroom before the authority of Judge Temple, but this key episode is made possible by this quasi-legal conflict with Brom, which reduces the old frontiersman in the eyes of Templeton's citizens. Approaching Natty's hut to serve him with a warrant for the illegal shooting of a deer, Doolittle encounters an indignant Leatherstocking who aims his rifle at the magistrate, keeping him at a distance.

Alarmed by this "disrespect" for the law, Judge Temple laments the fate of a society, his Templeton, "where the ministers of justice are to be opposed by men armed with rifles. Is it for this that I have tamed the wilderness?" Consequently, Sheriff Jones "collected his troop"—two deputies and seven constables—and led them in pursuit of one who "has set an example of rebellion to the laws, and has become a kind of out-law."[51]

The aftermath of the trial is a paradigmatic episode for the novel's exposition on freedom and whiteness; subjugating Natty and robbing him of his spirit, the legal order puts him in bondage. On his way to the stocks, where Temple has ordered him confined, Natty "bow[s] his head with submission to a power that he was unable to oppose." Back in the cell, Natty's restlessness signals his fate: "[Natty] paced their narrow limits, in his moccasins, with quick, impatient treads, his face hanging on his breast in dejection."[52] This fugitive, possessing no liberty and lacking political agency, resembles the African-American figures in the novel. Cooper appropriates the tragic histories of these figures in order to inject a moving pathos into the depiction of an alienated white man experiencing the sudden loss of independence. As a free white man, he cannot bear the humiliation of confinement; his sense of freedom, his indignation at being rendered an equivalent to a slave, objectifies whiteness in *The Pioneers*. Unlike Aggy, whom the law terrorizes into submissiveness, and Freeborn, whom the law forces to appeal to his white benefactors, Natty bristles under the yoke of legal authority and the novel's dramatic action leads to an inevitable alternative that is reserved solely for the white man: Natty escapes from bondage.[53]

Restoring the privileges of Natty's whiteness, his escape also reasserts the town's racial borders in a way unique to the novel's exploration of the racialized identities central to U.S. imperialism. According to Cheyfitz, when Edwards reveals he is actually an Englishman masquerading as an Indian, the novel moves toward its "happy ending" of the union of the two white heirs. Cheyfitz rightly sees this dynamic as one that justifies white settlement and ownership against the American Indians' prior or "natural" rights. The marriage of Edwards and Elizabeth "romances," or elides, the force of empire and dispossession—their union reassures readers of a legal fiction: land was "property" and American Indians willingly sold or surrendered it. Only by "slip[ping] off his Indian identity" can Edwards marry Elizabeth and take full possession of the property, a conversion that signifies the "legal power" invested in whiteness.[54]

Unlike Edwards's case, Natty's cross-racial identification has a different function. Despite the fact that Natty escapes, he cannot discard the signs of his black identity as casually as Edwards does his Indian character. Like Aggy or Freeborn, Temple's law does not recognize his civil rights and seeks to dominate him. His final refuge must be beyond Templeton, in the forest where natural law rules rather than the imperial authority of the stocks. If, as Cheyfitz says, the reunification of a white Templeton is based in the *Johnson v. M'Intosh* verdict on the American Indian's "unassimilability," then the fugitive Natty Bumppo evokes the latent threat of a free African-American population that the American Colonization Society argued must be removed if the United States was to realize the goal of revolutionary liberalism. As colonization discourse demonstrates, the presence of nominally free African-Americans, neither citizens nor slaves, undermined the notions of citizenship and natural law that were fundamental to an idealized republican society. In Priscilla Wald's study of how the United States legislates, or makes, subjectivity, slaves "profoundly troubled the concept of natural law—particularly the rights to own and inherit property, including property in the self." Due to their liminal status between slave and citizen, free African-Americans, I would add, posed an even more anxious threat than slaves did because of their closer proximity to white citizenship. The legal contingency of slaves or freemen, as Wald observes, reminds white Americans of the instability of national identity, which inspired fears, during moments of acute crisis, of dispossession as the white citizen's "potential fate."[55]

Before his jailbreak, Natty is experiencing this fate, the white fugitive in a story that Cooper sets, ironically enough, in the year of the first Fugitive Slave Law. If Cooper's previous representations of racial tension in Templeton were notable for their stark realism, his final rendering of Natty's flight backs away into the safety of historical romance. Unwilling to redress the grievances of the real victims of Templeton's imperial order—Aggy and Freeborn—Cooper invests all the drama of their plight in Natty. In the end, the metaphor of bondage, associated with the slave throughout the novel, sets up the white man's escape. This leads to a complete breakdown in social order, which Cooper represents in the setting of a suddenly anxious Templeton. While Natty is allowed to fight for his freedom, the novel does not allow Aggy to do the same. He cannot test Jefferson's warning about freed slaves possessing "freedom and a dagger" and looking for revenge.

Because the U.S. imperial imagination is preoccupied and distorted by racial violence, it rarely sees the past clearly. I suggest this is why, immediately prior to the disorder caused by Natty's declaration of his natural rights, the slave is neutralized. There is no other outcome possible for Aggy because the cultural assumption of the early 1820s was that the slave rather than the aging white frontiersman embodied this insurrectionary threat. As if sensing the link to the slave, Sheriff Jones, for no apparent reason, seeks out Aggy at the height of the crisis. As Jones approaches the barn, his call for Aggy conflates the slave with a dog: "'Holla! Aggy!' shouted the Sheriff when he reached the door; 'where are you, you black dog? will you keep me here in the dark all night?'"[56] In the dark and unaware of his slave's actions, Jones alternates his call for Aggy with a call for his dog Brave: "'Holla! Aggy! Brave! Brave! hoy, hoy—where have you got to, Brave . . . Holla! you, Agamemnon! where are you? Oh! here comes the dog at last.'" Almost as if by magic, the word play in his summons produces a metamorphosis:

> By this time the Sheriff had dismounted, and observed a form, which he supposed to be that of Brave, slowly creeping out of the kennel; when, to his astonishment, it reared itself on its two legs, instead of four, and he was able to distinguish, by the star-light, the curly head and dark visage of the negro.[57]

Often arising in response to African-American characters in U.S. literature, "metaphysical condensation," as Toni Morrison calls this rhetoric of debasement, works by "collapsing persons into animals and prevents human contact and exchange."[58] Of course, in this tenuous moment of social disorder, where the slave constitutes a potent threat to imperial order, this is the desired effect of the collapse of Aggy into the dog Brave, loyal and friendly. The potential for literary tropes to contain and articulate themes of social justice made Angus Fletcher pause and reflect on the way in which metamorphosis emerges from the "idea of liberation or imprisonment that it conveys," converting "humans into their bestial equivalents somewhere on the Great Chain, or frees them to live as humans, with free will."[59] The rhetoric of debasement is simultaneously the rhetoric of erasure, removing Aggy from a scenario designed to highlight the white man's revolutionary ethos.

Taking the place of the dead Brave as the low species on the Great Chain, Aggy is certainly not granted the freedom of natural law, not the type accorded to the great white hunter. Aggy's bondage, the law that subjugates him, thus casts a shadow over Natty and accentuates the drama of his eventual imprisonment in Templeton. The daring escape exemplifies the rebirth of Natty's expanding imperial consciousness:

> This was the last they ever saw of the Leatherstocking, whose rapid movements preceded the pursuit which Judge Temple ordered and conducted. He had gone far toward the setting sun,—the foremost in that band of Pioneers, who are opening the way for the march of the nation across the continent.[60]

Natty breaks his identification with a fettered slave by running into the west and renews the fundamental principle of the Revolution, that an oppressed individual should fight for freedom from tyranny. But Natty, as the figure of the (white) slave, can't outrun the shadow of slavery and U.S. imperialism. Thus, he communicates his aversion for a civilization that uses the law to invade his home, to humiliate him in the stocks, and to imprison him. One might bristle at Cooper's limited treatment of race in *The Pioneers,* and critics do, though more out of sport than anything. Nevertheless, his representations of slaves and free African-Americans and the unsafe border spaces they occupy effectively expose the dangers of an American empire that was beginning to move toward what it perceived as its Manifest Destiny. At the same time, Cooper's efforts to represent the culture of American slavery resemble the political philosophy being honed by the colonization movement. On his "march" across the continent, Cooper's pioneer was bound to confront an expanding slave system and a growing class of free African-Americans who had no place in the nation. Hadn't the Missouri controversy and the colonization movement both made it clear that as long as slavery existed in the United States, westward expansion would threaten to divide the union? Thus, buried within the fantasy of Natty running to the west is the deportation of African-Americans to a colony in the east.

EXPORTING "AMERICA"

The embryonic colony of Liberia allowed advocates of colonization to dream of a white America. The presence of free African-Americans in the United States was, as an early leader claimed, "a monument of reproach to those sacred principles of liberty"; colonizationists tirelessly pointed out that deportation would cure "American civil institutions, morals, and habits" by removing a significant political contradiction from the nation.[61] And in a remarkable rhetorical maneuver, advocates of colonization attempted to transform a history of slavery into a valuable learning experience for African-Americans. Viewed through the colonizationist's looking glass, a racially segregated society appeared as a republican campus where Africans learned the American principles that they would now implant in Africa. The American Colonization Society included in their annual report an 1811 letter written by Thomas Jefferson. He argues that African-Americans will "carry back to the country of their origin the seeds of civilization, which might render their sojournment here a blessing." Another advocate suggested that slaves inherited the very political forms denied them. Out of gratitude, emigrants would help build a colony modeled on the United States that will "attest [to] the extent of their obligations to their former master." Thus, the African colony becomes a redemptive site where the United States could not only relocate an alien population but also remove the stain of slavery and empire from American history.[62] This site promised to restore the classical and philosophical idea of imperial expansion, while conveniently forgetting the violent legacy of European and American imperialism.

Compared to these fantasies, Cooper's mediations on race relations in *The Pioneers* are those of a sober, if conservative, realist. The author does not shy away from depicting the effects of racial division on the domestic order of Temple's house, the novel's central metaphor for the American nation. Rather, Cooper establishes a correspondence between the social interior of Temple's house and its physical exterior. While interior scenes such as the community dinner and the fireside chat articulate social and race relations in Templeton, the stylistic flaws of the structure itself evoke a larger criticism of incompetence in the U.S. Congress. Following their own theory of "composite order," two amateur architects, Sheriff Jones and Hiram Doolittle, fail to adhere to the classical principles of balance, proportion, and order as they construct a house that, as the narrator admits, is "lucky" to be standing. The bricolage of the "composite order" is useful because it allows Jones and Doolittle to assimilate American materials and helps them to conceal their amateurish mistakes.

If we position this comic fable within the contexts of Missouri Compromise debates and the persistent dilemma of free African-American subjectivity, then the house represents an evolving democracy put together too haphazardly, its unbalanced nature assured by the problem of slavery spreading across the country. Jones and Doolittle resemble the meddlesome legislators whom Pennsylvania Supreme Court Justice Henry Brackenridge lamented as limited thinkers; lacking a classical vision, they use the Constitution recklessly and distort the republican edifice as they try to cover up their mistakes. Consider the misshapen roof of Temple's house; the two architects earnestly "essayed to remedy the evil [of the roof] with paint." They experiment with different colors in order to conceal the deformity with an idyllic illusion:

> The first [color] was a sky-blue, in the vain expectation that the eye might be cheated into the belief, it was the heavens themselves that hung so imposingly over [Judge Temple's] dwelling: the second was, what he called, a cloud-colour, being nothing more nor less than an imitation of smoke: the third was what Richard termed an invisible green, an experiment that did not succeed against a back-ground of sky. . . . Richard ended the affair by boldly covering the whole beneath a colour that he christened "sunshine," a cheap way, as he assured his cousin, the Judge, of always keeping fair weather over his head.[63]

Ignorant of the "square rule," the two architects kicked a "few wedges" under the faulty pillars to "keep them steady."[64] Despite their incompetence, the narrator claims their "composite order" had become the "model" for every "aspiring edifice" in the region, a notion clearly evoking popular lore that held up the United States as an example for new republics across the globe. Yet we should not believe the colorful illusion, since as Vidler reminds us, a "fault line" cutting across an architectural structure is often a self-conscious attempt to "underplay the monumental."[65] The color "sunshine," like the structural "gaps" and handy "wedges," attempts to prove that the "master's resources" have produced a secure, watertight roof. Yet buried beneath the colors is an American "fault line," created by the legislators of the Sixteenth Congress who devised the Missouri Compromise and upset the precarious balance between free and slave states. The house's original roof, hidden by both rhetorical "smoke" and legislative "sunshine," suggests the compromise line drawn across the United States at 36°30'.[66]

The issue of Missouri statehood unsettled Thomas Jefferson to such a degree that, as Peter Onuf has described, the crisis prepared the way for his radical disillusionment in the early 1820s.[67] So why have literary historians been reluctant to connect Cooper's novel, particularly Temple's house, to these momentous debates on race and nationhood? The general notion is that Cooper doesn't comment on the slavery question until 1828, when the polemical *Notions of the Americans* was published. One of the few critics who puts *The Pioneers* in dialogue with the politics of slavery, R. D. Madison, claims *Notions of the Americans* is Cooper's most comprehensive commentary on slavery, written "if not . . . in the absolute wake of the Missouri controversy, at least with that struggle in mind."[68] The book, a didactic and fictional travel narrative, has a curious history. Persuaded by the French revolutionary Lafayette to defend the United States against European charges of political hypocrisy, Cooper writes a long lecture for a European audience, in part about a democracy unmarked by imperial power or slavery. The racial tension that had come to characterize the 1820s— represented in Templeton—is absent in the 1828 narrative. Instead, Cooper invents a nation seemingly unfazed by racial difference and whose Constitution is sufficiently capacious to contain the contradiction of slavery. His self-conception as a strict constructionist makes Cooper, particularly in *The Pioneers,* a complex social critic of the competing interests of race, economics, and democratic idealism in the nationalist discourse. This chapter will conclude with a reading of *Notions of the Americans* that clarifies even more the complexity of Cooper's historical vision in *The Pioneers.*[69]

A blend of fact and fiction, *Notions of the Americans* relates the adventures of a European in the United States; he is known as the Bachelor, and Cadwallader, a native New Yorker, serves as his guide. The defensiveness of *Notions of the Americans* makes it a deeply troubled, argumentative text. As the mouthpiece for Cooper's patriotic declarations, Cadwallader spends a majority of his time revising allegedly inaccurate histories that Europeans have written about the United States. In the process of correcting these texts, Cadwallader teaches the Bachelor about democratic government so as to dispel the falsehood of an imperial America; as one might suspect, a very large part of defending American constitutionalism after the Missouri Compromise was finding a way to rationalize the existence of both slavery and oppressed free African-Americans. Consequently, *Notions of the Americans* has none of the realist depictions of racial tension that Cooper includes in *The Pioneers.*

For the first two hundred pages, *Notions of the Americans* celebrates America without mentioning race, but any discussion of the American system was forced to rationalize the cohabitation of slavery and the Declaration. At first, Cooper's polemic goes no further than a collective apologia for the institutions of slavery, but the need to address slavery and racial domination is unavoidable. In one paradigmatic passage, the European Bachelor's declaration of an honest America—like any number of statements about American exceptionalism that ignore slavery and racial segregation—deploys the parenthesis to suppress the reality of slavery:

> Europeans will not believe facts which have a daily existence before our eyes, prov[ing] nothing but their ignorance. In my own opinion, and this is but a matter of opinion, there is less falsehood uttered in the US, *(if you exclude the slaves)* than in any Christian country.[70]

The American Colonization Society preached political fitness in the United States through African-American expatriation; in the same way, this polemic uses the parenthesis to enable the depiction of a nation untainted by political "falsehood." As the narrative proceeds, the outline of a nation divorced from race gradually takes shape, but a remarkable parallel narrative necessarily appears as Cooper continually deposits qualifiers, facts, and observations regarding race in a series of parentheses and footnotes. One particular footnote is attached to a passage in the body of the text in which Cooper assures the reader that the free African-American population in New York will not increase. He includes the census report, as evidence, in the footnote that lists the numbers of cattle, horses, sheep, hogs, idiots, and lunatics currently residing in New York, a grouping that exemplifies the inferior status of free African-Americans in the United States.

Just as Freeborn's resistance interferes with Natty's gunplay in *The Pioneers,* race persistently counteracts Cooper's desire to construct a patriotic epic of the American republic. Declaring an exceptional America, Cooper discovers, means displacing slaves and free African-Americans downward into subordinate positions in *Notions of the Americans,* a move symbolic of the African-American's absent presence in the Constitution. In one footnote devoid of Cooper's usual political astuteness, he points to the reason why his polemic surrenders no space to race or slavery:

It is manifestly unsafe to found any arguments concerning the political institutions of this country on the existence of slavery, since the slaves have no
more to do with government than inanimate objects.[71]

Cooper's footnote articulates the rationale that traditionally enables American historiography and political science to exclude slavery from its focus.
The ambivalence of *The Pioneers,* however, demonstrates the presence and
function of race in larger structures symbolic of national government, such
as Temple's house, in the legal language Judge Temple and Sheriff Jones
rely on to create a hierarchical "order," and in the notion of democratic
government that excludes slaves from the table. Indeed, the Missouri controversy clarified everyone's worst fears: slaves, while lacking political identity, influenced the shape of national institutions. And now an increasing
number of free African-Americans joined the slaves and convinced political leaders to invent a vast number of local, state, and federal statutes aimed
at repressing the mobility and agency of African-Americans.

When the narrator takes the Bachelor down South, as we saw last chapter with Arthur Mervyn, the parallel narrative closes, and Cooper can no
longer dodge the slavery question through footnotes and parenthetical
commentary. Yet the author chooses to forget how his own novel grapples
with racial antagonism.[72] Instead, traveling into the South with his audience of American detractors in mind, Cadwallader chooses to downplay
the divisive aftermath of both the Missouri controversy and the Vesey conspiracy, while celebrating the uniqueness of the American experiment.
Cooper uses Cadwallader to explain how the president can appropriate the
Constitution in a state of national emergency in order to preserve the union.
The ambivalence of *The Pioneers* regarding slavery vanishes before the pro-
pagandistic impulse in *Notions of the Americans.* Where in its pages are
the incompetent architects of *The Pioneers?* The expansion of slavery, the
heightened oppression of free and bonded African-Americans, the lingering conundrum of emancipation, and the sectional divide at 36°30' all disprove his claim in *Notions of the Americans* that the United States has
passed the "ordeal of durability" occurring a few years earlier.

Cooper tries to invent a nation unfazed by issues of race and slavery, a
nation that can benevolently snuff out dissent by the nature of its Constitution, that can effortlessly remove the "blot" of blackness spreading across
the continent, and that, if necessary, can overcome any slave insurrection.

Directing his defense to America's detractors, Cooper does not forecast insurrection (he simply describes the constitutional machinery that would wipe it out) or sound Jefferson's "knell of the union." He guarantees that the sheer power of whiteness will magically subsume blackness: "There is no doubt, that the free blacks, like the aborigines, gradually disappear, before the superior moral and physical influence of whites."[73]

But this immense effort to suppress racial contradictions finally wears Cooper down; at the end of *Notions of the Americans,* when slavery should be sufficiently buried beneath a happy ending, he repeats a well-worn defense most famously used in an early draft of the Declaration of Independence. The United States is not responsible for slavery, since European empires imposed its institutions in the colonies and perpetuated the slave trade:

> Is it not a fact that the [slave] policy of all America was for more than a century controlled by Europe, and was not this scourge introduced under that policy? Has that policy in Europe been yet abandoned? . . . It is as puerile as it is unjust, therefore, for these two countries [France and England] . . . to pretend to any exclusive exemption from the sin or the shame of slavery.[74]

Cooper is willing to admit to the American republic's shame for perpetuating slavery, but only if England and France share the burden of what Cooper implies is the remnant "scourge" of empire that afflicts U.S. culture. Urging the reader to "think calmly" about immediate emancipation, Cooper claims that this oft-stated solution of Europe would have dangerous consequences in the United States. Until the French and English are ready to "contribute" to full emancipation (does he mean helping the United States to invest more resources in Liberia?), Cooper scolds, they should stop castigating America for a slave system that Europeans created.

As a way to express his conversion to American constitutionalism, the European Bachelor creates a national shield. Replacing an outdated, imperial European coat of arms, the new shield "is a constellation of twenty four stars, surrounded by [a] cloud of *nebulae,* with a liberty cap for a crest and two young negroes as supporters."[75] The symbol fixes the dynamic between slave and white American; unlike the architecture of Temple's house, defined by racial anxiety, the symbolic shield ignores the inherent tension in the relationship between their two worlds. In *The Pioneers,*

African-Americans repeatedly bisect homogeneous spaces intended to be symbolic of the larger political community—the dinner table, the forest trial, the house's interior architecture. Every discussion in the novel about civic or national identity, about the use of power or social order, stutters and pauses as participants qualify the exclusion of African-Americans. Like the slaves "snug stored below" in the cellar, the two figures represented in the shield are subordinate to an idealized democratic community. Yet Cooper's trenchant defense of the Constitution and denial of empire in *Notions of the Americans,* requiring the exclusion of slavery from the American story, erases the ambivalence of the novel. Unlike Jefferson's image of a former slave armed with "freedom and a dagger," a fearful slogan defining the representation of race in *The Pioneers,* Cooper's shield refuses to replay for his European audience Jefferson's apocalyptic prophesy of insurrection, white flight, and disunion. The slaves and free African-Americans depicted in *Notions of the Americans* are passive and fail to strike fear in the America's imperial imagination. On the contrary, Cooper's African-American figures refuse the dagger in order to hold the liberty cap with both hands.

chapter 5

William Apess and the Nullification of Empire

By the early 1820s, as a result of the joint public and private project of colonization, several thousand ex-slaves and free African-Americans left the United States for the new African colony of Liberia. Over the course of the decade, the notion that the United States could relocate American Indians west of the Mississippi gradually seemed like an attainable goal. With free African-Americans being deported and American Indians about to be pushed into the western territories, the emerging democratic citizen might finally dream of possessing a racially homogeneous nation. The twinned ideologies of colonization and Indian removal, each reinforcing the other, exposed the imperial workings of the United States. Like the previous British empire, the United States envisioned the subjugation of American Indians and African-Americans as a necessary sacrifice to the extension of white dominion. Liberia was supposed to strengthen slavery by eliminating the halfway freedoms embodied by both free African-Americans and Northern states. And Indian removal, under the guise of an enlightened national policy, needed the full arsenal of imperial strategies—military might, broken treaties, destitution, and disease—to remove tribes west of the Mississippi River and take possession of ancestral lands. Both removal plans rendered the United States as purified racial space endangered by the presence of African-Americans and American Indians.

Unlike European practices of imperialism, U.S. imperial activity did not necessarily have to establish overseas colonies in order to expand its geopolitical borders. For example, in 1816, General Andrew Jackson invaded

Spanish Florida by simply crossing the southern border in pursuit of Seminole Indians and the fugitive slaves to whom they granted refuge. Backed by his forces in Spanish territory, Jackson named himself commander of northern Florida and executed two Englishmen whom Jackson believed were inciting the Seminoles and former slaves to attack southern settlements. The First Seminole War was a watershed moment in American imperialism. The war instigated an international conflict among the United States, Spain, and England that negotiators ultimately resolved by selling Florida to the United States, including American assurances that the United States would make no future claim on Texas and Cuba.[1] With the Florida territory, the United States inherited two defiant populations—Seminoles and escaped slaves—who were unwilling to leave their homes for the American West. For over two centuries, Southern slaves had looked to Spanish Florida as English Puritans had once looked to New England: as an asylum from tyranny.[2] Seminoles and slaves played prominent roles in previous imperial conflicts and border skirmishes. Since slavery remained in the new United States, independence did not change the master class's fear that fugitives would cross the border and spark a slave insurrection. Once General Jackson took possession of Florida (which apparently took President Monroe by surprise), the United States moved to reverse centuries of what they perceived as Spanish evils. They implanted a policy to remove the Seminoles from the peninsula and to return the fugitive slaves to their former masters. Such a policy was intended to strengthen imperial authority by removing threats to slavery and by opening Florida to white immigration.

The Spanish cession of Florida to the United States, and its subsequent attempts to establish white dominion, demonstrates a critical intersection between the histories of U.S. imperialism, American Indians, and African-Americans. If maintaining slavery and racial domination had revealed the remnants of empire intrinsic to the United States, then Jackson's pursuit of runaways and Seminoles exhibited how such decisions could lead the nation into illegal actions and an unpopular war. Spanning twenty-six years and bracketed by the First and Second Seminole Wars (1816–1818 and 1835–1842), the conflict was a costly guerilla conflict marked by massacres and ambushes on both sides, leading military historians to refer to it as a nineteenth-century precursor of Vietnam.[3] The Battle of New Orleans at the end of the War of 1812 might have made General Jackson a national hero, but his assault on Spanish Florida demonstrated that this was a man willing to start a war, quite literally, over slavery. At least the slave powers held this perspective in the presidential election of 1829. A frontier war hero who envisioned an expanding national domain that included slavery, the new president carried every Southern and Western state.[4]

The subject of this final chapter, the nineteenth-century American Indian writer William Apess, was a veteran of the War of 1812, a key experience that shaped his criticism of white power. Of racially mixed heritage (white, Native, and African), Apess was brought up as a Pequot Indian in New England, but he spent much of his youth as an indentured servant in white households. After visiting a Methodist camp meeting as a thirteen-year-old boy, Apess experienced a vision calling him to "go in peace and sin no more." Acting in a way that would typify his later fusion of religion and an egalitarian politics, Apess translated the vision as a divine command to escape from a classic body of American owners—farmer, judge, general—who responded by putting the unmanageable boy up for sale or, when he inevitably ran, by placing a bounty on his head. His days as a fugitive read like a picaresque novel: finding a temporary refuge in the military during the War of 1812 and then fleeing; wandering along the northern frontier and living with sympathetic Natives across the border in Canada; working his way back south, earning subsistence wages as a cook, a baker's assistant, and a farmhand; arriving in Connecticut, which surprised his relatives who thought him dead; and becoming the most prolific Native author of the early nineteenth century. Apess published six works between 1829 and 1838, all of which addressed the problems of racial inequality in the United States: *A Son of the Forest* (1829), *The Increase of the Kingdom of Christ: A Sermon* (1831), *The Indians: The Ten Lost Tribes* (1831), *The Experience of Five Christian Indians of the Pequot Tribe* (1833), *Indian Nullification of the Unconstitutional Laws of Massachusetts Relative to the Marshpee Tribe, or The Pretended Riot Explained* (1835), and *Eulogy on King Philip* (1836). Taken collectively, the six texts constitute one of the period's most powerful rebukes to U.S. imperial authority. Over the course of his brief career, Apess fashioned a racially inclusive democracy that challenged mainstream Jacksonian America and its practices of racial domination.[5]

If his contemporaries were not familiar with this body of work, they knew Apess both as a lecturer on Indian affairs and as the notorious leader of the resistance movement he organized and led on behalf of the Mashpee

Indians of Massachusetts in 1833. Unlike the Seminoles' ongoing resistance and the previous year's Black Hawk War—two struggles against the federal government—the Mashpee opposed the exploitation of their labor and lands by the State of Massachusetts. Despite the obvious differences in scale, however, Native and white participants and onlookers understood the Mashpee revolt within the context of Indian removal, the federal policy of relocating Native peoples west of the Mississippi. Furthermore, like the protracted Seminole wars, the Mashpee revolt revealed the convergence of Native and African-American histories of resistance and subjugation. Both the Seminoles and Mashpees were racially mixed peoples who welcomed other survivors of colonization and slavery into their communities. Such a threatening mix, from the perspective of white power, would ultimately shape public perception of the Mashpee revolt.

The bulk of this chapter studies how Apess represents this event in *Indian Nullification of the Unconstitutional Laws of Massachusetts Relative to the Marshpee Tribe*. Apess did not simply forge his narrative practices or his political rhetoric out of thin air; this chapter, taking an unusual approach to the question, argues that William Lloyd Garrison and a defiant abolitionism offered him a useful model for attacking the racial prejudice that underpinned the state's oppression of nonwhites and the period's racist ideology of white nationalism as well as justifying the twinned ideologies of removal. Specifically, I consider the influence of William Lloyd Garrison's *Thoughts on African Colonization* on Apess's history of the Mashpee revolt, *Indian Nullification*. Both authors question a presumed national genealogy and demonstrate how U.S. imperial culture maintains its system of racial domination and privilege through an elaborate set of racial fictions, all of which invent the nation as a homogeneous site in which nonwhites have no legitimate place and are destined to disappear. Finally, I follow Apess's evolving political and narrative practice to its logical end. By placing King Philip's War (1676–1677), which pitted English colonists against a coalition of Native tribes, in the context of the American Revolution, Apess makes use of the past in order to tell an alternative history of Native sovereignty in the United States. Before moving toward those overtly collective narratives, however, this chapter begins by exploring how Apess's autobiography, *A Son of the Forest*, highlights the historical residue of colonization, which continually disrupts the rhetoric of personal salvation. Whether composing autobiography or historical narrative, Apess depicts a nation rooted in the historical trinity of U.S. imperialism—war, slavery, and territorial expansion—rather than the American Revolution.

SECOND SIGHT IN *A SON OF THE FOREST*

The tendency among critics has been to see two sides to Apess's career: his Christian salvationism and his political activism. On one side of the divide is *A Son of the Forest*, which has been read as a Christian conversion narrative that Apess wrote, in part, to earn an exhorter's license. Considered to be the first book-length autobiography written by an American Indian, it recounts Apess's religious awakening. Critical approaches often reduce Apess to the sum of his conversion narrative, lament his Christian voice, his dispersed community, his seeming ignorance of American Indian traditions, and his racial hybridity. This criticism ultimately concludes that Apess did not speak like an "authentic" American Indian. Over the last few years, however, critics have begun to see Apess as something more than a Christian convert, inventing new ways of reading his extraordinary body of work. For instance, Robert Allen Warrior, taking Apess as his central subject, claims that "little work exists that posits Native writings and Native history as existing within the complexities of the modern and the postmodern condition"; he urges critics to restore "Native realities [to] the crucible of modernity."[6] If we consider the historical complexity of a figure like Apess, whose narrative practice drew from religious, indigenous, and political currents, then Warrior suggests that we can reassess the value of a rediscovered writer who "subverts the usual, accustomed categories of who and what Indians are."[7]

To this end, I read Apess's *A Son of the Forest* as something more than a Christian conversion narrative; it is also a poignant story about the political awakening of an American Indian to the practices of U.S. imperial power. My reading reveals how the conversion narrative initiates Apess into abolitionism and antiremoval, the two great democratic struggles of the 1830s. Furthermore, the conversion narrative reveals how Apess's movement among several heterogeneous positions—indentured servant, soldier, preacher, laborer, and civil rights activist—produced a profound and agile narrative practice that drew materials from all corners of American society. Nineteenth-century narratives written by American Indians east of the Mississippi or from urban centers, migrant labor circuits, or under evangelical tents simply do not use the same narrative modes as their more traditional western counterparts who are more apt to speak from an identifiable tribal base.

Part of the challenge of reading *A Son of the Forest* is making sense of Apess's ironic sensibility. While he tells a story that, on the surface, is about the author's conversion to Christianity, he also represents a political, to go along with his personal, awakening. Apess is the title character—a son of the forest—born of natural law, governed by a just God. At the same time, Apess celebrates this lineage because he is decidedly not the son of the Great White Father, President Jackson, and an ambitious state that has robbed and enslaved his people. Apess's historical conscience evolves over the course of the 1830s, apparent less in his personalized conversion narrative than in his measured criticism of Massachusetts in *Indian Nullification* and in his scathing denunciation of Puritan New England in *Eulogy on King Philip*. Interwoven with the story of Apess's spiritual awakening is a remarkable tale about his awareness that the legacy of colonization still marked his life in New England. Apess narrates his life story with the moral force of Frederick Douglass's *Narrative of the Life of Frederick Douglass, an American Slave*. While *A Son of the Forest* might be the story of a Christian convert, it also blends religious and egalitarian politics, a mixture characterizing democratic struggle in the nineteenth century. Methodism appealed to Apess because it presented a God who recognized the American Indian, a God different from the one worshipped by his white masters: "I felt convinced that Christ died for all mankind—that age, sect, color, country, or situation made no difference. I felt assurance that I was included in the plan of redemption with all my brethren. No one can conceive with what joy I hailed this *new* doctrine."[8] Combining this "*new* doctrine" with his personal battles against racial prejudice, Apess wrought a new scriptural typology that called on the United States to grant freedom to all of its peoples.

Working within the conversion narrative's conventions, Apess must first realize his own sinfulness before finding salvation. The agonizing part of the story, the quality that makes it sound more like a slave narrative than a story of personal salvation, occurs when Apess relates his childhood fear of Indians. For Apess the conversion narrative does not end with his spiritual rebirth. First, Apess must overcome his self-alienation by forging a healthy connection to his Pequot relations, a move that is fundamental to the evolution of his democratic politics. Renee Bergland, one of the few to note Apess's racial awakening, suggests that by "acknowledging his own early hatred of Indians, Apess is able to construct *A Son of the Forest* as a narrative of enlightenment, of progress from childhood fears of his own Indianness to adult pride in his Indian identity."[9] The beginning of *A Son of the Forest* dramatizes the moments when young Apess confronts an American society that looks on him with scorn. The placement at the beginning is strategic, since it enables Apess to convey his temporary surrender to the nation's psychic violence. Unless he reconciles his own alienation, there can be no conversion to a religious faith by which the conflict between the Pequot and the American can be pacified.

His indenture to a white family, the Furmans, typified his efforts to forge a self out of broken circumstances. Literally born-again in the Furman home, Apess developed a curiosity for "the state of existence beyond the grave," and he begins to attend church, where he "receive[d] instruction in divine things."[10] However, members of the congregation engaged in a ritual of naming to marginalize him, ruining any solace gained from Scripture. "To this day I remember that nothing scarcely grieved me so much," Apess recalls, "than to be called a nickname."[11] The "improper name" that burdens him is "Indian":

> I thought it disgraceful to be called an Indian; it was considered as a slur upon an oppressed and scattered nation, and I have often been led to inquire where the whites received this word, which they so often threw as an opprobrious epithet at the sons of the forest. I could not find it in the bible and therefore concluded that it was a word imported for the special purpose of degrading us.[12]

Apess finds no justification for the racial hostility in Scripture, a simple episode that conveys his conviction that white people misused the Bible to justify continued subjugation of the American Indian. The episode epitomized the place of Scripture in his politics. Scripture, as much as democratic principles, defined public morality. Apess developed alternative interpretations that demonstrated how the social connotations of "Indian"—not divine inspiration—made it sound like a "slur."

This lesson about strategic white racism—"imported for the special purpose of degrading us"—prepares the reader for two noteworthy episodes told from the perspective of an Indian child not yet aware of how white society has alienated him from his history. For a time young Apess lived with his grandmother, apparently broken down by alcoholism and poverty. After she beat Apess on one occasion, state authorities removed him from his grandmother's home and indentured him. Too young to reconcile his grandmother's destitution with her violence toward him, Apess fears returning to his Pequot relations. This feeling makes him seek protection within his master's household:

> [S]o completely was I weaned from the interests and affections of my brethren that a mere threat of being sent away among the Indians into the dreary woods had a much better effect in making me obedient to the commands of my superiors than any corporeal punishment that they ever inflicted.[13]

The passage establishes a correspondence between the physical violence of his Native family and the psychological violence of a white culture that gradually alienates him. Serving white masters, Apess is gradually "weaned" from his family, so far removed from his past that he no longer remembers the "affections" of his Pequot relations. In fact, they terrify him, and his masters exploit his alienation by terrorizing him with the "mere threat" to send him back to his Pequot family's "dreary woods."

Using the second episode to elaborate his alienation in more detail, Apess explained the threat's force. On a walk in the woods, picking berries with some others, "the dread which pervaded [his] mind" about a forest possibly concealing "savages" distorts his perception:

> We had not been out long before we fell in with a company of white females, on the same errand—their complexion was, to say the least, as *dark* as that of the natives. This circumstance filled my mind with terror, and I broke from the party with my utmost speed, and I could not muster enough courage to look behind until I had reached home. By this time my imagination had pictured out a tale of blood.[14]

The sight of the two "dark" women reminds Apess, as Bergland points out, of the mother who abandoned him and of the grandmother who abused him; the ambiguity of the encounter attests to a racial code that is as superficial as variations of skin color.[15] The childhood "tale of blood" mocks the

power of "whiteness" in a society where the young Indian comes to identify with the "white fears of Indians."

In fact, the "tale of blood" receives more emphasis than any other event
in his childhood because it gives *A Son of the Forest* its structure of racial
awakening. After relating the tale, Apess interrupts the narrative with a
critical digression that will become the basis of his later efforts both to
contest Indian removal and to disprove imperial histories that depict American Indians as mindless killers:

> It may be proper for me here to remark that the great fear I entertained of
> my brethren was occasioned by the many stories I had heard of their cru-
> elty toward the whites—how they were in the habit of killing and scalping
> men, women, and children. But the whites did not tell me that they were
> in the great majority of instances the aggressors—that they had imbrued
> their hands in the lifeblood of my brethren, driven them from their once
> peaceful and happy homes—that they introduced among them the fatal and
> exterminating diseases of civilized life. If the whites had told me how cruel
> they had been to the "poor Indian," I should have apprehended as much
> harm from them.[16]

Replacing the legendary "savage" Indian as the source of terror with the
racial fictions of U.S. imperialism, Apess demonstrates the symbolic nature
of colonial and imperial history by invoking a home very different from
that of the Furmans. The imagery of contagion figures the destructiveness
of American civilization, represented by the bond of indenture that has
permanently replaced natural familial connections. Instead of "once peaceful and happy homes," American Indians occupy a haunted landscape of
colonial violence. Home casts a dark shadow, as the young Pequot flees
from dangerous "dark" figures who live only in imperial fictions, and must
seek protection in an abusive master's home.

Stranded between two domestic sites, Apess describes his alienation as
being released into a vast nothingness, a "cast-off member of the tribe"; the
title for his life story, *A Son of the Forest,* ultimately invokes the perspective of the older writer who has learned to resist white supremacy. With
the title, Apess captures the experience of growing up in New England, a
land torn apart rather than improved by the arrival of American civilization. Its allusion to the myth of the noble savage at home in the romantic

wilderness ironically depicts the vast distance between myth and an orphaned Apess, rendered homeless by a "fatal" America. Given the previous critical focus on a religious awakening in *A Son of the Forest,* I want, in contrast, to establish Apess's equally important racial (and thus political) awakening, particularly because these two impulses are mutually compatible in the evolution of his anti-imperial practices. His social gospel inspires visions of a single humanity, which will link his work to abolitionist discourse.[17] Perhaps alluding to Tom Paine's use of biblical Adam as a premise of revolutionary liberalism, Apess's autobiography posits that Americans are "in fact but one family; we are all descendents of one great progenitor—Adam"; the stories of racial prejudice that follow are designed to demonstrate to the reader how racial enmity breaches the democratic contract by dividing naturally equal persons.[18] For example, after relating the above episodes, Apess makes a transition that addresses the connection between color prejudice and religious morality: "shortly after this occurrence I relapsed into my former habits."[19]

What I want to suggest is that Apess's backsliding is always tied to networks of racial domination. His deliverance demands that he collapse the racial hierarchies of U.S. imperialism and envisage an inclusive democracy. Otherwise the evils of rum and other vices will continue to obstruct his path to salvation. Thus by the end of *A Son of the Forest,* Apess effaces the horror stories of his youth with the force of his egalitarian gospel, providing a larger vision of a racially harmonious future that rescues Natives from removal. Such an anti-imperial, democratic vision defines his Methodism: "One evening as I was preaching to some colored people, in a schoolhouse, the power of the Lord moved on the congregation, both white and colored—hard hearts began to melt and inquire what they must do to be saved."[20] Significantly, this revelation occurs in the schoolhouse, and from this place Apess believes the nation can realize its true moral creed. "I rejoice sincerely in the spread of the principles of civil and religious liberty—may they ever be found 'hand in hand' accomplishing the designs of God, in promoting the welfare of mankind." By coming to know the "tales of blood" and other racial fictions that maintain U.S. imperial culture, Apess, through his analysis, gains both freedom and a view of his human equality. The metaphor he employs to represent imperial power is the nation's prison house of racial hierarchies: "I can truly say that the spirit of prejudice is no longer an inmate of my bosom."[21] In contrast to earlier descriptions of American civilization as a "fatal and exterminating disease," afflicting primarily Natives, Apess sermonizes that only an antiracist, anti-imperial democracy can deliver all Americans from God's wrath. This fusion of his religious and political agendas—"hand in hand"—marks the direction his democratic politics will take in the 1830s.

An "inmate" to white America's contempt no longer, Apess devoted the rest of his career to demonstrating for Native rights and to obstructing the racial codes intrinsic to U.S. imperialism. Turning away from first-person forms like the conversion narrative, Apess wrote polemical histories of colonization and essays against racial prejudice, engaged in local activism on behalf of the Mashpee Indians, and traveled the New England lecture circuit to voice his objections to government intent on dispossessing American Indians. *A Son of the Forest* focuses attention on how white racism underpinned the psychological subjugation of American Indians in New England. In addition, the memoir presents his personal awakening as an allegory for an inclusive democratic politics, just the type of reform movement that was beginning to emerge as radical abolitionism.

WILLIAM LLOYD GARRISON AND THE EXAMPLE OF ABOLITIONISM

A defiant new model of abolitionism, led by William Lloyd Garrison, was one vital source for Apess's evolving literary and political perspective.[22] In 1829, the same year Apess published *A Son of the Forest* and announced his conversion, Garrison was on the cusp of his own conversion to immediate abolitionism. The doctrine of African-American colonization still monopolized theories of racial reform, and even Garrison believed it provided the safest solution to the nation's racial crisis. As the population of free African-Americans topped three hundred thousand by 1830, the number of state and local auxiliaries of the American Colonization Society (ACS) exceeded two hundred, and they worked to spread the gospel of removal throughout the country. But their vision of a nation freed of African-Americans was not unopposed. Spurred by the founding of Liberia, African-American intellectuals led a sustained offensive against the bulwark of general opinion that promoted colonization as the only solution to the nation's "race problem." As President Monroe, Henry Clay, and other American luminaries lobbied in Washington for support for colonization, the *Freedom's*

Journal, the first African-American newspaper, initiated its campaign against removal. While black freemen developed a response to colonization, David Walker's incendiary *An Appeal to the Coloured Citizens of the World* (1829) ignited a national emergency (such a text had to be smuggled into the South, often stitched into clothing or used as merchandise packing). Stunned by Walker's manifesto, and educated through countless discussions with his African-American allies in Baltimore, such as William Watkins, Garrison published *Thoughts on African Colonization* (1832). The book became both a conversion tale of Garrison's political awakening and a guide for a radical abolitionism calling for immediate emancipation. Not many people recognized at this time the significance of Garrison's conversion to immediate abolitionism. In the six years following *Thoughts on African Colonization,* abolitionists published the movement's founding texts and, in the process, writes Goodman, developed "the most extensive defense of racial equality in American history."[23]

Apess's work shows an affinity for abolitionism's agenda that is hard to ignore; since so much about Apess's life is a mystery, however, we don't know who may have mentored him or if he attended anticolonization meetings in Boston, New York, or Providence. One suspects that the most vocal activist for Native rights in the early nineteenth century read the *Liberator, Freedom's Journal,* and Walker's *An Appeal to the Coloured Citizens of the World* because the basis of their protest rhetoric—to convince white America that racial prejudice underpinned both the slave system and the separatist ideology of colonization—was also the basis of Apess's democratic politics. We do know, however, an essential fact: Apess and Garrison were aware of each other's political activities. Garrison published editorials supporting Apess and the cause of the Mashpee, and Apess included Garrison's defense of Mashpee rights in *Indian Nullification.* Even though Apess fought for racial equality, often unifying the struggle of Natives and African-Americans in a single phrase—"colored people"—he is not yet considered a key contributor to a burgeoning movement that articulated, for the first time since the intoxicating days of the Revolution, a vision of racial justice. Positioned within the context of abolitionism, Apess appears less like a regional or ethnic writer, more like an individual whose anti-imperial voice contested the racial limits of American democracy in its crucial decade.[24]

Thus one can safely assume Apess's familiarity with the groundbreaking publication of Garrison's *Thoughts on African Colonization*, published a year earlier, widely distributed, and affordable at sixty-two cents a copy or two copies for a dollar. Taking his evidence from the annual reports of the American Colonization Society, Garrison wrote a comprehensive report of the colonizationist doctrine, and then proceeded to expose its falsehoods. The first part refuted the racist reasoning that supported the American Colonization Society. For example, he exposed the public claim that colonization would not interfere with the property relations of slavery by introducing evidence from the annual reports, which assured slaveholders that the removal of an allegedly disruptive class of free African-Americans would actually help to assure the value of their slaves. The second part reprinted commentary of African-Americans voiced in anticolonization meetings. The simple format exhibited Garrison's "radical assumption" that the nation should consider the opinion of African-Americans; he effectively "converted a crucial core of early white abolitionist leaders and rank and file" and also "triggered an extensive debate between partisans of the ACS and abolitionists that shortly sidetracked colonization as a popular movement."[25] *Thoughts on African Colonization* immediately became a guide for abolitionists; in the words of Henry Mayer, its vision of a society free of racial distinctions "captured the attention of the humanitarian public with a force unmatched in American journalism since Tom Paine's *Common Sense.*"[26]

Garrison's *Thoughts on African Colonization* established two key rationales for opposing colonization and advocating immediate emancipation. First, Garrison exposes the ideological nature of white power by revealing the differential power relations at the core of racial prejudice. By attacking the notion of innate racial inferiority, gaining credence during this era through the growing popularity of raciology, Garrison rejects the fiction of racial difference. In chapter 9, "The American Colonization Society Denies the Possibility of Elevating the Blacks in This Country," Garrison condemns the opinions of colonizationists "in almost every instance by reputedly the most enlightened, patriotic and benevolent men in the land," who forbid the education of slaves and even withhold it from free African-Americans.[27] Education and achievement, of course, were the ultimate refutations of the racist notion that African-Americans were an inferior people, and Garrison accuses America of acting less on republican virtues than other European nations. Unlike these countries, where educated blacks have crashed through the supposedly "impassable barriers of nature," the colonization movement "proclaimed to the world . . . that the American people can never be as republican in their feelings and practices as Frenchmen, Spaniards or Englishmen!"[28]

Second, Garrison and the abolitionists of the 1830s nationalized the effects of slavery and racism. Just because slavery had disappeared from the North did not mean its peoples were free from its corrosive values—Garrisonian abolitionists tirelessly voiced this position as the movement surged over the course of the decade. Racial prejudice, often seen as the unenlightened blight of the Southern slaveocracy, also afflicted Northern merchants who profited from slave-produced commodities. Financial exchange blurred the boundaries between free and slave states, thus allowing Garrison to link racial apartheid in the North with slavery in the South. Attempting to inspire remorse and support from the merchant middle class, Garrison ends his preface to *Thoughts on African Colonization* with a conclusive statement on the economic value of free African-American labor: "In the great cities, and in various parts of the southern states, free persons of color constitute a laborious and useful class. In a pecuniary point of view, the banishment of one-sixth of our population—of those whom we specially need—would be an act of suicide. The veriest smatterer in political economy cannot but perceive the ruinous tendency of such a measure."[29] Garrison would not allow middle-class Americans—the very social class he most needed to persuade to support the break from colonization—to miss his point. He introduced the African-American as a vital agent in the national economy, a middling group out of which an American middle class would ultimately emerge. He knew merchants, many working productively together with free African-Americans in those "great cities," and he trusted they would heed this lesson.

The acceleration of abolitionism in the years between Walker's *An Appeal to the Coloured Citizens of the World* and Garrison's *Thoughts on African Colonization*—which became known as "immediatism" for their defense of immediate emancipation—presented an aggressive politics of racial equality to Apess, who adapted its agenda to the particular plight of American Indians in New England.[30] By exposing the ideological nature of white power and by nationalizing the effects of slavery, Garrison provided a means for connecting the plight of New England Indians to the histories of slavery. Furthermore, Garrison demonstrated the importance of writing counternarratives that could challenge the imperial fictions. Apess realized the need for publicizing his childhood "tale of blood" so that whites could see injustice with their own eyes: "My people have had no press to record their sufferings or to make known their grievances; on this account many a tale of blood and woe has never been known to the public."[31] In an effort to challenge the white public's low opinion of American Indians, Apess delivered versions of *An Indian's Looking-Glass for the White Man* on the New England lecture circuit. Like Garrison, Apess defines illiteracy among American Indians as a tool of empires that both perpetuated the subjugation of American Indians to England and America and alienated them from their past. Moreover, both Garrison and Apess remind their audience that the education of each citizen is perhaps the key republican tenet, since it can foster self-improvement and create an informed citizenry. Extending Garrison's use of literacy to include economic practice, as well as republican principle, Apess claims literacy is a commodity unavailable to Natives. The results are predictable. If a "mean, abject, miserable race of beings" live on the reservations of New England, Apess writes in the introduction to *An Indian's Looking-Glass for the White Man,* it is because "they have nothing to make them enterprising."[32] For Apess education will inevitably lead to enterprise and equality; without it, they know only the inverse of economic and moral improvement—the self-degradation that comes through alcoholism, prostitution, migrant labor—all pursuits in the service of white America.

Thus Apess delivers risky social criticism of U.S. imperial culture; he discovers no natural law, only a corrupt social hierarchy where the color white creates a nation of individual despots, a hierarchy that compels the Native's powerlessness. Forcing the reader to consider literacy within the Franklinesque myth of American enterprise, Apess calls attention to Native oppression caused by harsh legal fictions and national indifference rather than by a "natural barrier" of racial inferiority. To prove this idea, Apess must repudiate two fundamental components of U.S. policy toward American Indians. First, he blames the United States for a policy of paternalism that "made [American Indians] believe they are minors and have not the abilities given to them by God to take care of themselves" (155). By following the theme of enterprise with another statement connoting economic self-improvement—"take care of themselves"—Apess correlates illiteracy with the poverty of New England Indians, who then inevitably sink deeper into a dependence on whites. Second, Apess reveals the tautology caused by whites believing their own racial fictions. If whites deem Natives to be incapable of improvement, lacking God-given abilities and eternally child-like, then his people will never be given the opportunity to escape oppression and become true Americans.

While Garrison reveals how white power worked to deny African-Americans their civil rights, Apess adapts this point to the disposed and exploited Natives of New England. *An Indian's Looking-Glass for the White Man* does not limit his rebuke to white men who prey on Indian women while their men are away, laboring on whaling ships or on New England farms. Instead, Apess exposes greed and betrayal at the core of American paternalism, which deliberately dispossessed American Indians by refusing to educate them. Withholding instruction thus benefited white New Englanders who wished to profit from the natural resources of Native reservations. American Indians are "much imposed upon by their neighbors, who have no principle. They would think it no crime to go upon Indian lands and cut and carry off their most valuable timber, or anything else they chose; and I doubt not but they think it clear gain" (156). These neighbors are blind to their crimes and their crimes' origin in the British colonial period. Inventing the racial fiction of a lazy, nomadic Indian, colonists not only recast themselves as enterprising white farmers but also justified taking Native lands. If the American Indian wouldn't improve the "resources God had provided," colonists reasoned, then they "should forfeit those resources."[33] To make the issue even more distasteful to land-hungry New Englanders, Apess boldly asserted the Native desire to hold on to their property. He spoke possessively about "our property" in need of protection, implying that colonists had stolen Native lands. Even more radical, however, is the move Apess makes to join the Native "person" to the land. Making a point that echoes Emerson in *Nature,* published three years later, Apess argues that possession of self, as well as property, can only be accomplished through citizenship. Apess's emphasis on enterprise is thus a racially coded concept in the New England of 1833.

"WE ARE NATIVES OF THE UNITED STATES."

I would like to turn to the convergence between Garrison and Apess, abolitionism and the Mashpee revolt, a convergence that demonstrates a particular democratic ideology defined by racial justice. The equality of white men—and the networks of racial domination necessary for guarding such privilege—was fundamental to the social vision of mainstream Jacksonian democracy. A movement that championed political independence and economic opportunity for ordinary (white) Americans could hardly suppress alternative expressions of egalitarianism. Traditionally left out of the grand narrative of Jacksonian democracy, abolitionism was just such an expression and was instrumental to fashioning a racially inclusive United States. From this perspective, the principal achievement of Garrison's *Thoughts on African Colonization* was its introduction of a hitherto suppressed African-American perspective to the democratic movement, challenging the monopoly possessed by Garrison and other white spokespersons. In part 2—"Sentiments of the People of Color"—the reader encounters the views of African-American anticolonization societies from all parts of the country. The societies shared a unifying belief: "we claim, *this country, the place of our birth, and not Africa,* as our mother country."[34] Attacking the depiction of African-Americans as foreigners with no legitimate roots in the nation, this introductory statement brought the contradictions between democratic liberty and race to the surface. The anticolonization society of Rochester, New York, put it simply: "This is the land our fathers have tilled before us; this is the land that gave us our birthright."[35] In addition to making a solid claim on citizenship, the societies voiced a unique heritage rooted in the land, a fundamental characteristic of nationalist ideologies. For example, in Wilmington, Delaware, African-Americans who opposed expatriation wrote: "We are natives of the United States; our ancestors were brought to this country by means over which they had no control; we have our attachments to the soil, and we feel that we have rights in common with other Americans."[36] In order to gain possession of civic equality, anticolonization discourse repudiated the imperial symbol of Africa as the homeland of African-Americans.

Driven by a market revolution that demanded cheaper land and labor, the Jacksonian movement saw Indian removal and slavery as two parts of the same issue. Removing American Indians from the Southeast, as well as exiling free African-Americans to Liberia, would clear the way for the expansion of slavery and cotton.[37] Viewing Indian removal and slavery as an intertwined moral and political issue, Garrison regularly blamed proslavery apologists in the *Liberator* for the injustice of Indian removal. Apess shared this view, identifying racial prejudice and white power as the reasons Americans accepted the two knotted ideologies of removal: "It is this wicked distinction of color in our land which finds so many strenuous advocates even among professing Christians, that has robbed the red men of their rights."[38] Thus, the allusion to land has a unique meaning in Apess's writing, evoking the "dreary woods" of colonization and the Mashpee's exploited forest; however, his use of land to defend Native rights is also indebted to the rise of the abolitionist movement. It served as a model of political resistance for Apess, particularly as he led the Mashpee fight for political sovereignty.[39] The emergence of abolitionism had made it possible to challenge the Constitution's racial restrictions; without removal as the solution to the race "problem," social reformers, such as Garrison and Apess, could argue for extending civil liberties to free African-Americans and American Indians.[40]

In 1833, Apess was traveling throughout New England giving lectures on Native issues; when he arrived in Mashpee that year, the four hundred members formally adopted the newcomer, and a resistance movement quickly formed around him. Mashpee was one of the original Christian Indian districts of colonial New England, a place historically governed by a board of white overseers that had grown accustomed to exploiting their legal wards. The board profited from leasing the Mashpee out as indentured laborers, neighboring whites habitually stole timber from the Mashpee's Cape Cod lands, and their Harvard-sponsored minister, Phineas Fish, was disinterested in their spiritual lives. He had taken over the meetinghouse and preached mainly to whites. The crimes that white society had committed against American Indians, which Apess catalogs in *An Indian's Looking-Glass for the White Man,* refer specifically to the Mashpee experience.

Identifying white governance as an egregious violation of their civil rights, the Mashpee movement alluded to a revolutionary tradition in American politics. Even more concretely, by politicizing their struggle, the Mashpee countered narrow conceptions of democracy with an egalitarian vision that rejected racial and economic privilege. With Apess as their leader, the Mashpee delivered a series of resolutions to Governor Lincoln based on these democratic principles, including the right to resist an abusive government. "The situation was volatile," writes James Clifford in his study of identity in Mashpee. "Apess, a firebrand with a vision of united action by 'colored' peoples against white oppressors, stimulated a Mashpee 'Declaration of Independence' in 1833 on behalf of a sovereign Mashpee tribe."[41] This declaration was followed by their call for a "new government," run by themselves, so they could "shake off the yoke which galled them"—the metaphor Apess applied to the board of white overseers.[42] The proposed government would embody the classical expression of natural rights as put forth in the Declaration of Independence. One essential difference would distinguish the Mashpee's proposed government from the United States: "There was but one exception, viz., that *all* who dwelt in our precincts were to be held free and equal, *in truth,* as well as in letter."[43] Until the courts could resolve the matter, the Mashpee declared their Cape Cod land off-limits to their white neighbors. Two white men, the Sampson brothers, tested Mashpee resolve for independence by entering the reservation on July 4 and loading a wheelbarrow with firewood. When Apess commanded them, one of whom was the justice of the peace, to unload the firewood, he and other Mashpee were arrested for inciting riot.

Many white liberals in the region had been sympathetic to the Cherokee cause a few years earlier, and a local trial of Apess and six other collaborators in the Mashpee revolt unsettled New England. After the court found them guilty and sentenced Apess to prison for thirty days, white liberals contested the public's negative perception of the unlawful, riotous Mashpee. The *Boston Advocate* exposed the hypocrisy of New Englanders who fought for the Cherokee "abroad" but turned a blind eye at "home" to the exploitation of the Mashpee: "the law which takes this wood from the Indian proprietors, is as unjust and unconstitutional as the Georgia laws, that take the gold mines from the Cherokees."[44] Benjamin Franklin Hallett, the social reformer and editor of the *Advocate,* interpreted the wheelbarrow incident as a revolutionary act by Apess and the Masphee, comparing their resistance to the Boston Tea Party: "The persons concerned in the riot, as it was called, and imprisoned for it, I think were as justifiable in what they did, as our fathers were, who threw the tea overboard."[45]

The challenge for Apess and the Mashpee was to counter the public perception of Mashpee resistance as disorderly and savage. Prosecutors and anti-Mashpee opinion identified Apess as the key agitator for Mashpee defiance, even though Mashpee discontent with dependence and exploitation predated Apess's arrival. Critics have also attempted to identify the models of political resistance available to Apess and the Mashpee, as well as to interpret the meaning of their resistance. O'Connell wonders about the source of Apess's "militant consciousness," particularly since historians have recorded no instances of Native rights movements or actions in New England during the nineteenth century. "From what sources or experiences might Apess' consciousness have come," O'Connell asks, "a consciousness which anticipates so strikingly pan-Indianism?"[46] The tendency in Apess criticism has been to see his involvement in the Mashpee revolt as a collective action for cultural autonomy. For example, Sandra Gustafason concludes that Apess and the Mashpee "resist an American national identity that might subsume" them; such a perspective, however, overlooks both the democratic practices and rhetoric that are fundamental to Apess's leadership.[47] Writing in a similar vein, but more precise in linking Apess and the Mashpee with a contemporary historical struggle, Lepore identifies the ways in which Apess and the Mashpee "were quick to employ the rhetoric of anti-Indian removal sentiment to further their own goals."[48]

Apess and the Mashpee certainly drew on the example of the Cherokee and the rhetoric of anti-Indian removal, and one can safely speculate that the example of the Seminole resistance and the previous year's Black Hawk War emboldened the Mashpee. When Apess decides to write the history of the Mashpee revolt, however, the abolitionist movement and its anti-imperial blueprint of racial egalitarianism in Garrison's *Thoughts on African Colonization* provided him with a successful narrative model. A public history was essential to the cause, since Apess correctly realized that Mashpee resistance would have little effect if New England believed in the imperial fiction of an outside agitator riling up a normally placid Indian town. Apess needed to find a textual form to relate the history of a democratic movement that whites viewed as an insurrection. In the early 1830s Garrison had searched for a form that could communicate the cross-cultural makeup of the new abolitionism; in the final version of *Thoughts on African Colonization,* Garrison achieved a form that voiced a collective politics and, even better, successfully intervened in mainstream political discourse. Searching for a suitable form to describe the Mashpee revolt, Apess may have perceived the structure of his *Indian Nullification* in Garrison's *Thoughts on African Colonization.* The second half of Garrison's book exposed the network of racial domination underpinning the American Colonization Society by giving African-American voices against colonization center stage. Done to exemplify the principle of equality, the tactic also demonstrated widespread, cross-cultural resistance. This extraordinary move must have appealed to Apess, whose *Indian Nullification* adapted the dialogic form of *Thoughts on African Colonization.* Apess writes his own introductory essay to the volume, which Bernd Peyer calls a "complex ethnohistorical collage."[49] He then arranges a wide selection of documents such as the resolutions, minutes, and letters of the Mashpee Indians, his own commentary that contextualizes the fragments and makes them cohere, and the few newspaper editorials sympathetic to the cause.

In addition to the formulaic similarities between *Thoughts on African Colonization* and *Indian Nullification,* the title Apess chooses establishes a symbolic correspondence between abolitionism and Mashpee independence. He might have created a title that referred to the Black Hawk War, Indian removal, or the beginning of the Second Seminole War that same year. Instead, *Indian Nullification of the Unconstitutional Laws of Massachusetts Relative to the Marshpee Tribe* refers to the nullification controversy of 1832–33, the latest battle over slavery and the powers of the states. Spurred by a drop in cotton prices that South Carolina blamed on a federal tariff, senator and former vice president John Calhoun and his supporters fashioned a doctrine of nullification by which a state could nullify federal acts that went against its particular interests within the state. During the controversy, states' righters punctuated their exposition with threats to secede from the United States if the federal government insisted on enforcing the tariff, but the compromise tariff of 1833 satisfied the South Carolinians and dissolved the danger of secession.[50]

Why would Apess frame his account of the Mashpee revolt with a controversy that was primarily concerned about protecting a state's slave interests from the power of the federal government? Perhaps for the appeal of irony. The title playfully appropriates their explosive logic, that a minority group possessed certain rights in the framework of majority rule, while mocking spurious charges of Indian riot by the State of Massachusetts. Such transpositional rhetoric—replacing South Carolina and its "nullification" with the Mashpee and their "riot"—implies that the Mashpee had successfully defended their legitimate constitutional rights. In one sense, this is true, since the Mashpee had won a degree of self-government and political agency from Massachusetts, but there is deeper irony in the title evoked by the absent presence of President Jackson. His famous Nullification Proclamation of 1832 brushed off the states' righters, announcing that declaring federal acts null and void was an act of treason that would be punished. In the same manner, Jackson refused to recognize Justice John Marshall's ruling on behalf of Cherokee sovereignty in *Worcester v. Georgia* (1832). Jackson's decision thus granted Georgia the power to nullify the Cherokee Nation's laws. (The Cherokee would feel the full impact of the ruling in the winter of 1838–39, when federal troops under General Winfield Scott, reassigned after failing to subdue the Seminoles, drove the Cherokee out of Georgia along the infamous Trail of Tears.) In other words, Apess implies a miraculous David versus Goliath victory; this small band of New England Indians had been blessed with special providence and had managed, unlike South Carolina or the unfortunate Cherokee Nation, to defeat an all-powerful imperial state.

A second reason Apess frames his history with the nullification controversy is that the Southern strategy was a blueprint for defending minority rights within the framework of American constitutionalism. Apess develops a doctrine of Indian nullification that at once abolishes the state's unconstitutional laws over a minority group while declaring independence from a corrupt overseer system. Like Calhoun's doctrine, Apess does not wish to threaten secession—or, in our critical parlance, the Mashpee's cultural autonomy. He is committed to a position that enables the Mashpee to remain within the United States with specific constitutional rights. The only difference between the two doctrines is that whereas Calhoun advocates the minority interest of the state against the power of the federal government, Apess revises this logic to fit an even more localized minority interest, the Mashpee Tribe, against the power of an individual state. Recognizing the federal government's hostility to Native rights, Apess, unlike states' righters, does not invent a federal compact in defense of Mashpee interests. Instead, he adapts the main principle of nullification—that the people were the final arbiter—to the concept of Mashpee self-government.

Massachusetts's governance of the Mashpee had deteriorated by the nineteenth century into a board of white overseers whom Apess depicts as veritable slave masters concerned more about moneymaking than improving the lives of the Mashpee. If the title and form of *Indian Nullification* gives us two good clues about Apess's connection to abolitionism, then the rhetoric of slavery—which details the significance of these governors in a despotic system that stripped the people of their natural rights, sold their valuable timber, and exploited their labor—is another. Working under the assumption that Indians were ignorant and incapable of managing their own resources and civic affairs, the overseer ran a profitable economy (for whites) that dominated all facets of life in Mashpee. Apess writes:

> At one time, it was the practice of the overseers, when the Indians hired themselves to their neighbors, to receive their wages and dispose of them at their own discretion. Sometimes an Indian bound on a whaling voyage would earn four or five hundred dollars, and the shipmaster would account to the overseers for the whole sum. The Indian would get some small part of his due, in order to encourage him to go again and gain more for his white masters, to support themselves and educate their children with. And this is but a specimen of the systematic course taken to degrade the tribe from generation to generation. I could tell of one of our masters who has not only supported himself and family out of the proceeds of our lands and labors but has educated a son at Harvard, at our expense.[51]

British empire and colonization is clearly the historical basis of such an exploitative economy, but throughout *Indian Nullification* Apess draws on materials of slavery as a representational strategy for depicting the Mashpee's plight. He may have appropriated this strategy from the abolitionist defense of African-Americans, discriminated against and reduced to "slavery" in the Northern states. His scathing account of the Mashpee struggle against imperial power documents a "systematic course" of racial domination that resembled slavery. His descriptions of "bound out" labor, "white masters," and a tragic permanence achieve, in another manner, the abolitionist's principle aim: to convince the nation that slavery and its corrosive values were not enclosed in the imperial receptacle of the Southern states but afflicted the entire nation. To illustrate the culpability of Massachusetts, particularly its political leaders, Apess reports how the overseer's son attends Harvard "at our expense" while the state converts the education of the Mashpee into an illegal act, "dooming them to become chained under desperate laws." Apess thus justifies their nullification of state law: "what makes the robbery of my wronged race more grievous is that it is sanctioned by legal enactments."[52] The imperial laws of white racial privilege sanction the paradox, making it nearly impossible for the American Indian to rise up in "American" fashion, on merit and hard work. What myth celebrates as the essence of national identity—the meritocracy of natural talent that Tom Paine celebrated—Apess displays as a delusion of American imperialism, a delusion that translates "whiteness" as a sign of social and economic privilege.

Apess was not alone in connecting the Mashpee struggle for civil rights to a discourse of slavery. The few newspapers that did support the Mashpee cause viewed it as analogous to Southern slavery. Apess intends *Indian Nullification* "to mark out the state of public feeling" about the Mashpee revolt; a key part of the project is to demonstrate the "disposition prevalent among the editorial fraternity to prejudice the people at large against the rights and liberties of the Indians."[53] Inverting Garrison's use of African-American voices, Apess excerpts editorial opinion from white newspapers that explicitly call for racial justice. After a fact-finding visit to the reservation, the *Boston Advocate* reported that "we know how strongly and unanimously they feel upon the subject of what they really believe to be, their slavery to the overseers."[54] The *Daily Advocate* issued a more passionate plea to free the Mashpee from bondage: "But from that day [the Revolution], until the year 1834, the Marshpee Indians were enslaved by the laws of Massachusetts, and deprived of every civil right which belongs to man. White Overseers had power to tear their children from them and bind them out where they pleased. They could also sell the services of any adult Indian on the Plantation they chose to call idle, for three years at a time, and send him where they pleased, renewing the lease every three years, and thus, make him a slave for life."[55] Finally, Garrison and the *Liberator* described the situation of the Mashpee with an imagery of an oppressed slave: "Dreading lest they should run too fast, and too far, in an unfettered state, it [Massachusetts] has loaded them with chains so effectually as to prevent their running at all."[56]

Overshadowing the Mashpee cause, abolitionism established a persuasive rhetoric of democratic protest in the struggle for racial justice in New England. In part, this explains why both Garrison and Apess depict the Mashpee as slaves and the state as slaveholder, a necessary and effective strategy for joining the Mashpee cause to a surging abolitionist movement that was capturing public attention. For both movements, racial prejudice blocked their best efforts to win public support. While fighting against the colonization movement, Garrison had learned that the press inflamed these prejudices by depicting African-Americans as a national threat. Rather than an innate feeling of racial animus, Garrison found public discourse guilty of fabricating paranoia and fomenting white fears. Garrison devoted a chapter to the subject in *Thoughts on African Colonization*—"The American Colonization Society is Nourished by Fear and Selfishness"—and asserted that the public's "naked terrors" of African-Americans motivated the colonization movement. In addition to fomenting hysteria, white racism could also channel sympathy for the oppressed. For example, Lepore suggests that white liberals in New England, bolstered by their belief that the American Indian was vanishing, were able to rally behind the Cherokee Nation with mournful renderings of King Philip's heroic fight against Puritan tyranny.[57]

How do we reconcile this pull between the public's apparent fear and its sympathy for American Indians? Lepore's insight helps to explain the popular sentimentalism of *Metamora, or The Last of the Wampanoags,* one of the most popular plays of the nineteenth century; it was a gallant interpretation of the Native leader, Philip, who led his warriors against Puritan New England in one of the bloodiest wars of the North American colonial period. As Lepore suggests, white liberals increased sympathy for the Cherokee's plight by imagining a romantic Indian that colonization and American civilization had destroyed. While this romance of the vanishing Indian sheds some light on the motivations of Mashpee supporters, it can obscure our understanding of how the Mashpee revolt disturbed New England's sympathy for a "defeated" people. A fear of insurrection rather than sympathy galvanized opposition and caused the state to overreact. As Garrison did, Apess realized that the imperial fear of a Native uprising was the main obstacle to racial justice. The second clause of the title Apess chooses for *Indian Nullification—The Pretended Riot Explained*—hints at the effects of Mashpee defiance on the white imagination. Apess suggests that "it is time that the public should be made aware of our views and intentions."[58] While lecturing in neighboring towns on Native rights, he hoped to dispel white racism and hostility toward New England's Natives, particularly the approximately four hundred Mashpee; among the Quakers who came to hear him, Apess found friends and political allies, but he senses his politics only inflames others in his white audience. "Many of the advocates of oppression became clamorous, on hearing the truth from a simple Indian's lips, and a strong excitement took place in that quarter. Some feared that an insurrection might break out among the colored people, in which blood might be shed."

His reference to Mashpee's "colored people" is more than an accurate rendering of a town where intermarriage between American Indians and African-Americans had long made it a place of racial mixture. Anticipating the important anti-imperial work of critics like Michael Rogin, David Spurr, and Michael Taussig, Apess identifies a key catalyst of imperial violence: fears of savagery distort the imperial imagination.[59] Whites may have believed American Indians were fated to disappear, but Mashpee resistance reminded them that this dangerous combination of "colored people"—a dangerous combination evoking the fierce defiance of Seminoles and runaway slaves in the Florida territory—posed a grave threat to white power.[60] In addition to this reference, both the recent slave uprising led by Nat Turner and forceful abolitionist rhetoric had created a climate of racial anxiety in New England. Thus, like Garrison taking aim at the racist propaganda of the colonization movement, Apess knew his account of the Mashpee revolt would need to contest white New England's nightmare of insurrection; his history of what he calls a "pretended riot" needed to show how a Native uprising occurred only in an imperial imagination overwrought by its own racial demons.

The mainstream public may have felt pity for the romanticized struggle of Philip and his warriors, but if many shed tears for contemporary New England Indians, they dried their eyes while leaving the theater. Unlike the lionized Philip, Apess was marked as an instigator, who had disturbed the normally tranquil Mashpee. "At the time of Apes' [sic] coming among them, they were quiet and peaceable," wrote the *Barnstable Patriot;* "[here] comes this intruder, this disturber, this riotous and mischief-making Indian, from the Pequot tribe, in Connecticut . . . he stirs them up to sedition, riot, *treason!* Instigates them to declare their independence of the laws of Massachusetts, and to arm themselves to defend it."[61] Here the imperial nightmare of the savage Indian is invoked against the civilized state. The state's exaggerated response began after Apess and a Mashpee delegation deliver resolutions of independence to Governor Lincoln. At the same time, Gideon Hawley, one of the overseers, rushed to Boston to deliver an alarming report to Lincoln. Apess remembers the effects of Hawley's representation of Mashpee opposition:

> Those who had, as we think unlawfully, ruled us hitherto now awoke in astonishment and bestirred themselves in defense of their temporal interests. Mr. Hawley was dispatched to the governor at Worcester, to whom he

represented the state of affairs in colors which we cannot acknowledge to have been faithful. He stated that the Indians were in open rebellion and that blood was likely to be shed. It was reported and believed among us that he said we had armed ourselves and were prepared to carry all before us with tomahawk and scalping knife; that death and destruction, and all the horrors of a savage war, were impending; that of the white inhabitants some were clearly dead and the rest dreadfully alarmed! An awful picture indeed.[62]

The "awful picture" of "open rebellion" constitutes rational evidence: in *Indian Nullification,* before Apess can argue according to the logic of nullification, he must make the public aware of how its irrational fear of a "savage war" distorts their seemingly objective view of the Mashpee struggle for self-governance.[63] Despite the obvious personal investments Hawley and other overseers have in maintaining Mashpee economic and spiritual dependence—what Apess fittingly dubs "their temporal interests"— the deciding factor in Mashpee would be public opinion, presently dominated by white fears of impending "horrors." Apess parodies the imperial imagination, claiming that authorities actually believed the Mashpee had armed themselves with the legendary weapons of Native savagery. Embedded in the American state, these fears of racial threats produce historical amnesia, a forgetting of the imperial power that overwhelmed the "tomahawk and scalping knife" and was necessary to Indian removal. Such racial fictions cause amnesia and invert the actual history of colonization, converting the United States into a powerless victim, the Mashpee into powerful warriors.[64]

Apess identifies white fear as the catalyst for the unraveling of events, which nearly ended with military action. During a public meeting, the Mashpee voice their "bitter complainings . . . of the wrongs they had suffered."[65] White persons in the meeting, never hearing such criticism before, Apess writes,

> seemed very uneasy, often getting up, going out, and returning, as if apprehensive of some danger. The groundwork of their fears, if they had any, was this: Three of our people, who had been out in the morning hunting deer, had brought their guns into the meetinghouse, and this circumstance was thought, *or pretended to be thought,* by a few of our neighbors to portend violence and murder.[66]

Three guns lay at the root of white apprehension; but as Apess realizes, white antagonists may have simply faked such apprehension of the weapons in order to excite the public and perhaps end Mashpee opposition once and for all. For Apess this fabricated racial threat explains the "pretended riot." No matter whether the fear of a Mashpee conspiracy was truly felt or not, the imaginary fear of armed Mashpee ultimately persuades Governor Lincoln to ready the state militia. As Apess does throughout his history of the Mashpee revolt, he taunts the state and other opponents for demonizing the Mashpee as well as for betraying its alleged republican principles. For example, his political rhetoric condemns the governor for preparing an armed response. Events had

> put him [Governor Lincoln] in mind of his oath of office, to secure the Commonwealth from danger, and given him cause to call out perhaps fifty or sixty thousand militia; especially when the great strength and power of the Marshpee tribe was considered. To this supposed great demonstration of military power they might, possibly, have opposed a hundred fighting men and fifteen or twenty rusty guns.[67]

The ironic juxtaposition Apess draws between a militaristic Commonwealth and a law-abiding Mashpee exposes the falsehood inherent in the imperial imagination. What the state views as the weapons of a viable threat—perhaps not matching the Seminoles but still defying imperial authority—Apess reveals as rusty rifles. This misrecognition ultimately grants Governor Lincoln legal "cause" to act like a tyrant and muster the militia. Furthermore, this first stage of interpretation also produces public and historical knowledge of the Mashpee revolt, a situation that motivates Apess to write *Indian Nullification*. He includes an excerpt from the *Boston Courier* to demonstrate how the state's racial nightmare had become fact: "these deluded people [were] in a state of open rebellion against the government of the State, having with force, seized upon the Meeting-house, rescued from the Overseers a portion of property in their possession, chosen officers of their own, and threatened violence to all who should attempt to interfere with them, in the measures of *self-government* which they had assumed."[68] Since white racism held that the American Indian was inherently inferior, incapable of progress, and always verging

on savagery, Mashpee efforts for self-government (the newspaper emphasizes its disbelief in italics) were seen as a "delusion."

Contesting public delusions regarding the Mashpee revolt proved a stiff
challenge for Apess, but *Indian Nullification* succeeds on many levels. He
offers a rational theory of nullification in order to counter imperial perceptions of Native irrationality, exposes how racial prejudice both underpins
the state's overseer system and obscures the public perception of the Mashpee, interjects the Mashpee cause into both abolitionist and antiremoval
discourses, writes in an engaging style that balances political criticism with
a heightened sense of irony, and finally he recognizes the significance of a
form that could articulate cross-cultural viewpoints. As a result, *Indian
Nullification* is not only a documentary account of the Mashpee revolt but
also an essay on the political efficacy of historical narrative. Specifically,
the narrative's cross-cultural dialogue is one of the text's more remarkable
aspects, since it makes differential power relations—so often used to exclude
American Indians from the nation's historical understanding—the subject
of scrutiny. One example Apess employs to demonstrate this is his own
imprisonment. "It seemed to be the common opinion," he reports, "that
the imprisonment of Apess would frighten the rest of the tribe and cause
them to forego their efforts to recover their rights."[69] Arrested for riot,
assault, and trespass, Apess claims his false imprisonment as the inverse of
the Harvard degree of the overseer's son. Arrested with no evidence but
white hysteria, Apess posits his outlaw position as the only place where
one can capture a true sense of the Mashpee revolt. His false imprisonment for leading a politicized but nonviolent group of Mashpee against
the state stands in contrast to the horror stories propagated by white overseers, newspapers, and state officials.

In the process, Apess draws attention to the capacity of a revised national
history, told from the Native point of view, to forge cohesion among the
Mashpee. Consider, for instance, his seemingly impartial account of arriving in Mashpee and meeting the white minister and overseer, Phineas Fish,
whom Apess would replace as tribal spokesperson. In response to Apess's
request to speak to the Mashpee, Fish attempts to nullify Mashpee claims
for justice, as well as to censor Apess's remarks. Apess relates the conversation
with his typical balance of defiance and wit: "Mr. Fish cautioned me not
to say anything about oppression, that being, he said, the very thing that

made them discontented. They thought themselves oppressed, he observed, but such was not the case."[70]

The dialogue conceals the germ of the conflict, symbolizing the plight of the Mashpee—the minister assigned to their plantation is blind to their oppression. Apess uses Fish's warning to depict the larger discursive issue of the white public's inability to see the suffering of the Mashpee. The placement of Fish's warning at the beginning of the narrative is not simply an act faithful to chronology; rather, Apess delivers an effective rhetorical move that appeals to a reading public who might share Fish's opinion that the "case" of the Mashpee was not dire. The move also sets up Apess's refutation. Ignoring Fish's order, Apess speaks to the Mashpee about the "history of the New England Indians"; suddenly, "an individual among the assembly took occasion to clap his hands and, with a loud shout, to cry 'Truth, truth!' This gave rise to a general conversation, and it was truly heartrending to me to hear what my kindred people had suffered at the hands of whites."[71] The call-and-response between Apess and the audience establishes him as the public leader, the one entrusted to author a new truth. The actions of call-and-response form a new history, one linking the Mashpee's local struggles with other New England Indians, such as Apess's own Pequots. Voicing the difference between memory and history, the public shouts of "Truth!" also punctuate Apess's words, an apt illustration of the consensual nature of both the speech and the democratic and anti-imperial practices epitomized by Mashpee resistance.

A USEFUL PAST FOR A NEW NATION

In the center of their attack on the colonization movement, white and black abolitionists argued that military service was the African-American soldiers' collective sacrifice for democracy. In the introduction to the second section of *Thoughts on African Colonization,* Garrison records this strategy of invoking war: "large numbers of them were distinguished for their patient endurance, their ardent devotion, and their valorous conduct during our revolutionary struggle."[72] In addition to this standard allusion to the Revolution, abolitionists also pointed directly to the War of 1812 in order to make the point that the "Second War of Independence," like the first one, still shut black soldiers out. Garrison reminds his readers that African-American soldiers served courageously during that war, and he proceeds to charge the United States with a "pitiful . . . hypocrisy manifested in our conduct as a people toward our colored population!"[73] For proof of such shame, Garrison includes a proclamation issued during the war by General Andrew Jackson, which urged the continued service of free African-Americans during the second war with Britain. "I knew with what fortitude you could endure hunger and thirst, and all the fatigues of a campaign," Jackson writes. "*I knew well how you loved your NATIVE country,* and that you had, as well as ourselves, to defend what man holds most dear—his parents, relations, wife, children and property."[74] Garrison responds to Jackson's cynical use of nationalist rhetoric to manipulate the loyalty of his African-American troops with an argument for a racially egalitarian United States: "Yes—when peril rears its crest, and invasion threatens our shores, then prejudice is forgotten and the tongue of detraction is still—then the people of color are no longer brutes or a race between men and monkeys, no longer turbulent or useless, no longer aliens and wanderers from Africa—but they are complimented as intelligent, patriotic citizens from whom much is expected, and who have property, home and country at stake!"[75]

A patriotic citizen defended his home, and by extension his country, from foreign invasion. There is a simple reason Garrison emphasizes war as a nation-building trope: he is summarizing the commentaries by African-American anticolonization societies, many of which identified military service as an unassailable claim on the rights of citizenship. Military service exemplified the masculine revolutionary credo of Paine's *Common Sense,* to trust in the power of the people rather than an oppressive government and unjust laws. Perhaps most important, invoking war and loyal service of African-American troops humanized a population that many whites thought, as Garrison says, a "race between men and monkeys." It was a necessary tactic simply because appeals to the nation's founding documents were not effective. By stressing their exploits in battle, African-American abolitionists were able to bypass both a hostile government and laws that circumscribed them as "aliens and wanderers from Africa." War enabled them to appeal directly to alternative sources of national identity.

Denied the protections of civic identity, African-American abolitionists called attention to their history of sacrifice for the nation, while subtly claiming an American heritage that preceded the Revolution. For example, in Brooklyn, members declare that we are not strangers; neither do we come under the alien law. Our Constitution does not call upon us to become naturalized; we are already American citizens; our fathers were the first that peopled this country; their sweat and their tears have been the means, in a measure, of raising our country to its present standing. Many of them fought, and bled, and died for the gaining of her liberties; and shall we forsake their tombs, and flee to an unknown land?[76]

In another meeting at the African church in Middletown, Connecticut, its members concurred with the statement issued from Brooklyn. In New Haven, at a meeting of the "Peace and Benevolent Society of Afric-Americans," the society resolved, with no sense of irony,

That we know of no other place that we can call our true and appropriate home, excepting these United States, into which our fathers were brought, who enriched the country by their toils, and fought, bled, and died in its defense, and left us in possession—and here we will live and die.[77]

These nationalist statements call forth a period preceding the American Revolution, a period when every slave embodied a true revolutionary. They did the epic work of nation-building, according to members in Brooklyn, who represent their ancestors' "sweat and tears" as the real lifeblood of a great nation, their labor "raising the country to its present standing." In both Brooklyn and New Haven members dispute their status as "strangers" by implying that the slave was the "other" pilgrim and by repeating the simple expression that the American nation is "our true and appropriate home." Even more stunning, however, was the way in which these societies, quintessentially democratic in their aims, transformed slavery from a violent and oppressive institution, which threatened national stability and degraded both slaves and slave owners, into a positive source. The societies invoke the histories of slavery—the slaves "who enriched the country by their toils"—which *precede* in both cases the reference to fighting for independence. Such a rhetorical maneuver depicts the slaves as founding fathers on a par with their revolutionary masters.

Employing the trope of war was the surest way to convince a white public that African-Americans possessed an equal claim on an American civic identity, a strategy not lost on William Apess. Throughout his career, as early as *A Son of the Forest,* Apess told war stories as a means to argue for racial justice. Battles during the War of 1812 had forged Apess's patriotism, most notably in the pivotal defeat of the British at Plattsburgh. "This was indeed a proud day for our country," Apess recollects. "We had met a superior force on the lake, and 'they were ours.' Our army did not lose many men, but on the lake many a brave man fell—fell in the defense of his country's rights."[78] Apess's use of the possessive "our" establishes his claim on American identity and its promise of citizenship. He paid for this claim long ago, Apess believes, by surviving the "sublime horrors of war." Nevertheless, the country refuses to extend political rights to its nonwhite soldiers:

> But I could never think that the government acted right toward the "Natives," not merely in refusing to pay us but in claiming our services in cases of perilous emergency, and still deny us the right of citizenship; and as long as our nation is debarred the privilege of voting for civil officers, I shall believe that the government has no claim on our services.[79]

He accuses the U.S. government of two crimes. First, it reneged on its guarantee to pay Native veterans money and land for their services to the country, a betrayal that Apess views as egregious considering the hazardous circumstances. Second, serving in the war gave Apess the idea that he possessed the right of citizenship. Such a move, I would argue, proves that Apess believed American Indians needed to establish rather than sever ties with the state. Christopher Castiglia has argued that abolitionists "conceived citizenship in opposition to the state," exhibiting, in the case of William Lloyd Garrison, a "conscientious anti-institutionalism" and desire to "divorce citizenship from the state."[80] To position one's self outside a corrupt state and preach universal rights, in Castiglia's reading of white abolitionists, is to be truly American. Together with Apess's experience, Castiglia's reading reveals how white racial privilege enabled a conception of stateless citizenship by concealing the universal power of whiteness. For Apess the only citizenship that mattered was tied to the United States, since to live in exile within it still meant that one could not escape racial domination. Thus, despite the government's refusal to compensate them with property or political rights, Apess continually roots his conception of American identity in the collective history of U.S. imperialism. While his conversion narrative relates a spiritual awakening open to all people, no matter their color, the veteran's narrative contained within it conveys subjugation to white power and an ongoing political struggle to be recognized within the logic of empire. When Apess arrives in Mashpee in 1833, invoking the experiences of Native veterans who fought for the United States had become a regular part of his critical practice, allowing Apess both to challenge the romantic view of an Indian past and to argue for civil rights. In *Indian Nullification,* he includes an editorial from the *Daily Advocate* written by a white writer in order to draw the connection between military service and the suppression of Native rights. The writer lists each of the Mashpee men who served with Colonel Bradford, and this act of remembrance becomes a monument to those Mashpee men who died fighting during the Revolution:

> Francis Webquish, Samuel Moses, Demps Squibs, Mark Negro, Tom Caesar, Joseph Ashur, James Keeter, Joseph Keeter, Jacob Keeter, Daniel Pocknit, Job Rimmon, George Shawn, Castel Barnet, Joshua Pognit, James Rimmon, David Hatch, James Nocake, Abel Hoswit, Elisha Keeter, John Pearce, John Mapix, Amos Babcock, Hosea Pognit, Daniel Pocknick, Church Ashur, Gideon Tumpum. In all twenty-six men. The whole regiment, drawn from the whole county of Barnstable, mustered but 149 men, nearly *one-fifth* of whom were volunteers from the little Indian plantation of Marshpee, which then did not contain over one hundred male heads of families! No white town in the County furnished anything like this proportion of the 149 volunteers. The Indian soldiers fought through the war; and as far as we have been able to ascertain the fact, from documents or tradition, all but one, fell martyrs to liberty, in the struggle for Independence.[81]

Many of the surnames repeat, coming in groups of two and three, none too subtly evoking the tragedy of Mashpee's sacrifice of its brothers, sons, and fathers for the rewards of universal freedom. Their willingness to fight was no doubt influenced by their hope that the new United States would grant them the equality and justice that the British empire had denied them. In the above quotation, the white writer delivers the exclamation point with astonishment and indignation but without any sense of irony. However, while the white writer can express indignation without irony, Apess resorted to other, less obvious tactics. He expresses less surprise that descendants of these Mashpee revolutionary soldiers still lacked the protection of U.S. citizenship.

By placing Mashpee resistance within the context of the Revolution, Apess, like African-American opponents of colonization, once again imbues their fight with the blood of independence. In a letter to the *Barnstable Journal,* Apess and the Mashpee coalition exploit this distinctly patriotic language, asking the "good people of Massachusetts, the boasted cradle of independence," for liberty. They finally realize that they possess a uniquely American right to defend their natural freedoms from tyranny:

> there was no other alternative but like theirs, to take our stand, and as we have on our plantation but one harbor, and no English ships of tea, for a substitute, we unloaded two wagons loaded with our wood. . . . And now, good people of Massachusetts, when your fathers dared to unfurl the banners of freedom amidst the hostile fleets and armies of Great Britain, it was then that Marshpee furnished them with some of her bravest men to fight your battles. Yes, by the side of your fathers they fought and bled, and now their blood cries to you from the ground to restore that liberty so unjustly taken from us by their sons.[82]

The Mashpee delegation calls attention to the irony of the American Revolution. Even though they sacrificed their men for the cause, the Mashpee actually suffered more oppression after independence. They tell New Englanders that the Revolution was nothing more than "your battles," not the Natives', and the passage returns to the revolutionary script in order to highlight the fighting of this Mashpee revolution against yet another imperial state. By equating the wheelbarrow incident at Mashpee with the Boston Tea Party, Apess and the coalition invests the Revolution's appropriation of the Indian image with the political content of the Mashpee revolt. In other words, by revising the Boston Tea Party, they depict the real bodies of Mashpee men who fought for independence in contrast to the American Indian as a purely symbolic element in the Revolution—whites in red-face throwing tea into the harbor. The blood of "white" and "red" fathers bleeding together in the soil contributes to this revision, destabilizing the racial purity on which the imperial memory of the Revolution depends. Instead of ensuring their freedom, the Revolution robbed the Mashpee of the limited rights that they did possess. Thus, having "no English ships of tea," the Mashpee attempt to bring the nation's unfinished revolutionary struggle to a close around two wagons of stolen wood. In the end, this strategy helped the

Mashpee gain a limited victory over the State of Massachusetts; the Mashpee Act of 1834 granted the Mashpee limited powers of self-government, a remarkable victory in the decade of Indian removal.[83]

When Apess finally turned to King Philip's War as a subject, he did so with the intent of transforming white sympathy for an imagined Indian into support for an inclusive democracy. As a result of the removal debates of the 1830s, white liberals had recast King Philip's War as a revolutionary conflict in which oppressed Natives, led by the heroic Philip, fought for their natural rights to be free from the British Empire.[84] The first New England Native to write about King Philip's War, Apess approached the subject after years of incorporating the experience and trope of war into his writing. In his brief, remarkable career, one can trace how Apess worked out an anti-imperial theory of democracy tethered to war and military service, the Native veteran's strongest argument for civil rights. First delivered as a public lecture in 1836, Apess's *Eulogy on King Philip, as Pronounced at the Odeon, in Federal Street, Boston* marked the last time Apess appeared in the "public eye" before being forgotten.[85] In his last published text, Apess overturns a patriotic history of American imperialism by denouncing the settlers' "Christianity" as one of the most depraved instruments of colonization; settlers used the Bible as a means to shame and to subjugate Natives and to justify holy wars against them. There are few voices of racial justice in the 1830s that sound as righteous and pained as Apess's in *Eulogy on King Philip*. After a career spent acquiring literacy and advancing the revolutionary principles of natural rights, Apess appears to lose faith altogether.

The sentimental narrative of Philip's gallantry took place in a by-gone period when Native warriors almost drove the Puritans into the sea. Such a narrative reinforced the notion that contemporary Natives, as impoverished wards of the state, had no fight left in them. Apess exposes how this sentimental narrative conceals the historical progression of British to American imperialism. Writing American history through the eyes of a Pequot survivor, Apess sees the outlines of an epic crime, beginning at a founding moment of Puritan deception and winding its way through the revolutionary period and into the era of Indian removal. The Puritan forefathers commit the original crime during King Philip's War, which colonists were able to win only by reneging on a deal made with Philip's Native enemies. The Puritans hired them to fight, Apess writes, with [the] promise of their enjoying equal rights with their white brethren; but not one of those promises have as yet been fulfilled by the Pilgrims or their children. . . . It was only, then, by deception that the Pilgrims gained the country, as their word has never been fulfilled in regard to Indian rights.[86]

Here is the symbolic origin of American empire in Apess's revisionist history, an origin of deception that gets replicated throughout the text. Unlike the Puritan forefathers, New England Indians were the civilized ones who honored the authority of the word, what would later become the sacred social contract of an idealized American civilization. Apess depicts this culture's progress as marred by repeated violations of the Pilgrim's unfulfilled promise of equal rights. The broken treaties, unjust wars, and white racism that tarnish the course of U.S. imperial culture—all of it, in Apess's history, originates in the Puritan's broken promise, which allowed them to defeat Philip and "[gain] the country." Alluding to a national genealogy as a way to show how the past's great crime persists into the present, Apess claims that the "doctrines of the Pilgrims has [sic] grown up with the people."[87]

This view displays none of the optimism of Apess's final awakening in *A Son of the Forest* or his enthusiasm for anti-imperial democratic struggle as represented in *Indian Nullification*. Did his protest against white power, whether in Mashpee or on the lecture circuit, wear him down? Had he simply grown disenchanted with the irreconcilability of republican principles and American imperialism? Had the unstoppable force of Indian removal eclipsed the once successful glow of the Mashpee's partial victory? Did he lose faith in the American "doctrine" once it became clear that an imperial president like Andrew Jackson could simply ignore the Supreme Court's law that Indian sovereignty be honored? In *Eulogy on King Philip* Apess has no use for the American democratic practices on display in *Indian Nullification* or in his evangelical rhetoric of liberation, a staple of much of his writing. Lacking any information about Apess, one can only speculate. *Eulogy on King Philip* invokes the sacred doctrine of American civilization only to discard it immediately as its greatest lie. In place of the word, Apess substitutes the symbol: "It will be well for us to lay those deeds and depredations committed by whites upon Indians before the civilized world, and then they can judge for themselves."[88] Apess certainly knew how to write a good speech, which partially explains why he prefers visual language. Yet this strategy also permits him to turn to the colonists' "deeds and depredations" and to reject the doctrine of freedom and equality, which had fueled his egalitarian politics and contributed to his greatest successes.

With his symbolic history of American imperialism, Apess does not let his readers forget the historical basis of the United States. He refuses to appropriate the American doctrine and its myths—or to dress the revolutionary Indian in the Yankee's clothes—as he did in documenting the Mashpee revolt. Instead, Apess inverts the British empire's racial hierarchies and shows them as the essential truths underlying an American patriotic rhetoric. As a result, the "doctrine" passed down to all Americans, one that had "grown up" with the country, is not a vaunted republicanism but a "holy war" of a racially motivated imperialism, an offspring of a ruthless Christian and political faith. Consistent with his aim to write a symbolic history, Apess begins his narrative with an appeal to the eye: "Now let us see who the greatest savages were."[89] If, as a boy, he admits feeling wounded by the "slur" of being called an Indian, here he redefines savagery as synonymous with being American. He paints a *tableau vivant* of colonization for the audience: gun, powder and ball, rum, disease, broken treaties and stolen land, massacres and dismembered bodies, slavery and families torn apart, and a Bible that justified all of it. Even the colonists' prayers, instead of offering love or universal salvation, were instruments of colonization. "It is also wonderful how they prayed," Apess remarks with his characteristic graveyard wit, "that they should pray the bullet through the Indians' heart and their souls down into hell. . . . if this is the way they pray, that is, bullets through people's hearts, I hope they will not pray for me."[90]

This Pequot's archival memory contains the instruments and technology of conquest and imperialism rather than a doctrinal belief in the Puritans' "special providence," an archive that finds its symbolic hero in the figure of Philip, "the greatest man that ever lived upon the American shores."[91] Philip was also the most civilized man, Apess says, a point reinforced by the Puritans who savagely mutilated his body after executing him and then sold his family members into slavery. In this contest of America's origins, Apess resembles his fellow African-American abolitionists who forge a useful past from the tragedy of colonization; Apess writes a history that both rejects the American doctrine as imperialism's most powerful fiction and promises the birth of a new union built on the principle of equality rather than racial domination. If Nietzsche urged nations to forget the past in order to gain freedom from its "monumental history," then Apess offers a different vision by transforming it. For example, in *Eulogy on King Philip,* Apess tells the audience about an "act in King Philip that outweighs all the princes and emperors in the world":

> when his men began to be in want of money, having a coat neatly wrought with mampampeag (i.e. Indian money), he cut it to pieces and distributed it among all his chiefs and warriors, it being better than the old continental money of the Revolution in Washington's day, as not one Indian soldier found fault with it, as we could ever learn; so that it cheered their hearts still to persevere to maintain their rights and expel their enemies.[92]

Although the fable ostensibly traffics in Native lore, its politics evoke the contemporaneous subjugation and struggles of American Indians, from the Mashpee struggle against Massachusetts and its overseer system to the Seminoles and their adopted runaways who struck U.S. forces a year earlier and began the Second Seminole War. Philip's act provides the basis for a distributive ethic that opposes a political system born of an American Revolution that maintains the privileges of "whiteness" at the expense of Native veterans—this time, veterans of colonization as well as of wars of independence. As a symbol of a nation built on the principle of racial justice, Apess substitutes a revolutionary King Philip for the slaveholder George Washington. King Philip forces the audience to reconsider an American genealogy in which justice was freely distributed to all peoples, regardless of race, as long as they were willing to die for America and its promise of equality.

epilogue

Troopers in the Saddle: The Histories of American Empire

In the early 1990s, I immersed myself in the works of Latin American poets and novelists, such as Ernesto Cardenal, Rubén Darío, José Carlos Mariátegui, José Martí, Gabriel García Márquez, Luisa Valenzuela, and José Enrique Rodó, whose histories, fictions, and poetry, *escriben en el otro lado,* challenged my nationalist perspective by repositioning it in the hemispheric context of *Las Americas.* I remember being unsettled by the presence of U.S. imperial power throughout García Márquez's *El Otoño del Patriarca,* a remarkable, gut-wrenching novel about an evil regime and its puppet dictator who murders dissidents and disappears his country's children while, outside the palace windows, a U.S. gunboat sits anchored in the harbor.[1] That image of American empire would come back to me at many points while writing this book and thinking about the historical and cultural trajectories of U.S. imperialism. Time after time I encountered histories and stories that led me into transnational borderlands. During the War of Jenkins's Ear, English warships carried colonial militia to the West Indies to fight Spain and search for gold-laden Spanish traders in the Atlantic; and following the conspiracy trials of 1741, colonial authorities contracted merchant vessels to carry banished slaves to the Caribbean slave markets so the colony could be free of a population it had come to see as an internal threat. At the end of the eighteenth century, an embattled Federalist government sent U.S. gunboats to intervene in the Haitian revolution. Further demonstrating the symbiotic relationship between military and economic goals, a fundamental quality of American imperial ventures,

these same gunboats escorted commercial vessels when they carried commodities into West Indian markets, which they had trouble opening and
holding without the support of naval power. This turbulent era infused
the mercurial career of Charles Brockden Brown, an American patriot who
understood prose and poetry as essential measures of national distinction.
For example, in *Arthur Mervyn* he depicts a nation afflicted by corruption and greed as a plague-infested Philadelphia and traces the epidemic
back to the importation of dirty money from the West Indies. Even James
Fenimore Cooper's *The Pioneers*—ostensibly a historical novel about nation-
building deep in the New York wilderness—is entangled with the imperial
histories of the global slave trade. Eschewing the republican rhetoric of
Judge Temple, the old sailor Ben Pump simply describes Judge Temple's
model house, with its body of slaves imprisoned in the basement, as a slave
ship. Finally, there is the ship that unexpectedly appears in William Apess's
historical lecture on race relations in colonial New England. Apess tells his
audience how colonial rulers, in an effort to root out Native resistance
once and for all after the first Pequot War (1636), captured his surviving
ancestors, put them on a boat, and carried the new slaves to the Caribbean
slave plantations. In an age before air supremacy, military and commercial
vessels were floating signifiers of imperial ambition, routinely violating
national borders in the pursuit of geopolitical advantages. The historical
antecedents of García Márquez's U.S. gunboat helped me to imagine the
hemispheric reach of American imperialism.

   U.S. military and economic intervention in Latin America has always
made ironic the humanitarian core of American republicanism. This dis-
crepancy between U.S. power and republican principles constitutes a fundamental theme of writers like Martí, Darío, and García Márquez. For
example, the display of U.S. imperialist power during the Spanish-American
War so distressed Darío that the Nicaraguan *modernista* began developing
an oppositional poetics. Addressing Theodore Roosevelt in the poem "To
Roosevelt," Darío depicts a volcanic American empire; when it begins to
rumble, the concussions are felt in "the enormous vertebrae of the Andes,"
the sacred nervous system of "our America." Running through the poem
is the theme of reckless U.S. power, and the imagery of fire, an eruption,
a bullet, comes to characterize, for Darío, the perversion of the U.S. republic's founding principles: "You believe that life is a fire / that progess is eruption / that where you put the bullet / you put the future."[2] After chastising

the figure of President Roosevelt for believing that life burns like a violent
fire, that Latin America's future will follow the bullet's flight, the speaker
condemns the practices and beliefs of U.S. imperialism with a word, a
resounding "No." Darío's bullet and García Márquez's gunboat expose the
nature of American imperialism and serve as a guide for future study. They
render visible the contours of state power, employ historical experience
against the pronouncements of American exceptionalism, and view U.S.
imperial action as a self-interested force that crosses and violates sovereign
national borders.

   While the historical trajectories of an American empire were central to
the political and fictional worlds imagined by the Latin American writers
I was reading, these same histories have been almost entirely absent from
developmental narratives of U.S. history. From the moment of its inception, American historiography hewed closely to the limits established by
republican ideology, particularly in the consensus view that its fundamental
precepts were antithetical to imperialism. As the political ideology of the
American Revolution, republicanism advanced the classical ideals of civic
humanism, national virtue, self-sacrifice, the general good, and freedom
from coercion. Unfortunately, viewing the American past through the lens
of republicanism produces a series of omissions around the subject of empire. Our republican traditions exert pressure on scholars at the most basic
levels of analysis and presentation. Working within the context of American
historiography, we are often unwittingly complicit with the production of
silences, even when we consciously try to qualify crucial distinctions. For
example, writing about New York under the British empire, I had the temporary freedom of being able to speak directly about imperial power; however, crossing the revolutionary Rubicon into the new United States and
the "republican period" required me to qualify whose republicanism I was
describing, since no discourse included African or Native Americans. Apparent each time a student of U.S. imperialism confronts the symbiotic relationship between republican visions and the practices of slavery and racial
domination, these qualifiers appear as *racialized* republicanism, a *white*
Republic, a *white* nation, and so on. These qualifiers shift the terms of
debate, to some degree, by recognizing the centrality of racial domination
to the republican project; but they also remind us how this project, which
takes republican ideology as a coherent and stable standard, undermines
our efforts to integrate the disordered and violent histories of imperialism.

Throughout these pages I have attempted to uncover these histories and interpret how they either challenge or uphold republican visions about the nonexistence of an American empire. Scholars have extended the chronology of U.S. imperialism beyond wars in Southeast Asia, Central America, and the Middle East, beyond the 1898 wars in Spanish Cuba, the Philippines, and Puerto Rico, and up to the Mexican–American War (1848) and the flowering of Manifest Destiny. My intention was to extend this chronology into an earlier historical epoch, before a republican revolution was said to have replaced imperial society and initiated a supposedly more progressive civilization. For this reason, my historical critique paid little heed to the tenets of republican ideology, such as civic responsibility, enlightened individualism, and political progress, which resemble political dreams more than political realities. In these pages my principal aim has been to measure how war, racial domination, white racism and power, territorial expansion, slavery, and other forms of imperial power infused early American writing. This writing demonstrates, in my eyes, both the continuity between British and American imperial activities and the hemispheric reach of an American empire.

Rather than adhere to the conventional critical divide between colonial and republican periods, I reconstructed a context for early American writing out of the imperial practices that lay at the roots of U.S. historical development. The texts covered in this book consistently manifest the interconnections between domestic and foreign territories. The meaning of the United States exists in tension with transnational geographies and along the axis of imperial action in places like Cuba, Saint-Domingue, and Liberia. U.S. and Latin American writers alike teach this lesson about national identity in the Western Hemisphere. Like García Márquez, whose anchored gunboat translates the sea into a geopolitical grid of expansive U.S. power, Herman Melville rendered the sea as a shifting center of American empire in "Benito Cereno" (1855). The tale recounts a slave insurrection aboard a Spanish vessel captained by Benito Cereno. After overthrowing the Spanish crew and renaming their free vessel the *San Dominick*, in honor of the Haitian war of independence occurring that same year, 1799, the slave leader, Babo, and his army of rebels encounter a U.S. ship captained by Amasa Delano. Not suspecting a slave revolt but thinking the Spanish vessel might be in distress, the American captain requests permission to board and offer assistance. Seeking to hide the fact of revolt, the liberated slaves maintain the fiction of a Spanish slaver with the white crew seemingly in charge of an obedient slave cargo. Having terrorized the Spanish sailors into playing their roles in the masquerade, the slaves pose submissively and engage in habitual chores and appear to follow the orders of their Spanish masters, and the ignorant and benevolent Captain Delano fails to see that Babo and his rebels have overthrown the Spanish crew. Only when Delano proposes to take Cereno back to the U.S. ship, causing Babo to leap into the dinghy to assassinate his Spanish master, does the American captain realize that he has stepped into the middle of a slave revolt. Thus begins Melville's ironic allegory of a nation blind to an imperial past that had not only undercut the highest values of its republican revolution but had also made slavery and racial domination essential elements of national consciousness.

For good reason, "Benito Cereno" has been a favorite text for scholars interested in issues of race, slavery, and national identity. Strengthened by commercial and territorial expansion, practices of racial domination, military action, and a U.S. Constitution protective of slave property, the institutions of slavery could no longer be lamented and reasoned away as an intractable remnant of the British empire. Beginning in the 1790s, the United States moved to make slavery vital to national stability and prosperity. With these historical experiences in mind, critics have built a thick national context for "Benito Cereno"; they have connected Melville's fictional world to the domestic politics of the 1850s, particularly abolitionism, racial violence, and expansionism. Placed in the context of a domestic world splitting apart, critics render "Benito Cereno" as an antislavery, antiracist narrative in which the innocent, oblivious American Captain Delano is offensive because he is blind to the slave conspiracy taking place before his eyes. Viewed within the domestic context of a looming Civil War, Melville composes a prophetic tale of American obtuseness.[3]

I want to offer a reading of "Benito Cereno" that considers its hemispheric context and locates the story's larger meaning in the foreboding domain of U.S. imperial history. What interpretations might be possible if, following García Márquez, we anchor our interpretations off the South American coast, the setting for "Benito Cereno"? What if one treats the sea and the *San Dominick less* like a universal microcosm emitting allusions to U.S. domestic politics and *more* like a geography of empire that cannot be easily relocated within the country's borders? Such a reading assumes that slavery is not reducible to a national tragedy and that institutions were essential to a global economy; slavery's human commodities hailed from Africa as well as North and South America, its profitability spurred continental expansion and wars, and its entrenchment instigated practices of racial domination. Slavery crossed the national boundaries of the United States and established political and cultural cross-currents throughout North and South America. Unlike Brown's *Arthur Mervyn,* where contact with racial unrest in the West Indies returns to the national domain in the form of the yellow fever, the revolt aboard the *San Dominick* in the Southern Hemisphere does not come back to the United States to wreak havoc.

For critics, part of the ease and indisputable logic of returning "Benito Cereno" to a domestic context is the real fear during the 1850s that the slavery crisis was pushing the United States toward civil war. In addition to the story's historical context, the tale's narrative structure has led critics to locate the meaning of "Benito Cereno" within the United States.[4] The narrative consists of three parts: the story proper, the depositions, and the concluding flashback. The story proper follows Delano's movements over the course of a single day, from his ignorance at dawn to his illumination at night. Since the story proper centers on the events aboard the *San Dominick*—and the unlocking of Melville's mystery—critics have almost too automatically focused on a slaveholding world that the insurrectionary slaves have turned upside down.

Enlightening as these readings continue to be, the critical attention paid to the spectacle of insurrection aboard the *San Dominick* risks overlooking a narrative fragment hidden in the interstices of the story's three main parts. The fragment I have in mind, technically the end of the story proper, centers on the *Bachelor's Delight,* the U.S. ship, which is generally not considered a key to the story. This fragment, I argue, links Delano's revelation with the rise of the American empire, which makes the fragment essential to the narrative's spatial and temporal concerns. With his boot across Babo's neck, pinning him to the boat's floor, Captain Delano has seen through the masquerade, but the implications of his epiphany only become clear *after* the American's pursuit of the *San Dominick* and *before* the reader encounters the depositions. In my reading, the *Bachelor's Delight* becomes the true focus of the story. Once Delano is safely aboard the U.S. vessel, he becomes a potent force. He organizes his men for the attack on the *San*

Dominick, and then he initiates a succession of imperial power from Spain to the United States. Sailing at the southernmost extremity of the hemisphere and captained by a New England Yankee, the *Bachelor's Delight* symbolically links North and South America; moreover, the U.S. vessel constitutes a mobile national base, an extension of the state's power and ideology. If the floating island of the *San Dominick* is a decayed and vanquished Spanish empire, then the *Bachelor's Delight* is a more powerful and entrepreneurial American empire. With our focus on Captain Delano's vessel, the meaning of "Benito Cereno" is necessarily tied to a resurgent U.S. power, a fact often missed in the aftermath of the mutiny, as readers move to the depositions. As a result, the U.S. imperial trajectories that stretch, in this case, from Roxbury, Massachusetts, to Patagonia, Chile, displace the trans-Atlantic routes of the Spanish empire. In addition, if we acknowledge the succession of imperial power from the skeletal Cereno to the suddenly emboldened Delano, then the slave mutiny takes on a different meaning. It was a price of empire-building that Spain is no longer prepared to pay but that Delano and the Americans embrace with gusto. Replacing the exhausted Spanish imperialist Benito Cereno, Delano will ultimately prove himself, in his ambition and lust for wealth and power, to be an equal to the first Spanish conquistadores.[5]

Moving the story to the *Bachelor's Delight*, Melville reveals Captain Delano's peculiar disposition, a mix of republican rhetoric and imperial practices. By locating this imperial activity within the American ship's national domain and alongside the revolutionary events aboard the *San Dominick*, Melville undercuts the idea that the United States cannot act like a rapacious empire because of its republican heritage. There is a single direct reference to republican ideology in "Benito Cereno" and it takes place on board the *San Dominick*, prior to Delano's illumination, when casks of water and provisions are loaded onto the deck. Having asked Cereno for the honor of performing the service, Delano aims to play the part of virtuous republican, condescending equally toward all members of the motley crew. "The casks being on deck, Captain Delano was handed a number of jars and cups by one of the steward's aids, who, in the name of his captain, entreated him to do as he had proposed: dole out the water. He complied, with republican impartiality as to this republican element, which always seeks one level, serving the oldest white no better than the youngest black."[6] Delano's classical republican character changes when he undertakes his next duty, to serve the food: for the slaves, "wilted" minced pumpkins; for the whites, "soft bread, sugar, and bottled cider." This scene clarifies Delano's American brand of *racialized* republicanism and predicts the imperial power his men will ultimately wield against the fugitive slaves. At Babo's urging, one can assume, Cereno orders Delano to stop the unequal distribution of the provisions and give all members an equal share. While Delano's aim was to convey his humanitarian spirit, his version of republicanism conceals an ideology of white power, which in American society shaped every facet of African-American life, particularly in the slaveholder's management of the slave's physical body. Alongside Babo, Captain Delano's concern for racial order fares poorly. Like the Haitian revolution to which the liberated slaves pay homage, Babo offers the American captain an alternative model for a republic, one free of racial hierarchies and white supremacy. The ritual of a color-blind republicanism aboard the *San Dominick* reveals an unforeseen layer of irony in racial masquerade: next to the slave rebel and the symbol of Haitian independence, the American captain is a counterfeit of republican values. Thus, Delano's symbolic handling of the casks establishes the link between imperial and republican authority: "[For] the time oblivious of any but benevolent thoughts," Delano detaches from a racially mixed site that he no longer understands, no longer exhibiting his prized "good order," and he loses himself in self-congratulatory reflections about his humanitarian intervention.

Such thoughts are a prerogative of empire; resistance, in the form of Babo's leap into the boat to assassinate his master, abruptly halts Delano's reflections. For years I believed this pivotal scene was Melville's triumph, both a denunciation of the crippling racial ideology undergirding American slavery and national division, and a forecast of civil war. Read with an eye on this turbulent domestic background, the remainder of the narrative after Delano's awakening seemed anticlimactic. Melville's skillful dramatic irony had apparently, at least in my case, hit its mark: the reader upbraids the ignorant republican protagonist for his racism, for arrogantly stumbling into a slave conspiracy, and for being unable to interpret the vocabulary of revolt. Lost in this space between the second and third parts of the narrative is the presence of U.S. imperial power. I understand Delano as performing a version of Jeffersonian republicanism, which is precisely the crux in interpreting Delano's mistaken vision aboard the *San Dominick* but also in interpreting his astute and ruthless statecraft once back in command of the *Bachelor's Delight.* The reader comes to discover that in Captain Delano the republican and the imperial coexist; he is republican in word, imperial in action.

So why does Melville send Captain Delano back to the *Bachelor's Delight* to plan the attack? By returning the story to the deck of the U.S. vessel, Melville makes the exercise of U.S. imperial power the story's central subject. No longer the benevolent, ineffectual republican, Delano plans to seize the *San Dominick* and its cargo of gold, silver, and slaves. As Delano ascends into the role of commanding imperialist, Cereno, "whose spirit has been crushed by misery," urges him not to risk his life in pursuit of the fugitive slaves.[7] Symbolically taking the place of the timorous Cereno, Captain Delano, the American, becomes the bellicose spirit of a new imperial force. No reason is given for Delano's decision to send armed boats in pursuit of the escaping slaves. The Americans have no claim on the property, expressing neither loathing for the slaves nor love for the Spanish sailors still held captive on the ship, nor do they justify their quest with republican rhetoric of liberating their fellow white men. On the contrary, Delano's plan to seize the rich Spanish vessel joins military and economic power in a single mission. It is the essence of U.S. imperialism.

Unlike the republican ritual of the casks aboard the *San Dominick,* Delano refrains from a similar performance aboard his ship. Since Delano has taken the place of the defeated Cereno, an equivalent transfer of Spanish wealth is necessary if the symbolic substitution is not going to be drained of history. Planning the attack on board the *Bachelor's Delight,* Delano does not rely on republican rhetoric to conceal the Americans' rapacious goals. The *Bachelor's Delight* fiduciary voyage moves the officers to ask Delano to stay behind rather than to lead his men into battle, "for reasons connected with their own interests," to maintain his command aboard the *Bachelor's Delight,* and to safeguard their investment. Delano employs a similar fiscal appeal—the golden vision of the Spanish "prize" and equal shares in the booty—to attract volunteers and rally them in pursuit: "The more to encourage the sailors, they were told, that the Spanish captain considered his ship good as lost; that she and her cargo, including some gold and silver, were worth more than a thousand doubloons. Take her, and no small part should be theirs. The sailors replied with a shout."[8] In addition to Catholic terrors and depravity, the Spanish Black Legend included this vision of seizing a fortune. (In chapter 1, we saw how Governor Clarke employed the same recruiting pitch in New York to attract volunteers to fight Spain in the War of Jenkins's Ear.) Cereno's concession that "his ship [is as] good as lost" is the key phrase, surrendering the Spanish property claim and ensuring the succession of imperial power from Spain to the United States. With their future stake in the booty protected by law, the sailors punctuate the recruitment pitch and their impending mission with a spirited shout, a striking contrast to the dispirited Cereno.

The shout forecasts the Americans' seizure of the *San Dominick,* and the passage of the ship's possession—from Spain, to the slaves, to the United States—alters its meaning. Much has been made, for good reason, about the racial masquerade, which conceals the inversion of the master-slave relationship and is, after all, the principal source of Melville's irony. The masquerade's conclusion, however, does not end the story proper. If we stop the narrative and pause to consider the fugitives' flight, then the revolt is no longer a masquerade to deceive Delano, no longer stalled between freedom and slavery. For a fleeting moment, Babo and his fellow slaves have overturned the master-slave hierarchy and constitute a free people. Their flight temporarily suspends the meaning of the *San Dominick.* In pursuit, the Americans see only abandoned property, a windfall. In their eyes, the *San Dominick* is a floating microcosm of the Spanish conquest, of the legendary *galleon* that carried the riches of the New World across the Atlantic to Spain. Again, as I have tried to demonstrate throughout, the American imperial imagination becomes a lethal force, particularly its demonizing of racialized others. In this case, racial ideology converts the freed slaves into "cargo," and the Americans, dreaming of a thousand doubloons, kill indiscriminately while taking possession of the *San Dominick.* Stripped of republican sentiments, the scene reveals the military and commercial power of a burgeoning American empire.

Yet the meaning of this new force, and the champions of it, is open to question, particularly since Melville insinuates that U.S. power in the South American seas is indistinguishable from piracy. The histories of empire are intrinsic to the meaning of privateering and piracy, both sharing their origins in the European state's imperialist policies. The difference between piracy and privateering was that the privateer held a commission from a "civilized" nation-state to capture merchant vessels, particularly those sailing under the flag of a hostile state. Moreover, piracy was a form of terror both widely condemned *and* exploited by European powers, depending on whose colonial economies were being disrupted. Deliberately blurring the line between privateer and pirate, "Benito Cereno" is enmeshed in their conflicting versions of colonialism and empire. The telling moment occurs when Delano chooses his chief mate—"an athletic and resolute man, who had been a privateer's-man"—to lead the attack. By Delano's order, the chief mate officially possesses the privateer's figurative letters of marque to seize the *San Dominick*, and in the wake of the horrific attack, the official distinction between piracy and privateering collapses. We saw in Brown's *Arthur Mervyn* how money infected with the violence of Caribbean slavery is symbolically buried at the new nation's foundation. Writing over fifty years later, Melville also reveals the imperial roots of U.S. culture and national institutions; but while Brown marks the Philadelphia setting as the center of U.S. power, Melville detaches this force from American territory and relocates it at the southernmost edge of the hemisphere.

The diseased money in *Arthur Mervyn* demonstrates the rebirth, in the new United States, of the British Empire's old imperial networks in her North American colonies. Taking possession of the Spanish vessel in "Benito Cereno," on the contrary, evokes the evolving hemispheric ambition of the United States, its so-called Manifest Destiny and the catastrophic violence that was essential to realizing it. Sailing away from the Americans is a rich ship formerly of the Spanish empire, piloted by slaves whom, by nature of their race and lack of affiliation to a Western nation-state, imperialists deem acceptable prey. Although Babo and the slaves invoke the eighteenth-century right of revolution, they are illegitimate in the eyes of Cereno and Delano—the two figures of Spanish and American imperialism—like the revolutionary Haiti that the slaves honor by rechristening the Spanish vessel the *San Dominick*. Indeed, Cereno sounds the alarm with the phrase, "this plotting pirate means murder," robbing Babo and his "desperados" of their newfound freedoms.

What might have Melville been thinking in placing the slave pirate and the American privateer side-by-side? Among other reasons, the sea narrative inspired Melville because his experience had shown him how rapidly a ship's society could swing between a despotic regime and an egalitarian democratic community. No ship society was more notorious for its brand of a radically color-blind democracy than a pirate ship, a space often free of race, class, national, and religious hierarchies. In this sense, Babo, the "plotting pirate," is threatening because of a democratic vision that has no home, at least not within the American state or on its periphery. Thus, Delano's mission implies a new masquerade, in which American power is not what it seems. Pursuing a democratic band of slaves, the veil of Delano's official commission is lifted, revealing privateering to be yet another prerogative of empire, nothing more than a sanctioned form of piracy. ("There is but a slight step from the privateersman to the pirate," Washington Irving once commented. "[B]oth fight for the love of plunder" *[Oxford English Dictionary]*.)

During his visit to the *San Dominick,* Delano suspected the Africans and Spaniards of being pirates and of having formed a conspiracy to seize the *Bachelor's Delight.* Delano's fear of this piratical threat exemplifies how political and racial demonization work together in the American imperial imagination. After the slave mutiny is revealed, however, the American's pursuit of the fugitive vessel transforms a previously foreign seascape into a mythic American frontier. Armed with their muskets and sealing spears, while the fugitive slaves have only their hatchets, the American militia fire their muskets upon approaching the ship's quarters. "Having no bullets to return, the negroes sent their yells. But, upon the second volley, Indian-like, they hurtled their hatchets. One took off a sailor's fingers. Another struck the whale-boat's bow, cutting off the rope there, and remaining stuck in the gunwale like a woodman's axe."[9] When the attack intensifies, the narrator describes the Americans as "fighting as troopers in the saddle, one leg sideways flung over the bulwarks."[10] The rhetoric and tropes of the American frontier wilderness permeate the description of the attack.

As an imperial metaphor, the attack is significant. It detaches the American frontier from its legendary place in the West, even as it appropriates a new imperial space with familiar expansionist rhetoric.[11] No longer a foreign setting, the Chilean sea is rendered a frontier American outpost: the solitary woodsman, the Indian and hatchet, a cavalry soldier. Thus the stark picture pits the figure of a solitary woodsman against a terrifying mass of screaming African savages. This nightmare scenario of a massacre in the Americans' mind ultimately fuels the killing of the slaves. By negating the imaginary gulf between domestic and foreign territories, the attack thus extends U.S. racial hierarchies to a new site of empire. This new grid of geopolitical power has implications for the American sailors, whom the narrator, for the first time in the story, describes as a unified band of white men. At the height of the attack, the fugitive ship's bow comes around—

both slowly and ominously—and displays the white skeleton of Don Alexandro Aranda, Babo's former master. "One extended arm of the ghost seemed beckoning the whites to avenge it." The American chief mate, the ex-privateer, responds with Babo's earlier call to arms, "Follow your leader!"[12] Finally, the narrator's description of the Americans as "whites" is no accident. The representation of the attack clearly registers the connection between race and U.S. imperial power in no uncertain terms: "nearly a score of the negroes were killed" and "many were mangled," the narrator remarks, if they were fortunate enough to escape the volley of musket balls. As for the American and Spanish forces, the whites, some were wounded but none were killed.

The terror of the American attack alludes to violent struggles of colonialism and imperialism, and we are left with the uncomfortable notion that the key to unlocking the mystery of "Benito Cereno" is in the savage display of U.S. power. Departing New England as whalers and sealers, the Americans end up repeating the history of Spain's conquest of South America. The voyage of the *Bachelor's Delight* enhances U.S. imperial power by claiming a larger geographical dimension and by defeating key competitors, both the Spanish imperialists and the slaves who have reclaimed their freedom as well as the fruits of their labor. Like the Spanish imperialists before him, Captain Delano both conquers nature, imposing the state's domain, and subjugates racialized others. Perhaps most important, the Americans suppress resistance to their rule, towing the *San Dominick* and its survivors back to port, while taking possession of the riches and slave labor. Their seizure of the Spanish vessel adds another layer of irony to Delano's epiphany upon seeing Babo brandishing the knife against Cereno: "All this, with what proceeded, and what followed, occurred with such involutions of rapidity, that past, present, and future seemed one."[13] In the chaotic space of Spanish empire's collapse, the Americans have seen the future and revolutionized the hemisphere, creating new spaces of U.S. empire and a new future for humanitarian intervention.

The study of war, imperialism, and national identity has been central to the evolution of American studies, and considering the ideological and economic investments made by the United States in Afghanistan, in Iraq, and in the "War on Terror," we can safely assume that the debate over the nature of U.S. imperialism has just begun and will not abate during the first decades of the twenty-first century. In his 1976 lectures *Society Must Be Defended,* Michel Foucault wondered if the phenomenon of war could not be considered a primary mode of power relations in society: "If we look beneath peace, order, wealth, and authority, beneath the calm order of subordinations, beneath the State and the State apparatuses, beneath the laws, and so on, will we hear and discover a sort of primitive and permanent war?"[14] His question gets to the core of my understanding in this book of how the critical paradigm of American exceptionalism veils the practices of early American imperialism, namely, slavery, trade wars, and territorial expansion. The American writers covered here anticipated Foucault's insight into the nature of power in the modern nation-state. Looking beneath Captain Delano's peace, order, and authority, for instance, Melville discovers the imperial authority of white power that coexists with the "calm order" of the American captain's republican values.

I began this book by investigating how imperial warfare heightened racial tension in colonial New York and found that the "primitive and permanent war" between slavery and freedom had, by 1741, produced a culture of terror. One of the consequences of the war with Spain was the increasing fear among whites that the city's slaves were serving as Spain's proxy militia, a charge the courts upheld during the conspiracy trials of 1741. Writing the history of these events has always been an act distorted by terror, both the terror of white colonists who feared for their lives and of slaves who were coerced, tortured, and mutilated at the gallows. I end this book with Melville because he recognized how white power had caused an epistemological crisis in U.S. culture. What was the legacy of the American Revolution if systemic racial domination lay beneath the grand order of a free republic? Confronted by the strange events aboard the *San Dominick,* Captain Delano figures the crisis as a narrative problem: "He recalled the Spaniard's manner while telling his story. There was a gloomy hesitancy and subterfuge about it. It was just the manner of one making up his tale for evil purposes, as he goes. But if that story was not true, what was the truth?"[15] Rather than treat the depositions as Melville's revelation of truth, we might remember, as I've discussed throughout this book, the irony inherent in many early American texts: white power leaves its imprint. All "facts" are open to counterfeit.

I often turn to these counterfeit histories because within them lay buried the keys to resisting the silences they so often impose. For instance, Daniel

Horsmanden's narrative of the New York Conspiracy trials is an artifact of white power that exposes how narrative was essential to the state's strategies of domination. Horsmanden can teach readers how to approach the question of truth in "Benito Cereno." The key tactic in his *Journal of the Proceedings in the Detection of a Conspiracy* resembles that of the official narrative that Melville integrates into his fictional account: to link the text with imperial authority. Melville's narrator explains the purpose of the court depositions: "The following extracts, translated from one of the official Spanish documents, will, it is hoped, shed light on the preceding narrative, as well as, in the first place, reveal the true port of departure and true history of the San Dominick's voyage, down to the time of her touching at the island of St. Maria."[16] At this point in the narrative there is no good reason to trust the narrator's confidence that Spain's viceregal courts will arrive at a "true history." The English and Spanish courts provide both narratives with the stamp of authenticity, of a thorough investigation undertaken by the judges. Strikingly enough, the conclusion of both Horsmanden's and Melville's conspiracy narratives are identical. Horsmanden's final chapter is a ledger, organizing the convicted, confessed, burned, hanged, and transported into logical columns. This is one of the text's symbols of a revived imperial authority, and it reaffirms the relation between terror and the state. In the same vein, Melville concludes "Benito Cereno" with the gruesome image of Babo's head on a pike, surveying the plaza and meeting "unabashed, the gaze of the whites."[17]

Babo chooses not to speak after the Americans capture him and carry him to the Spanish authorities, a problem of interpretation familiar to students of slave conspiracies. In the moments suspected slave rebels did speak, torture and coercion distorted their testimony, and more often, convicted slaves made no confessions and bore their execution in silence, which was the case in New York. Melville invests these histories of slavery and imperial culture with symbolic power, turning his narrator's neutral forecast of truth into an unbelievable notion. Read alongside each other, Melville's ironic narrative casts suspicion on Horsmanden's assuredness in the court's discovery of truth. Refusing the claim on truth made possible by the court's coercive tactics and the faulty memory of its defendants, Melville focuses the reader's attention on the slave leader's dishonored body, "dragged to the gibbet at the tail of a mule" and burned to ashes. Like the thirty executed slaves in New York, Babo meets his "voiceless end."[18]

At the conclusion of Horsmanden's ledger, a reader encounters a list of their names under the heading "Negroes Indicted Who Were Not to Be Found": Hanover, London, Ben, Pedro, Ben, Jack, and Joe. They, too, met a voiceless end. Since first encountering the ledger, I considered their escape from New York City, their erstwhile presence in historical memory, essential to any interpretation of the historical text. The six fugitives appear at the end of the document as the court's errata, the mistakes that literally escape the notice of colonial authority. As victims of white power, they bear a relation to the executed suspects that both Horsmanden and Melville depict in their narratives. Some bodies, particularly those hung in chains or burned, are visible, a fearful spectacle intended to quell resistance and to strengthen state power; other bodies, like the six fugitives, remain invisible, their history in New York City translated as, and reduced to, a blemish on the official record. While none of the six apparently wound up in Philadelphia and wrote down their experience (one can perhaps imagine that their oral histories circulated widely), critics can recapture a version of their histories by coming to understand how white power both interpreted their presence and silenced their resistance. By investing Horsmanden's fugitive errata with humanity and the desire for freedom, Melville does as much in "Benito Cereno."

And yet his rendering of the American ship in pursuit of the Spanish prize, the symbol of a new imperial force in South America, reveals how the same racial fictions that sanctioned slavery and white power at home enabled the international expansion of an American empire in the nineteenth century. The dynamic between these two readings, in my eyes, makes "Benito Cereno" a significant text for American studies as the field attempts to reconcile the reach of American empire with other forms of transnationalism. The context of the slavery crisis, which drives interpretations of "Benito Cereno," is only part of a larger story about the historical succession of American power in the Western Hemisphere. Melville suggests that slavery's inevitable collapse in the United States would fail to curtail imperial expansion. The same racial ideology that prohibited Delano from seeing either the slave rebel's humanity or his true intentions would come to justify U.S. military and economic intervention in foreign places like Nicaragua, Cuba, the Philippines, Mexico, and Haiti. Melville's prescient observation challenges us to locate the current crisis of American empire in a historical continuum and to resist the prevailing perspective that the foreign and domestic "war on terror" is a new, unprecedented conflict. As it had been in the past, the terrorist threat has been racialized, which has both dehumanized and demonized Arabs and Muslims. Many Arab and Muslim detainees are incarcerated against their will, presumed guilty by virtue of their culture and their color, denied the protections of the Geneva Convention and basic human rights, and subjected to forms of torture. In approving and implementing these abuses, civilian and military authorities have implicitly invoked the legal precedents of the old slave codes. Armed with this arbitrary and racist power, the U.S. military has created its own fugitives, called "ghost detainees," disappeared so as to avoid the supervision of human rights organizations. The most egregious abuses are rationalized as the unavoidable excesses of a new global conflict against terrorism that obscures, regrettably, the distinctions between good and evil. When these same narratives emerged from the Vietnam War, American studies contested their authority by initiating a historical critique of U.S. imperial power. The foreign and domestic "war on terror" compels American studies to keep adding to this alternative historical memory. It remains one of the few critical spaces to present a politics of anti-imperialism. We can continue to challenge the historical tensions between America's progressive ideals and its imperial practices, and to deepen our understanding of how American writing both sanctions and resists U.S. imperialism.

Notes

INTRODUCTION

1. In particular, Amy Kaplan discusses how American exceptionalism denies the reality of empire in U.S. culture. See Kaplan, "'Left Alone with America': The Absence of Empire in the Study of American Culture," in *The Cultures of United States Imperialism,* ed. Amy Kaplan and Donald E. Pease (Durham, NC: Duke University Press, 1993).

2. Fred Anderson makes a similar statement about the legacy of British imperialism in his important study of war and the politics of empire: "To see the Seven Years' War and the Revolution together as epochal events that yoked imperialism and republicanism in American political culture may therefore enable us to take another step toward understanding a national history in which war and freedom have often intertwined. For ours is, in the end, an inheritance shaped no less by the quest for power than by the pursuit of happiness." *Crucible of War: The Seven Years' War and the Fate of Empire in British North America, 1754–1766* (New York: Vintage Books, 2001), 746. While I am indebted to Anderson for elaborating the significance of colonial warfare and British imperialism in the formation of American nationhood, I do not find imperialism and republicanism to be, more or less, equal on the scale that weighs them. To be fair, this difference may be due to the different periods that we cover (Anderson's book ends in 1766), as well as the material we study. Since I am interested, among other things, in the interrelationships between slavery and imperialism, my subject has made me more uncertain about the capacity of republicanism to balance out the violence of imperialism. The historian Richard Van Alstyne also argued that the new United States was defined by imperial expansion. See his *The Rising American Empire* (New York: Norton, 1960) and *Empire and Independence: The International History of the American Revolution* (New York: John Wiley and Sons, 1965).

3. I am alluding to Kaplan's discussion of this apparent contradiction. See "Left Alone with America," 12. That American imperialism is no longer viewed as a contradiction is a subject Kaplan takes up in her 2003 address to the American Studies

Association. See "Violent Belongings and the Question of Empire Today," *American Quarterly* 56, no. 1 (March 2004): 1–19.

4. Particularly since September 11, 2001, the number of books on the subject has risen dramatically, and there are literally thousands of articles. A representative sample would include Chalmers Johnson, *The Sorrows of Empire: Militarism, Secrecy, and the End of the Republic* (New York: Metropolitan Books, 2004); Niall Ferguson, *Empire: The Rise and Demise of the British World Order and the Lessons for Global Power* (New York: Basic Books, 2002); Patrick Buchanan, *A Republic, Not an Empire: Reclaiming America's Destiny* (Washington, DC: Regnery, 2002); Joseph Nye, *The Paradox of American Power: Why the World's Only Superpower Can't Go It Alone* (New York: Oxford University Press, 2002); Michael Ignatieff, "The American Empire: The Burden," *New York Times Magazine*, January 5, 2003; Max Boot, *The Savage Wars of Peace: Small Wars and the Rise of American Power* (New York: Basic Books, 2002).

5. There are notable exceptions, such as Chalmers Johnson, who, in his latest book, makes cursory mention of the early nineteenth-century roots of U.S. imperialism, when the "US declared all of Latin America its sphere of influence and busily enlarged its own territory at the expense of the indigenous people of North America, as well as British, French, and Spanish colonialists, and neighboring Mexico" (*The Sorrows of Empire*, 2).

6. On process versus place in U.S. imperial culture, see Eric Hindraker, *Elusive Empires: Constructing Colonialism in the Ohio Valley, 1673–1800* (Cambridge: Cambridge University Press, 1997).

7. A number of important studies have influenced my thinking about U.S. imperialism. See Fred Anderson, *Crucible of War: The Seven Years' War and the Fate of Empire in British North America* (New York: Vintage, 2001); Amy Kaplan, *The Anarchy of Empire in the Making of U.S. Culture* (Cambridge: Harvard University Press, 2002); Richard Drinnon, *Facing West: The Metaphysics of Indian-Hating and Empire-Building* (Minneapolis: University of Minnesota Press, 1980); Reginald Horsman, *Race and Manifest Destiny* (Cambridge: Harvard University Press, 1981); Annette Kolodny, *The Lay of the Land: Metaphor as Experience and History in American Life and Letters* (Chapel Hill: University of North Carolina Press, 1975); Michael Rogin, "'Make My Day!': Spectacle as Amnesia in Imperial Politics [and] the Sequel," in *The Cultures of United States Imperialism*, ed. Kaplan and Pease; Lisa Lowe, "The International within the National," in *The Futures of American Studies*, ed. Donald E. Pease and Robyn Wiegman (Durham, NC: Duke University Press, 2002); John Carlos Rowe, *Literary Culture and U.S. Imperialism: From the Revolution to World War II* (New York: Oxford University Press, 2000); Richard Slotkin, *Regeneration through Violence: The Mythology of the American Frontier, 1600–1860* (Middletown, CT: Wesleyan University Press, 1973); Jan Radway, "What's in a Name?" in *The Futures of American Studies*, ed. Pease and Wiegman; George Lipsitz, *The Possessive Investment in Whiteness: How White People Profit from Identity Politics* (Philadelphia: Temple University Press, 1998).

8. In historical accounts of the early United States, the conflict between republicanism and imperialism is often centered on the career of Thomas Jefferson and generally divided by his adherence either to republican ideals or to imperial expansionism. A comprehensive and helpful analysis of Jefferson's political theory of a "republican

empire" is Peter Onuf's *Jefferson's Empire: The Language of American Nationhood* (Charlottesville: University of Virginia Press, 2000). For accounts of Jefferson that focus more on the policy and practices of expansionism, see Robert Tucker and David Hendrickson, *Empire of Liberty: The Statecraft of Thomas Jefferson* (Oxford: Oxford University Press, 1990) and Alex Deconde, *This Affair of Louisiana* (Baton Rouge: Louisiana State University Press, 1979). Hisorians of diplomacy in the new United States provide a useful counterweight to current reformulations of empire, such as Michael Hardt and Antonio Negri's *Empire* (Cambridge: Harvard University Press, 2000). While I learned from them, I depart from both their European model and developmental thesis, which recasts U.S. power in the late eighteenth and early nineteenth centuries as an ambiguous force but not essentially a form of imperialism. However, when their discussion arrives in the twentieth century, they look back, cautiously, on the past: "Perhaps what we have presented [are not] *exceptions* to the development of imperial sovereignty within the history of the U.S. Constitution. In other words, perhaps the root of these imperialist practices should be traced back to the very origins of the country, to black slavery and the genocidal wars against Native Americans" (177). The undeniable histories of U.S. imperial *practices*—what I am calling the historical trinity of U.S. imperialism—cause the authors to doubt the *theoretical* division they posit between European and American imperialism.

9. Kaplan, *The Anarchy of Empire in the Making of U.S. Culture*, 17.

10. Focusing on 1848 popular culture, the Mexican War, and other imperial ventures, Shelley Streeby has also made an impressive contribution to this history of American empire building. *American Sensations: Class, Empire, and the Production of Popular Culture* (Berkeley: University of California Press, 2002).

11. Ellison, "Perspective of Literature," *The Collected Essays of Ralph Ellison* (New York: Modern Library, 1995), 778.

12. Gary Nash, *Race and Revolution* (Madison: University of Wisconsin Press, 1990), 77–78.

13. James Roger Sharp, *American Politics in the Early Republic: The New Nation in Crisis* (New Haven, CT: Yale University Press, 1993).

14. Rogin, "Make My Day!" 503.

15. Mahmood Mamdani argues that Western notions of "good" (secularized and modern) and "bad" Muslims (fundamentalist and tribal) are a result of a collective failure to understand the political origins of terror. Mamdani demonstrates how Cold War politics, particularly the active support given to terrorist movements by the U.S. government, fostered the growth of "political Islam," a term the author hopes will shift public attention to the historical and political reasons for violence. See Mamdani, *Good Muslim, Bad Muslim: America, the Cold War, and the Roots of Terror* (New York: Pantheon, 2004).

16. Teresa Goddu, *Gothic America: Narrative, History, Nation* (New York: Columbia University Press, 1997).

17. Joan Dayan fittingly calls these practices the "sorcery of law," an idea that I return to in chapter 1. See Joan Dayan, "Legal Slaves and Civil Bodies," in *Materializing Democracy: Toward a Revitalized Cultural Politics*, ed. Russ Castronovo and Dana D. Nelson (Durham, NC: Duke University Press, 2002), 1.

18. The current debate about the slave conspiracy allegedly led by Denmark Vesey in Charleston, South Carolina, has once again focused attention on an enduring issue in the historiography of slavery. Thus, even the supposed legitimacy of trial manuscripts, as James Sidbury finally concludes in his response to the recent controversy of the Denmark Vesey affair, are "at worst . . . a collective fiction . . . a fiction about slavery and freedom" ("Forum," *William and Mary Quarterly* 59, no. 1 [2002]: 182).

19. This is the moment in colonial writing, as Homi Bhabha suggests, when narratives exercise command and become essential to the reconstruction of white power. Bhabha, "Of Mimicry and Man: The Ambivalence of Colonial Discourse," in *The Location of Culture* (London: Routledge, 1994).

20. Michel-Rolph Trouillot, *Silencing the Past* (Boston: Beacon Press, 1995); Carl Sandburg, *Abraham Lincoln: The War Years, 1861–1864* (New York: Dell, 1974).

21. On the national narrative, see Castronovo, Goddu, and Wald, whose definition encompasses many recent studies. "Viewed as an amalgamation of stories, the narrative of 'America' resists being told in terms of an intelligible story of uncontested descent; on the contrary, the nation's genealogy is inhabited by lost members, dispossessed bastards, forgotten orphans, and rebellious slaves." Russ Castronovo, *Fathering the Nation: American Genealogies of Slavery and Freedom* (Berkeley: University of California Press, 1995), 6. See also Teresa Goddu, *Gothic America: Narrative, History, Nation* (New York: Columbia, 1997); and Priscilla Wald, *Constituting Americans: Cultural Anxiety and Narrative Form* (Durham, NC: Duke University Press, 1995).

22. The American Revolution dominates scholarly study of eighteenth-century America, as well as the emergence and later development of the United States. As Fred Anderson has pointed out, virtually all modern accounts of the Revolution accept the 1763 Peace of Paris, which ended the Seven Years' War, as the common starting point for studying the foundations of the United States. This watershed moment gives the impression that key events preceding the 1763 treaty were simply seeds of an inevitable revolution, and Anderson claims that selecting a different starting point can produce an "alternative understanding" of the period. Beginning his story of the United States in the 1750s, with the Seven Years' War and the British empire's demise, Anderson's history casts events in imperial as well as revolutionary terms (*Crucible of War*, xx).

23. Dana Nelson, "Consternation," in *The Futures of American Studies,* ed. Donald Pease and Robyn Wiegman (Durham, NC: Duke University Press, 2002).

I. WAR FOR EMPIRE AND THE NEW YORK
CONSPIRACY TRIALS OF 1741

1. For the history of slavery in colonial New York, see Herbert Aptheker, *American Negro Slave Revolts* (New York: International Publishers, 1977); Joseph Carroll, *Slave Insurrections in the United States, 1800–1865* (1938; repr. New York: Negro Universities Press, 1968); Graham Russell Hodges, *Root and Branch: African-Americans in New York and New Jersey, 1613–1863* (Chapel Hill: University of North Carolina Press, 1999); Michael Kammen, *Colonial New York* (New York: Scribners, 1975); Winthrop Jordan, *White over Black: American Attitudes toward the Negro* (Chapel Hill: University of North Carolina Press, 1968); Edgar McManus, *A History of Negro Slavery in*

New York (Syracuse, NY: Syracuse University Press, 1966); Edwin G. Burrows and Mike Wallace, *Gotham: A History of New York City to 1898* (Oxford: Oxford University Press, 1999); Sherril D. Wilson, *New York City's African Slaveowners: A Social and Meterial Cultural History* (New York: Garland, 1994).

2. Thomas J. Davis, "Conspiracy and Credibility: Look Who's Talking, about What—Law Talk and Loose Talk," *William and Mary Quarterly* 59, no. 1 (2002): 169.

3. From Charleston, South Carolina, Denmark Vesey was allegedly the leader of a slave conspiracy in 1821 and 1822 to attack the city. The plot was betrayed and the court arrested 131 slaves and free African-Americans and ultimately executed Vesey and 37 of his accused coconspirators, a sum exceeding those executed during the New York Slave Conspiracy trials. Claiming that Vesey was wrongly accused, Michael Johnson has argued that historians accepted the court's verdict and misread the trial manuscripts. Michael Johnson, "Denmark Vesey and His Co-conspirators," *William and Mary Quarterly* 58, no. 4 (2001): 915–77.

4. In addition to Horsmanden's documentation of the legal workings of Negro evidence, see Edwin Olson, "The Slave Code in Colonial New York," *Journal of Negro History* 29, no. 2 (April 1944): 147–65; and Carl Nordstrom, "The New York Slave Code," *Afro-Americans in New York Life and History* 4, no. 1 (1980): 7–26. For comprehensive studies of colonial slave law, see Leon Higginbotham, *In the Matter of Color: Race and the American Legal Process, the Colonial Period* (Oxford: Oxford University Press, 1980); and Alan Watson, *Slave Law in the Americas* (Athens: University of Georgia Press, 1993). Watson documents both the local development of slave statutes and the tendency of colonies to appropriate particular codes from each other.

5. Daniel Horsmanden, *A Journal of the Proceedings in the Detection of the Conspiracy Formed by Some White People, in Conjunction with Negro and Other Slaves, for Burning the City of New York in America, and Murdering the Inhabitants*, ed. Thomas Davis (Boston: Beacon Press, 1971); hereafter cited as Horsmanden, *Journal of the Proceedings*. Philip Morgan, "Conspiracy Scares," *William and Mary Quarterly* 59, no. 1 (2002): 164.

6. Thomas Davis, *A Rumor of Revolt: The "Great Negro Plot" in Colonial New York* (New York: Free Press, 1985); Marcus Rediker and Peter Linebaugh, *The Many-Headed Hydra: Sailors, Slaves, Commoners, and the Hidden History of the Revolutionary Atlantic* (Boston: Beacon Press, 2000), 193.

7. Peter Charles Hoffer, *The Great New York Conspiracy of 1741: Slavery, Crime, and Colonial Law* (Lawrence: University Press of Kansas, 2003), 8.

8. Davis (*A Rumor of Revolt*) deserves much of the credit for reviving interest in the New York Slave Conspiracy. For other early and important commentators, see Apetheker, *American Negro Slave Revolts;* Jordan, *White over Black;* Leopold Launitz-Schurer, "Slave Resistance in Colonial New York: An Interpretation of Daniel Horsmanden's New York Conspiracy," *Phylon* 41, no. 2 (1980): 137–51; and Ferenc M. Szasz, "The New York Slave Revolt of 1741: A Re-Examination," *Journal of Negro History* (July 1967): 215–30. Recent interpretations include Hoffer, *The Great New York Conspiracy of 1741;* William J. Moses, "Sex, Salem, and Slave Trials: Ritual Drama and Ceremony of Innocence," in *The Black Columbiad: Defining Moments in African American Literature and Culture,* ed. Werner Sollors and Maria Diedrich (Cambridge: Harvard

University Press, 1994), 64–76; and Rediker and Linebaugh, *The Many-Headed Hydra*. Serena Zabin's *The New York Conspiracy Trials of 1741: Daniel Horsmanden's Journal of the Proceedings* (New York: Bedford/St. Martin's, 2004) is an abridged version of Horsmanden's text designed for classroom use, but my chapter went into print before I could consult it. Both Zabin and Jill Lepore are at work on monographs on the conspiracy trials.

9. My analysis of the effects of imperial warfare on colonial culture is indebted to George Lipsitz's "Whiteness and War," in *The Possessive Investment in Whiteness: How White People Profit from Identity Politics* (Philadelphia: Temple University Press, 1998). Lipsitz examines the dual function of U.S. military action over the past five decades. Armed conflicts function geopolitically and domestically in order to control contested markets and raw materials, as well as to reinforce white citizenship. Nationalist rhetoric, military spectacles, and patriotic displays complement military ventures and reveal the "particular rewards of white identity" (70–71). As I see it, the historical seeds of Lipsitz's insight are buried in the formative decade of the 1740s, when imperial warfare contributes to the production of a nascent "American" identity.

10. *Dictionary of National Biography*, ed. William Cosby (London: Oxford University Press, 1975), 249.

11. Michael Warner, *The Letters of the Republic: Publication and the Public Sphere in Eighteenth-Century America* (Cambridge, MA: Harvard University Press, 1990), 18, 19.

12. Horsmanden, *A Journal of the Proceedings*, 5; emphasis in original.

13. Hayden White has argued that all historical narratives, even the chronicle, are "verbal fictions, the contents of which are as much *invented* as *found*" and that the historian, more poet than scientist, uses a combination of tropes—metaphor, metonymy, synecdoche, and irony—to craft the narrative's style and perspective ("The Historical Text as Literary Artifact," in *Tropics of Discourse: Essays in Cultural Criticism* [Baltimore: Johns Hopkins University Press, 1978], 83; emphasis in original). Moreover, at the root of every history is a specific plot structure, rooted in historical consciousness, which converts the historical details into a narrative. For White this operation of "emplotment," which all historical writing must undergo, is "precisely the way that [Northrop] Frye has suggested is the case with 'fictions' in general" (83)—except that White disagrees with Frye on a key point. White believes the fictional aspect of historical writing, rather than producing a "bastard genre," is precisely what distinguishes all histories and gives them their "explanatory effect" (83). There is no consensus on the proper number or types of plot structures, although both White and Frye believe in a limited number. Unlike White and Frye, I am not concerned with classifying a particular plot structure as romantic, comic, tragic, or satirical (or some combination of the four), or with matching a pregeneric structure with its classical or Judeo-Christian precursor. Although both White and Frye trace underlying plot structures and story types back to a "deep level of consciousness," my primary aim is to locate these fictive elements in sociopolitical discourse, or the realm of public consciousness (82). Despite this distinction, White's approach to historical writing as well as Frye's approach to historical myths are useful aids in understanding the role the imagination plays in writing history.

14. Horsmanden, *Journal of the Proceedings*, 27.

15. Mikhail Bakhtin, *Rabelais and His World,* trans. Helene Iswolsky (Bloomington: Indiana University Press, 1988).

16. Rediker and Linebaugh, *The Many-Headed Hydra,* 193.

17. Philip Morgan, "Conspiracy Scares," 166.

18. Davis, "Conspiracy and Credibility," 173.

19. David Shields, *Oracles of Empire: Poetry, Politics, and Commerce in British America, 1690–1750* (Chicago: University of Chicago Press, 1990), 187, 179.

20. For studies of the war, see Berkeley, "The War of Jenkins' Ear," in *The Old Dominion: Essays for Thomas Perkins Abernethy,* ed. Darrett B. Rutman (Charlottesville: University Press of Virginia, 1964); Howard Peckham, *The Colonial Wars, 1689–1762* (Chicago: University of Chicago Press, 1964); Albert Harkness, "Americanism and Jenkins' Ear," *Mississippi Valley Historical Review* 37 (1950): 61–90; Douglas Leach, *The Northern Colonial Frontier, 1606–1763* (New York: Holt, Rinehart, and Winston, 1966); Joseph Devine, "The War of Jenkins' Ear: The Political, Economic, and Social Impact on the British North American Colonies," PhD diss., University of Virginia, 1964; and John T. Lanning, *The Diplomatic History of Georgia: a Study of the Epoch of Jenkins' Ear* (Chapel Hill: University of North Carolina Press, 1936).

21. Richard Pares, *War and Trade in the West Indies* (London: Frank Cass, 1963), 253.

22. Ibid., 72.

23. For a study of the economic foundations of eighteenth-century warfare in the West Indies, see ibid. For a larger study of Stono's Rebellion and the history of slavery in South Carolina, see Peter Wood, *Black Majority: Negroes in Colonial South Carolina from 1670 through the Stono Rebellion* (New York: Norton, 1974). He makes the observation that New York's treatment of its own slave population was influenced by the eruption of rebellion in South Carolina.

24. Wayne Booth, *The Rhetoric of Fiction* (Chicago: University of Chicago Press, 1983), 196.

25. Horsmanden, *Journal of the Proceedings,* 27.

26. Ibid., 28, 29.

27. Ibid., 30.

28. Ibid., 30; emphasis added.

29. Ibid., 31; emphasis added.

30. Benedict Anderson, *Imagined Communities: Reflections on the Origins and Spread of Nationalism* (London: Verso Press, 1991), 198.

31. Bernard Bailyn and Philip D. Morgan, introduction to *Strangers within the Realm: Cultural Margins of the First British Empire* (Chapel Hill: University of North Carolina Press, 1991), 13.

32. Homi Bhabha, "Of Mimicry and Man: The Ambivalence of Colonial Discourse," in *The Location of Culture* (London: Routledge, 1994), 87.

33. Horsmanden, *Journal of the Proceedings,* 38.

34. Ibid., 66.

35. Szasz, "The New York Slave Revolt of 1741," 221.

36. Horsmanden, *Journal of the Proceedings,* 273.

37. Ibid.

38. Cotton Mather's *Pillars of Salt* (1699) transformed into text what was significant

social ritual in the American colonies and helped to spawn a publishing revolution by which the gallows confession became a highly popular text. See also Richard Slotkin, "Narratives of Negro Crime in New England, 1675–1800," *American Quarterly* 25, no. 1 (March 1973): 3–32. For a larger study of execution as one of New England's "repertory of rituals," see David D. Hall, *Worlds of Wonder, Days of Judgment: Popular Religious Belief in Early New England* (New York: Knopf, 1989).

39. Joan Dayan, "Legal Slaves and Civil Bodies," in *Materializing Democracy: Toward a Revitalized Cultural Politics,* ed. Russ Castronovo and Dana D. Nelson (Durham, NC: Duke University Press, 2002).

40. Horsmanden, *Journal of the Proceedings,* 276.

41. Ibid., 137.

42. Ibid., 185.

43. Ibid., 186.

44. Berkeley, "The War of Jenkins' Ear," in *The Old Dominion,* ed. Rutman, 46, 48. The detail about the handkerchief comes from Peckman, *The Colonial Wars,* 88–89.

45. Ibid., 52.

46. Harkness, "Americanism and Jenkins' Ear," 79.

47. Pares, *War and Trade in the West Indies,* 82. For a look at how trade and colonization became a key issue in the War of Jenkins's Ear, see pages 72–86.

48. In 1736 Clarke was appointed lieutenant governor under Governor William Cosby. When Cosby died in 1736, Clarke became acting governor and retained the position's full power and privilege. His contemporaries as well as historians use both titles when referring to him.

49. In his study of the political satires of the war, Shields aptly points out how they illustrate a "British infantry infected with a gold fever as virulent as that of the conquistadors seeking El Dorado" (*Oracles of Empire,* 193).

50. "Gold" stories filled the pages of colonial newspapers, particularly in the early stages of the war and were often viewed as marking the progress of the war as well as serving as an inducement for colonists.

51. Clarke to the Duke of Newcastle, May 15, 1741, *Documents Relative to the Colonial History of the State of New York,* vol. 6, ed. E. B. O'Callaghan (Albany, NY: Weed, Parsons, 1855), 187.

52. While Rhode Island, with its economy tied to the West Indian slave trade, was unusual in its support, Maryland, like New York, found it difficult to recruit volunteers because of a recent slave revolt as well as the presence of potentially subversive Catholics. See Harkness, "Americanism and Jenkins' Ear," 65.

53. Clarke to the Duke of Newcastle, June 20, 1741, *Documents Relative to the Colonial History,* 196.

54. Shields, *Oracles of Empire,* 187.

55. Clarke to the Duke of Newcastle, June 20, 1741, *Documents Relative to the Colonial History,* 196.

56. Clarke to the Lords of Trade, ibid., 198.

57. Ibid., 199.

58. McManus, *A History of Negro Slavery in New York,* 132.

59. Clarke to the Lords of Trade, June 20, 1741, *Documents Relative to the Colonial History*, 197.

60. See the *Dictionary of National Biography*, 966.

61. Quoted from Pares, *War and Trade in the West Indies*, 89.

62. In his studies of colonial violence and terror, Michael Taussig argues that a "colonial mirror" is a staple of all such cultures, "which reflects back onto the colonists the barbarity of their own social relations, but as imputed to the savage or evil figures they wish to colonize." See Taussig, "Culture of Terror—Space of Death: Roger Casement's Putumayo Report and the Explanation of Torture," *Comparative Studies in Society and History* 26, no. 3 (July 1984): 495.

63. Horsmanden, *Journal of the Proceedings*, 324.

64. Ibid., 321.

65. Newspapers, journals, and private and official correspondence provide the most revealing depictions of slave troops during the war. For a glimpse of slave troops in larger geographical and political contexts, see Peter M. Voelz, *Slave and Soldier: The Military Impact of Blacks in the Colonial Americas* (New York: Garland, 1993).

66. See ibid., 78–79.

67. Harkness, "Americanism and Jenkins' Ear," 89.

68. Quoted in ibid., 75. In "Lismahogo's Captivity: Transculturation in *Humphrey Clinker*," Charlotte Sussman reads Smollett's novel as a response to English imperial expansion. *ELH* 61, no. 3 (1994): 597–619.

69. As Bhabha puts it, the alienated "language of liberty" produces another form of knowledge that may be intolerable to the colonial subject precisely because it is defined by the absolute nature of colonial power. I am suggesting here that the war and conspiracy contribute to a redefinition of an "American" liberty marked by the ambivalence of racial identification, as well as the violence produced by the "slippage" of these "identity effects" ("Of Mimicry and Man," 86).

70. Horsmanden, *Journal of the Proceedings*, 211.

71. There is much work to be done on the role religious differences played in the events of 1741. For a recent interpretation of the trial of John Ury, see Hoffer, *The Great New York Conspiracy of 1741*, 130–51. I would disagree with his claim that the Ury trial brought an international dimension to the conspiracy trials. From the beginning, the war with Spain rendered this "local" crisis as a "global" conflict.

72. Szasz notes that the word "popery" first appears four months after the trials begin and after sixty witnesses had testified. "What had been Black Magic in Salem in 1692," Szasz writes, "became the Black Conspiracy in New York fifty years later" ("The New York Slave Revolt of 1741," 223).

73. Horsmanden, *Journal of the Proceedings*, 432.

74. Ibid., 440.

75. For many historians this conclusion to the investigations resembles what occurred in Salem. Szasz is representative of this school of thought, aptly remarking, "These fresh accusations served the same purpose in New York as had the accusation of Governor Phips's wife in Salem. The trials ceased abruptly" ("The New York Slave Revolt of 1741," 225).

76. Davis, "Conspiracy and Credibility," 173.

77. Horsmanden, *Journal of the Proceedings*, 386–89.

78. Underlying this discussion of what Walter Benjamin calls a "state of siege" is Taussig's use of Benjamin to describe the disciplinary power when the state deliberately uses disorder, uncertainty, and paranoia as tools of social control.

79. Horsmanden, *Journal of the Proceedings*, 442.

80. Ibid., 12.

81. Alexander Hamilton, "The Itinerarium of Dr. Alexander Hamilton," in *Colonial American Travel Narratives*, ed. Wendy Martin (New York: Penguin, 1994), 241–42.

2. UNREASONABLE DISCONTENT

1. Historians have attached many labels to the armed conflict between France and the United States—a quasi-war, an undeclared war, a defensive war, a limited war. Whatever its name, Americans understood it to be a war. Alex Deconde claims that the "limited war was the first armed conflict that Americans, as citizens of an independent nation, fought." DeConde, *The Quasi-War: The Politics and Diplomacy of the Undeclared War with France, 1797–1801* (New York: C. Scribner, 1966), vii. The anti-Federalist *Philadelphia Aurora*, in response to President Adams's hostile actions toward France, also claimed that the president's "harpies say it is not a declaration of war, although they know it amounts to the same thing." See Paul Rosenfeld, *American Aurora* (New York: St. Martin's Press, 1997), 47.

2. In addition to my own analysis of primary documents, my understanding of U.S. political culture at the end of the eighteenth century draws from a range of political, economic, and social histories. Some of the most useful studies include Saul Cornell, *The Other Founders: Anti-Federalism and the Dissenting Tradition in America, 1788–1828* (Chapel Hill: University of North Carolina Press, 1999); Stanley Elkins and Eric McKitrick, *The Age of Federalism: The Early American Republic, 1788–1800* (Oxford: Oxford University Press, 1993); Linda Kerber, *Federalists in Dissent* (Ithaca, NY: Cornell University Press, 1970); Richard Kohn, *Eagle and Sword: The Federalists and the Creation of the Military Establishment in America, 1783–1802* (New York: Free Press, 1975); Joyce Appleby, *Capitalism and a New Social Order: The Republican Vision of the 1790s* (New York: New York University Press, 1984); John Miller, *The Federalist Era* (New York: Harpers, 1960); Peter S. Onuf, *Jefferson's Empire: The Language of American Nationhood* (Charlottesville: University Press of Virginia, 2000); Thomas Slaughter, *The Whiskey Rebellion: Frontier Epilogue to the American Revolution* (New York: Oxford University Press, 1986); James Morton Smith, *Freedom's Fetters: The Alien and Sedition Laws and American Civil Liberties* (Ithaca, NY: Cornell University Press, 1956); William Earl Weeks, "American Nationalism, American Imperialism: Interpretations of U.S. Political Economy, 1789–1861," *Journal of the Early Republic* 14, no. 4 (1994): 485–95; Gary Nash, *Forging Freedom: The Formation of Philadelphia's Black Community, 1720–1840* (Cambridge: Harvard University Press, 1994); Douglas Egerton, *Gabriel's Rebellion: The Virginia Slave Conspiracies of 1800 and 1802* (Chapel Hill: University of North Carolina Press, 1993); DeConde, *The Quasi-War;* John Nelson, *Liberty and Property: Political Economy and Policymaking in the New Nation, 1789–1812* (Baltimore, MD: Johns Hopkins University Press, 1987); James Roger Sharp, *American Politics in the*

Early Republic: The New Nation in Crisis (New Haven, CT: Yale University Press, 1993); Wiley Sword, *President Washington's Indian War: The Struggle for the Old Northwest, 1790–1795* (Norman: University of Oklahoma Press, 1985).

3. Elkins and McKitrick, *The Age of Federalism*, 621.

4. Larzer Ziff, *Writing in the New Nation: Prose, Print, and Politics in the Early United States* (New Haven, CT: Yale University Press, 1991), 193.

5. Robert Levine, *Conspiracy and Romance: Studies in Brockden Brown, Cooper, Hawthorne, and Melville* (Cambridge: Cambridge University Press, 1989); Jared Gardner, "Alien Nation: Edgar Huntley's Savage Awakening," *American Literature* 66 (1994): 429–61. On the effects of Brown's commercial career on his politics, see Harry Warfel, *Charles Brockden Brown: American Gothic Novelist* (Gainesville: University of Florida, 1949), 203–4. Ziff offers a representative statement on Brown's famous transformation: "As it happens, Brown himself abandoned his Jeffersonian ideals at about the same time in his short life . . . that he abandoned the writing of fiction. . . . It is tempting, therefore, to suggest that Brown's political conversion was brought about by self-discovery implicit in his mode of fictional composition" (*Writing in the New Nation*, 145). I share Gardner's and Levine's unwillingness to accept this political conversion narrative; this chapter attempts to blur the border between the two supposed phases of Brown's public career.

6. Bill Christopherson, *The Apparition in the Glass: Charles Brockden Brown's American Gothic* (Athens: University of Georgia Press, 1993); Teresa Goddu, *Gothic America: Narrative, History, Nation* (New York: Columbia University Press, 1997); Shirley Samuels, *Romances of the Republic: Women, the Family, and Violence in the Literature of the Early American Nation* (Oxford: Oxford University Press, 1996); Steven Watts, *The Romance of Real Life: Charles Brockden Brown and the Origins of American Culture* (Baltimore, MD: John's Hopkins University Press, 1994). Three new studies on Brown were published in 2004; since this book was already in production, I did not have the opportunity to consult them. I attended two conferences sponsored by the Charles Brockden Brown Society and have benefited greatly from panel discussions there. See Michael Cody, *Charles Brockden Brown and the Literary Magazine: Cultural Journalism in the Early American Republic* (Jefferson, NC: McFarland, 2004); Peter Kafer, *Charles Brockden Brown's Revolution and the Birth of the American Gothic* (Philadelphia: University of Pennsylvania Press, 2004); Philip Barnard, Mark L. Kamrath, and Stephen Shapiro, eds., *Revising Charles Brockden Brown: Culture, Politics, and Sexuality in the Early Republic* (Knoxville: University of Tennessee Press, 2004).

7. In relation to Brown's novels, Gardner ("Alien Nation") and Philip Gould ("Race, Commerce, and the Literature of Yellow Fever in Early National Philadelphia," *Early American Literature* 35, no. 2 [2000]: 157–86) make a similar point about public anxieties revolving around contagion and the conflation of racial and national identities. A number of important studies, focused on U.S. imperial culture later in the nineteenth century, call attention to the metaphor of contagion, particularly in how it collapses borders (racial, geographic, sexual, national, and so on). See Cheyfitz, "Savage Law: The Plot against American Indians in Johnson and Graham's *Lessee v. M'Intosh* and *The Pioneers*," in *Cultures of United States Imperialism*, ed. Amy Kaplan and Donald Pease; Priscilla Wald, *Constituting Americans: Cultural Anxiety and Narrative Form*

(Durham, NC: Duke University Press, 1995); and Amy Kaplan, *The Anarchy of Empire in the Making of U.S. Culture* (Cambridge: Harvard University Press, 2002).

8. Kohn, *Eagle and Sword*, 252.

9. The origin of the Democratic-Republicans is the ratification debate over the Constitution. After ratification, Saul Cornell claims, Democratic-Republicans incorporated anti-Federalist objections to national power into their opposition to the Federalist party, who stuck them with the label "Democratic." See Cornell, *The Other Founders*. Jefferson and Madison are conventionally viewed as the founders of the Democratic-Republican party, which became known as the Democratic party when Andrew Jackson dropped "Republican." One can distinguish this institutional history from the Democratic-Republican societies of the 1790s, which offered both grassroots support for sympathetic elites and established their own oppositional agenda. As Philip Foner has observed, the societies grew out of the experience of many ordinary Americans who fought for independence but did not share in the rewards: "The immediate source of the popular societies go back to the day when the revolutionary soldiers returned to their homes to find them mortgaged, their families in debt, and the government in the hands of wealthy merchants and landed gentry who were piling up their wealth by speculating in land, in soldiers' certificates, in treasury warrants, and in Continental paper" (Foner, *The Democratic-Republican Societies* [Westport, CT: Greenwood Press, 1976], 5). See also his *History of the Labor Movement*, vol. 1 (New York: International Publishers, 1971). For the standard history of the societies during the Federalist period, see Eugene Link, *Democratic-Republican Societies, 1790–1800* (New York: Octagon Books, 1965).

10. Cornell, *The Other Founders*, 193.

11. Brown, *Monthly Magazine* 1, no. 1 (April 1799): 2.

12. While disagreements and factions existed within the Federalist party, I refer to a single agenda that, despite political differences, advanced martial measures, expansionism, and the restriction of civil liberties. Furthermore, I focus more on political actions and rhetoric during the war crisis, less on individual disagreements about policy and philosophy. For a closer look at Federalist political philosophies, see Cornell, *The Other Founders;* Miller, *The Federalist Era;* Elkins and McKitrick, *The Age of Federalism;* and Kerber, *Federalists in Dissent.*

13. John Adams, "Presidential Proclamation," in *The Rising Glory of America, 1760–1820*, ed. Gordon Wood (Boston: Northeastern University Press, 1990), 116.

14. Ibid.

15. Brown, *Monthly Magazine* 1, no. 2 (1799): 129.

16. Ibid., 130–31.

17. David Clark made an early claim that Brown took a "prudent approach" to avoid politics in the *Monthly Magazine*. Unfortunately, the praise stuck (Clark, *Charles Brockden Brown: Pioneer Voice of America* [Durham, NC: Duke University Press, 1952]; and Steven Frye, "Constructing Indigeneity: Postcolonial Dynamics in Charles Brockden Brown's *Monthly Magazine and American Review*," *American Studies* 39, no. 3 [Fall 1998]: 69–88). Most recently, Frye uses postcolonial theory to account for the construction of "indigeneity" in the journal, but he limits his discussion of national identity in the Federalist period to what takes place in an "intellectual environment" defined

by Hume, Gibbon, and Locke. Beneath Frye's postcolonial theoretical apparatus is a standard intellectual history that abstracts his reading from actual postcolonial political tensions that shaped cultural production in the period. For an innovative reading of how Brown's fiction is influenced by racial anxieties, a discourse I discuss in connection to the journal in the last section, see Gardner, "Alien Nation."

18. Elizabeth Barnes, *States of Sympathy: Seduction and Democracy in the American Novel* (New York: Columbia University Press, 1997), 4. My understanding of sentimentalism in American literary culture, in addition to Barnes, has benefited from Julia Stern, *The Plight of Feeling: Sympathy and Dissent in the Early American Novel* (Chicago: University of Chicago Press, 1997); and Bruce Burgett, *Sentimental Bodies: Sex, Gender, and Citizenship in the Early Republic* (Princeton, NJ: Princeton University Press, 1998).

19. The important work of Sacvan Bercovitch, Jay Fliegleman, Cathy Davidson, Michael Warner, and Steven Watts is crucial if one is to come to grips with the development of American rhetorical, intellectual, and literary traditions in the late eighteenth century. I contribute to this body of work by accounting for ways in which the potency of cultural items increases while in collaboration with institutional power. See Bercovitch, *The American Jeremiad* (Madison: University of Wisconsin Press, 1978); Fliegleman, *Prodigals and Pilgrims: The American Revolution against Patriarchal Authority, 1750–1800* (Cambridge: Cambridge University Press, 1982); Davidson, *Revolution and the Word: The Rise of the Novel in America* (New York: Oxford University Press, 1986); Warner, *The Letters of the Republic: Publication and the Public Sphere in Eighteenth-Century America* (Cambridge, MA: Harvard University Press, 1990); and Watts, *The Romance of Real Life.*

20. Fliegleman *(Prodigals and Pilgrims)* takes issue with mythic, psychohistorical, or rhetorical studies of George Washington eulogies that are flawed "by an overreliance on the apparatus of psychohistory at the expense of sufficiently coming to terms with relevant eighteenth-century intellectual history." He argues that the mythologization of Washington as the national father "enthroned the antipatriarchal values" of the ideology of the Revolution. According to Fliegleman, the glorification of Washington is derived from Locke's theory of virtuous exemplars. The power of Washington's example, however, was instrumental in the creation of Federalist institutions and laws that made the national father an exemplar of governmental coercion.

21. For data on George Washington eulogies and public rituals, see Margaret Bingham Stillwell, *Washington Eulogies: A Checklist of Eulogies and Funeral Orations on the Death of George Washington, December 1799–February 1800* (New York: New York Public Library, 1916).

22. Laurence Friedman (*Inventors of the Promised Land* [New York: Knopf, 1975]) and Fliegleman *(Prodigals and Pilgrims)* mischaracterize Brown's contribution to the Washington myth because they do not consider the entire text of the *Monthly Magazine.* Fliegleman believes Brown, under the mask of Monendus, is satirizing the national obsession with Washington. The last text in the preceding issue of the journal, however, which neither scholar mentions in their otherwise excellent studies, is Brown's heartfelt lament that follows here. His desire for "faithful pictures" of the greatness of Washington does not suggest Brown's unwillingness to glorify him. As I demonstrate, Brown is simply frustrated with inept orators who devalue the memory of Washington.

23. Brown, *Monthly Magazine* 1 (September–December 1799): 477.

24. Ibid., 104.

25. Ibid.

26. I am alluding to Fliegleman's well-known study of this dynamic, *Prodigals and Pilgrims.*

27. Quoted in Rosenfeld, *American Aurora,* 239.

28. Michael Walzer, "On the Role of Symbolism in Political Thought," *Political Science Quarterly* 82 (1967): 194–95.

29. Brown, *Monthly Magazine* 2 (February 1800): 103.

30. Ibid., 125.

31. Stern, *The Plight of Feeling,* 2–3.

32. Morse was certainly not alone in his crusade against subversives. John Robison's book on the Illuminati (*Proofs of a Conspiracy against All Religions and Governments of Europe Carried on in the Secret Meetings of Free Masons, Illuminati, and Reading Societies* [London, 1798]) was reprinted in New York City in 1798–99, and its thesis fortified the "paranoid style" of sermons preached by the New England clergy.

33. Brown, *Monthly Magazine* 2 (February 1800): 127.

34. Bercovitch, *The American Jeremiad,* 141. For accounts of Fourth of July addresses as instrumental rhetorical components of nationalism in postrevolutionary America, see Merle Curti, *The Roots of American Loyalty* (New York: Columbia University Press, 1946); Paul Goetsch and Gerd Hurm, *The Fourth of July: Political Oratory and Literary Reactions, 1776–1876* (Tubengen, Germany: Narr, 1992); Paul Nagel, *This Sacred Trust: American Nationality, 1798–1898* (New York: Oxford University Press, 1971); Len Travers, *Celebrating the Fourth: Independence Day and the Rites of Nationalism in the Early Republic* (Amherst: University of Massachusetts Press, 1997); Wilbur Zelinsky, *Nation into State: The Shifting Symbolic Foundations of American Nationalism* (Chapel Hill: University of North Carolina Press, 1988); David Waldstreicher, *In the Midst of Perpetual Fetes: The Making of American Nationalism, 1776–1820* (Chapel Hill: University of North Carolina Press, 1997).

35. Bercovitch, *The American Jeremiad,* 145.

36. Ibid., 135.

37. Brown, *Monthly Magazine* 5 (August 1799): 374.

38. Ibid., 373.

39. Ibid., 243.

40. Ibid., 244.

41. Matthew Davis, "An Oration Delivered in St. Paul's Church on the Fourth of July," 1800, New York.

42. Brown, *Monthly Magazine,* 3, no. 2 (August 1800): 144.

43. Stern, *The Plight of Feeling,* 9.

44. Brown, *Monthly Magazine* 4 (July 1799): 242.

45. Matthew Davis, "An Oration Delivered in St. Paul's Church on the Fourth of July," 1800, New York.

46. On the effects of warfare on nationalist thinking, see Bruce Porter, *War and the Rise of the State: The Military Foundations of Modern Politics* (New York: Free Press, 1994); and Weeks, "American Nationalism, American Imperialism."

47. Webster, *An Oration Pronounced at Hanover, N.H., the 4th Day of July, 1800; Being the 24th Anniversary of American Independence* [1800], 4, 10. See also Goetsch and Hurm, *The Fourth of July,* 58. For a recent and more precise study of the way July 4 is transformed into public ritual, see Len Travers, *Celebrating the Fourth.*

48. Fliegleman, *Prodigals and Pilgrims,* 197.

49. Webster, *An Oration Pronounced at Hanover, N.H.,* 12, 14, 24. Nagel's reading of Webster's speech illustrates patriotic symbolism, but he completes his analysis without considering the link of Webster's call for war (*This Sacred Trust,* 49). Instead of considering the way in which federal institutions and propaganda used the prospect of war to unify the nation, Nagel ignores the Federalist war measures and paints Republican and popular opposition as a dark threat: "In desperation the nation's leadership sought to control dissenting individuals and their evil abstractions by the Alien and Sedition Acts of 1798" (5).

50. Elijah Parish, *An Oration Delivered at Byfield* (1799), 9.

51. Ibid., 14–15.

52. Brown, *Monthly Magazine* i, no. 4 (July 1799): 243.

53. The ongoing challenge is to find fresh strategies for reconciling the political, social, and cultural histories of early America, such as Douglas Egerton has done in his study of the Virginia slave conspiracies of 1800 and 1802. More than a study of Gabriel's Rebellion and slavery, the book demonstrates how political arguments between Federalists and Republicans created the necessary conditions for insurrection, a thesis that sheds light on the interrelationships between republicanism, national politics, and slavery at the turn of the century. See Egerton, *Gabriel's Rebellion.*

54. Philip Foner, *History of Black Americans* (Westport, CT: Greenwood Press, 1975), 448.

55. Michael Rogin, "'Make My Day!' Spectacle as Amnesia in Imperial Politics [and] the Sequel," in *Cultures of United States Imperialism,* ed. Amy Kaplan and Donald Pease (Durham, NC: Duke University Press, 1993), 503.

56. Quoted in Deconde, *The Quasi-War,* 84.

57. In his seminal study of American abolitionism, James Brewer Stewart does not claim that these early abolitionists constituted a democratic movement even though his descriptions of their practices clearly is democratic: "To many African Americans, however, the Revolution's promises were hardly exhausted with the adoption of the Constitution. Politicized by the Revolution's struggle and empowered by increasing literacy, slaves and freedpeople now began collaborating extensively across regional boundaries. Throughout the North, from 1790 to 1820, legislative petitioning by African Americans was increasingly frequent. . . . African Americans worked to extend the 'spirit of '76' as incidents of localized slave resistance multiplied along with emancipation petitions from literate blacks to federal and state governments." Stewart, *Holy Warriors: The Abolitionists and American Slavery* (New York: Hill and Wang, 1976), 28–29.

58. Quoted in Egerton, *Gabriel's Rebellion,* 47.

59. For significant accounts of race relations during the 1790s, see David Brion Davis, *The Problem of Slavery in the Age of Revolution* (Ithaca, NY: Cornell University Press, 1975); Paul Finkleman, *Slavery and the Founders: Race and Slavery in the Age of Jefferson* (Armonk, NY: M. E. Sharpe, 1996); Winthrop Jordan, *White over Black:*

American Attitudes toward the Negro (Chapel Hill: University of North Carolina Press, 1968); Nash, *Forging Freedom;* and Nash, *Race and Revolution* (Madison: University of Wisconsin Press, 1990).

60. Gardner gives a particularly useful reading of the pamphlet. Looking at it within the context of the period's racial turbulence, Gardner challenges the literary historian to rethink how we weigh the putative historical transition from Federalism to Republicanism by investigating the racial component of American politics in the late eighteenth century that bridges the divide ("Alien Nation," 431).

61. Matthew Davis, "An Oration Delivered in St. Paul's Church on the Fourth of July, 1800, New York," *Monthly Magazine* 1, no. 6 (September–December 1799): 454.

62. Brown, *Monthly Magazine,* 82–83.

63. Ibid., 84.

64. Ibid., 129–30.

65. Brown, *Monthly Magazine,* 131.

66. Elkins and McKitrick, *The Age of Federalism,* 455.

67. Jordan, *White over Black,* 330.

68. Gary Nash, "Reverberations of Haiti in the American North: Black Saint Dominguans in Philadelphia," *Explorations in Early American Culture Pennsylvania History* 65 (1998): 44–73.

69. Ibid., 55.

70. Brown, *Monthly Magazine* 2, no. 4 (April 1800): 298.

71. Rush's theory that black skin was a product of leprosy contradicts Fredrickson, who argues that American thinkers immediately before and after 1800 were unwilling or unable to "defend anti-Negro predisposition by presenting anything that resembled a 'scientific' or philosophical case for the moral and intellectual inferiority of the black race." George Fredrickson, *The Black Image in the White Mind: The Debate on Afro-American Character and Destiny, 1817–1914* (New York: Harper and Row, 1971), 1.

72. Foucault's theory of diffusion is particularly useful for a study of how the United States attempted to control the free black population living in Northern cities before the Civil War.

73. Brown, *Monthly Magazine* 2, no. 4 (April 1800): 300.

74. Dana Nelson, *National Manhood: Capitalist Citizenship and the Imagined Fraternity of White Men* (Durham, NC: Duke University Press, 1998), 58.

75. Davis confirms Rush's conclusion. See *The Problem of Slavery in the Age of Revolution* (302) for his discussion of race as the central excuse for slavery.

76. Nelson, *National Manhood,* 58.

77. A fictional doctor, Royall Tyler's Updike Underhill, arrives at a similar conclusion after he survives his descent into slavery in Royall Tyler's *The Algerine Captive* (1797). Forgetting his earlier pledge to abolish the slave trade, Updike makes a plea for union: "Let us, one and all, endeavor to sustain the general government. Let no foreign emissaries inflame us against one nation. . . . Our first object is union among ourselves. For to no nation besides the US can that ancient saying be more emphatically applied; BY UNITING WE STAND, BY DIVIDING WE FALL" (226). Tyler, *The Algerine Captive; or, The Life and Adventures of Doctor Updike Underhill* (New York: Modern Library, 2002).

3. IMPERIAL GEOGRAPHIES AND *ARTHUR MERVYN*

1. Quoted from Franklin Knight, "The American Revolution and the Caribbean," in *Slavery and Freedom in the Age of the American Revolution,* ed. Ira Berlin and Ron Hoffman (Charlottesville: University of Virginia Press, 1983), 242.

2. William Earl Weeks, "American Nationalism, American Imperialism: Interpretations of U.S. Political Economy, 1789–1861," *Journal of the Early Republic* 14, no. 4 (1994): 486.

3. For the standard history of economic growth in the early national period, see Douglas North's *The Economic Growth of the United States, 1790–1860* (Englewood Cliffs, NJ: Prentice-Hall, 1961). Other economic histories, such as Gary Walton and James Shepard's *The Economic Rise of Early America* (Cambridge: Cambridge University Press, 1979), are notoriously blind to the role slavery played in economic expansion and even downplay the significance of the international slave economy in the commercial growth of the United States. Walton and Shepard want their analysis to stand as an economic model for developing nations in the late twentieth century. Their macroeconomic analysis, which intends to interpret the "behavior of the overall economy," claims that the adoption of the Constitution transformed a stagnant economy by protecting property, stabilizing contracts, and instilling confidence. They ignore the way economic policy in these years deepened the nation's involvement in the international slave economy. For example, North notes that between 1793 and 1808, commercial development was tied to international trade and shipping, particularly through "re-export" with the Caribbean (46–47). On a domestic front, exports increased by £30 million, with slave-manufactured cotton accounting for half this total (40). The best way to counter claims such as Walton and Shepard's, which bring forth statistics to reaffirm myths of a liberal economy based on the Constitution, is to consider the global and imperial aspects of the U.S. economy. For example, Richardson sees economic growth in early America much differently than Walton and Shepard: "[R]ecent studies have shown that although independence triggered the development of trade with new areas overseas . . . it was the slave economies of the European powers in the Caribbean and South America that continued to exercise the most powerful influence on New England trade in the decades after 1783" (David Richardson, "Slavery, Trade, and Economic Growth in Eighteenth-Century New England," in *Slavery and the Rise of the Atlantic System,* ed. Barbara Solow [Cambridge: Harvard University Press, 1991], 263). For perspectives on economic life during the early national period that attempt to comprehend the conflicts between economic liberalism and slave labor, see Jay Coughtry, *The Notorious Triangle: Rhode Island and the African Slave Trade, 1700–1807* (Philadelphia: Temple University Press, 1981); Elizabeth Fox-Genovese and Eugene Genovese, *Fruits of Merchant Capital* (Cambridge: Oxford University Press, 1983); Thomas Ott, *The Haitian Revolution* (Knoxville: University of Tennessee Press, 1973); Eric Williams, *From Columbus to Castro: The History of the Caribbean* (New York: Vintage, 1970); Philip Foner, *History of Black Americans,* 3 vols. (Westport, CT: Greenwood Press, 1975); Gary Nash, *Forging Freedom: The Formation of Philadelphia's Black Community, 1720–1840* (Cambridge: Harvard University Press, 1994); and Gary Nash, *Race and Revolution* (Madison: University of Wisconsin Press, 1990). I like *Fruits*

of Merchant Capital for the analysis of "the janus face of merchant capital," which includes the "resurrection" of slavery and the slave trade (6). Davis remarks how the Caribbean trade brought the sugar that was the fuel of New England economy; lacking a primary staple, the region had over sixty rum distilleries on the eve of the Revolution, and the Caribbean trade employed over ten thousand seamen; David Brion Davis, *The Problem of Slavery in the Age of Revolution* (Ithaca, NY: Cornell University Press, 1975), 262. New studies of the relationship between theoretical market capitalism and American culture, however, focus only on the magic of commerce. For example, Stephen Watts, in his highly regarded cultural biography of Brown and a commercial society, never even mentions slavery; *The Romance of Real Life: Charles Brockden Brown and the Origins of American Culture* (Baltimore: Johns Hopkins University Press, 1994).

4. Cheryl Harris, "Whiteness as Property," in *Critical Race Theory*, ed. Kimberley Crenshaw et al. (New York: New Press, 1995), 286. Looking at the "Second American Revolution" from the perspective of Absalom Jones or an anonymous member of the Free African Society, such a victory is limited, nothing more than, as Harris remarks, "a racialized version of republicanism [that] constrained any vision of democracy" (118).

5. See Jared Gardner, "Alien Nation: Edgar Huntley's Savage Awakening," *American Literature* 66 (1994): 429–61, for an extended study of Brown's twinned novels.

6. J. H. Powell, *Bring Out Your Dead: The Great Plague of Yellow Fever in Philadelphia in 1793* (Philadelphia: University of Pennsylvania, 1993), 63.

7. See Philip Gould, "Race, Commerce, and the Literature of Yellow Fever in Early National Philadelphia," *Early American Literature* 35, no. 2 (2000): 157–86. While Gould discusses how Brown employs the epidemic as a metaphor for such global phenomena in *Arthur Mervyn* (I will return to this reading later in the chapter), he gives a useful analysis of the "commercial jeremiad" that emerged to explain why the epidemic had afflicted Philadelphia. The jeremiad pointed to reckless speculation, stagnant trade, unscrupulous businessmen, and citizens living beyond their fiscal means as potential reasons.

8. See Powell, *Bring Out Your Dead,* for the seminal account of the 1793 yellow fever.

9. Goddu also positions *Arthur Mervyn* within the context of U.S.–Caribbean relations. She claims that Brown's *Arthur Mervyn* demonstrates a cultural anxiety that an American economy connected to the Caribbean slave economies cannot remain truly republican or healthy. For example, Goddu argues: "While the novel consistently displaces discussion of the nation's domestic economy onto the international scene, the specter of slavery lurks in every economic transaction. Money from slave societies ubiquitously circulates to America, revealing America's international and domestic economies dependence on slavery" (Teresa Goddu, *Gothic America: Narrative, History, Nation* [New York: Columbia University Press, 1997], 37). Her analysis of this antirepublican economy emphasizes how money, "tainted by disease and issuing from destruction," circulates in *Arthur Mervyn*. While my reading also traces the circulation of diseased currency, I focus less on the commercial economy and Gothicism and more on how such currency manifests histories of imperial violence and racial anxiety.

10. Bill Christopherson, *The Apparition in the Glass: Charles Brockden Brown's "American Gothic"* (Athens: University of Georgia Press, 1993), 104.

11. Brown, *Arthur Mervyn, or Memoirs of the Year 1793* (New York: Holt, Rhinehart, and Winston, 1962), 18.

12. John Seelye presents a helpful summary of this question. See Seelye, "Charles Brockden Brown and Early American Fiction," in *Columbia Literary History of the United States*, ed. Emory Elliott (New York: Columbia University Press, 1988).

13. Eliza Hinds, *Private Property: Charles Brockden Brown's Gendered Economics of Virtue* (Newark: University of Delaware Press, 1997), 91.

14. Brown, *Arthur Mervyn*, 43–44.

15. Ibid., 90.

16. Ibid., 89.

17. Ibid., 68.

18. In 1798 the United States had entered into an international war for control of the Caribbean, in large part because the Federalist government saw the crisis as an opportunity to uphold their flagging authority. For a discussion of Federalist politics, see chapter 2. The Federalist agenda in 1798–1800 included a series of legislative and emergency war measures aimed at increasing the power of their military and government, as well as silencing domestic opposition. These measures created a permanent army and navy, direct taxes to pay for the military, a Naturalization Act (tripling the residency requirement for citizenship) to undercut the influence of Irish and Germans sympathetic with rival Republicans, and internal security measures called the Alien and Sedition Acts to silence political opposition.

19. For accounts of the conflict that consider the combination of warfare and commerce, see Alex DeConde, *The Quasi-War: The Politics and Diplomacy of the Undeclared War with France, 1797–1801* (New York: C. Scribner, 1966); and Ott, *The Haitian Revolution*.

20. William Currie, *A Sketch of the Rise and Progress of the Yellow Fever* (1799), 60; Thomas Condie and Richard Folwell, *History of the Pestilence* (1798).

21. Daniel Defoe (both speculator and novelist) had provided in *A Journal of the Plague Year* (1722) a notable literary example of how a metaphor of contagion could articulate speculative fevers.

22. Brown, *Arthur Mervyn*, 88.

23. The literal and figurative significance of the yellow fever shaped the first accounts of the 1793 pestilence, including *Arthur Mervyn* and Matthew Carey's history of the epidemic, which found the meaning of the plague in the citizens' luxurious living. See Carey's *A Short Account of the Malignant Fever* (1793). The best critical essays have also explored the historical, literary, and theoretical aspects of contagion in Brown's novel. See Christopherson, *The Apparition in the Glass;* Robert Ferguson's "Yellow Fever and Charles Brockden Brown: The Context of the Emerging Novelist," *Early American Literature* 14 (1979–80): 293–305; Gardner, "Alien Nation"; Goddu, *Gothic America;* Gould, "Race, Commerce"; Levine, *Conspiracy and Romance;* Shirley Samuels, "Plague and Politics in 1793: *Arthur Mervyn*," *Criticism* 27, no. 3 (1985): 225–46.

24. Brown, *Arthur Mervyn*, 140.

25. Ibid.

26. Kaplan suggests that this dynamic is fundamental to the exercise of U.S. imperial power. See Amy Kaplan, "Left Alone with America," in *The Cultures of United States*

Imperialism, ed. Kaplan and Donald E. Pease (Durham, NC: Duke University Press, 1993), 14.

27. For many states, policing the alleged threat of slaves and free African-Americans included increased slave patrols, more inspections, restrictions on travel, prohibitions on the use of the U.S. mail, and restrictions on slaves purchased from the West Indies. See Foner, *History of Black Americans,* vol. 1; and Nash, *Forging Freedom.*

28. Brown, *Arthur Mervyn,* 140–41.

29. I am indebted to Michael Rogin for his analysis of historical amnesia in imperial culture; Rogin, "'Make My Day!': Spectacle as Amnesia in Imperial Politics [and] the Sequel," in *The Cultures of United States Imperialism,* ed. Amy Kaplan and Donald E. Pease (Durham, NC: Duke University Press, 1993). I take this subject up again in chapter 5.

30. While I call attention to the imperial context that converted Philadelphia's African-Americans into foreign enemies, Gould reads the public anxiety regarding black nurses as a sign of the depersonalization of market forces caused by the epidemic. Both perspectives, it seems to me, are evidence of how Brown, on a fundamental level, aligns anxieties of market capitalism and imperial expansion (Gould, "Race, Commerce").

31. Christopher Castiglia, *Bound and Determined: Captivity, Culture-Crossing, and White Womanhood from Mary Rowlandson to Patty Hearst* (Chicago: University of Chicago Press, 1995), 5.

32. Brown, *Arthur Mervyn,* 141.

33. For a broad study of how captivity became a central narrative in Britain's pursuit of empire, see Linda Colley, *Captives* (New York: Pantheon Books, 2002).

34. Brown, *Arthur Mervyn,* 142.

35. Levine, *Conspiracy and Romance,* 22.

36. Nash, *Forging Freedom,* 143.

37. Ibid., 175. For a contemporaneous history of these emergency measures, see Thomas Condie and Richard Folwell, *History of the Pestilence Commonly Called Yellow Fever, Which Almost Devastated Philadelphia* (Philadelphia: Press of R. Folwell, 1799).

38. Nash, *Forging Freedom,* 175–76.

39. Davis locates the origin of the Fugitive Slave Law in Article IV of the Constitution, which included the provision that no fugitive slave could be freed by the laws of any state into which he escaped (*The Problem of Slavery,* 125). Debates over the 1793 law hinged on the federal government's role. Does it become a seller of the slave and "repeat the crime" (135–36)? The compromise was that the recovered slave would be taken to the state or territory in which he had been bought (137). Philip Foner notes how slavery debates in the first Congress, particularly over taxes on "slave" commodities like rum and molasses and the importation of slaves, caused so much alarm among political leaders about the issue's volatility that the 1790 Naturalization Act (limiting naturalization to only "white" aliens) and 1793 Fugitive Slave Law were needed to pacify Southern legislators (*History of Black Americans,* 408–20). Finally, the 1819 Slave Trade Act debate, as P. J. Staudenraus relates, instigated debates on the federal government's participation in the "disposing of rescued Africans" (*The African Colonization Movement, 1816–1865* [New York: Columbia University Press, 1961], 50). The act authorized sending a naval squadron to African waters, a $100,000 budget, and a government

agency in Africa; the American Colonization Society lobbied for converting this agency into a "nucleus for a colony." Chapter 4 examines this discourse of colonization.

40. Goddu, *Gothic America,* 37.

41. For example, Stephen Watts, in an otherwise insightful study of Charles Brockden Brown and the American market economy, manages to discuss national expansion into foreign markets, commercial values, and a business revolution taking place in the 1790s without mentioning the contradictory or ironic effects of an international slave economy on his view of a theoretical market society. In *The Romance of Real Life: Charles Brockden Brown and the Origins of American Culture* (Baltimore: Johns Hopkins University Press, 1994), Watts constructs a "cultural biography" of Brown as artist, radical, and moralist, but slavery apparently leaves no impression on this life.

42. Brown, *Arthur Mervyn,* 217.

43. Ibid., 230.

44. Ibid., 240.

45. Ibid.

46. Ibid., 157.

47. Ibid., 232.

48. Gould, "Race, Commerce."

49. Brown, *Arthur Mervyn,* 319.

50. Ibid., 335.

51. Ibid., 354.

52. In Tyler's *The Algerine Captive, or The Life and Adventures of Doctor Updike Underhill* (New York: Modern Library, 2002), Updike Underhill's journey into the Southern slave states also brings him into contact with an alien world of racial difference and white power.

53. Brown, *Arthur Mervyn,* 355; emphasis in original.

54. Ibid., 361.

55. Ibid., 362.

56. Ibid., 367.

57. Samuels, "Plague and Politics in 1793," 20.

58. Brown, *Arthur Mervyn,* 370.

59. Ibid., preface.

60. Carey, *Short Account of the Malignant Fever* [1793, 3rd printing], 37, 78–79.

61. Ibid., 105.

62. J. M. Powell, *Bring Out Your Dead,* 55.

63. On Rush's appeal to Jones and Allen, see Gould, "Race, Commerce."

64. Powell, *Bring Out Your Dead,* 96.

65. Ibid., 93.

66. On the historic African-American opposition to the Fugitive Slave Law, see Benjamin Quarles, *Black Abolitionists* (Cambridge: Oxford University Press, 1969).

67. Jones and Allen, *A Narrative of the Proceedings of the Black People, During the Late Aweful Calamity in Philadelphia, in the Year 1793* (Philadelphia, 1794), 7.

68. On the relationship between Carey and Jones and Allen, see Gould, "Race, Commerce."

69. Jones and Allen, *A Narrative of the Proceedings of the Black People,* 8.

70. Ibid., 2.

71. Ibid., 15.

72. Carey, *Short Account of the Malignant Fever,* 78. Carey holds to this belief despite the fact that he records fifteen sick African-Americans admitted to Bush Hill, of whom three-fourths died, a statistical sampling that might have demonstrated to him that nobody was immune to the pestilence.

73. Warner, *The Letters of the Republic,* 12.

74. Jones and Allen, *A Narrative of the Proceedings of the Black People,* 14.

75. Ibid., 13. While measuring racism is notoriously difficult, certain artifacts of our political process can provide valuable insight about human emotions. For instance, during the crisis, Mayor Clarkson issued an official warning against racist assault and battery to stop an increasing number of white on black assaults (Powell, *Bring Out Your Dead,* 193).

76. Brown, *Arthur Mervyn,* 168.

77. Ibid., 169.

78. Powell, *Bring Out Your Dead,* 99.

79. Michel-Rolph Trouillot, *Silencing the Past* (Boston: Beacon Press, 1995), 26, 25.

80. Powell, *Bring Out Your Dead,* 113.

81. Norman Grabo, ed., introduction to *Arthur Mervyn* (Kent, OH: Kent State University Press, 1980), 449.

4. SNUG STORED BELOW

1. I am indebted to Gary Nash, who has written widely about the African-American experience during the postrevolutionary period. See especially his book *Forging Freedom: The Formation of Philadelphia's Black Community, 1720–1840* (Cambridge: Harvard University Press, 1988). For other useful histories of race relations during this period, see Herbert Aptheker, *American Negro Slave Revolts* (New York: International Publishers, 1977); Joseph Carroll, *Slave Insurrections in the US, 1800–1865* (New York: Negro Universities Press, 1968); David Brion Davis, *The Problem of Slavery in the Age of Revolution* (Ithaca, NY: Cornell University Press, 1975); Philip Foner, *History of Black Americans* (Westport, CT: Greenwood Press, 1975); and James Brewer Stewart, *Holy Warriors: The Abolitionists and American Slavery* (New York: Hill and Wang, 1996).

2. Jones and Allen, *A Narrative of the Proceedings of the Black People, During the Late Aweful Calamity in Philadelphia, in the Year 1793* (Philadelphia, 1794), 20.

3. Nash, *Forging Freedom,* 4.

4. My understanding of how national power can "reroute" democracy comes from Dana Nelson's "Frontier Democracy and Representative Management," *REAL: The Yearbook of Research in English and American Literature* 18 (2002): 215–29.

5. Thomas Jefferson, *Notes on the State of Virginia* (Chapel Hill: University of North Carolina Press, 1955), 46.

6. David Waldstreicher, *In the Midst of Perpetual Fetes: The Making of American Nationalism, 1776–1820* (Chapel Hill: University of North Carolina Press, 1997). While I am in agreement with Waldstreicher's claim about the pattern of white nationalism followed by the American Colonization Society, I do not believe, as Waldstreicher

does, that the American Colonization Society established this nationalist ideology in the wake of the War of 1812 and the national desire for consensus. I would push the beginning of this pattern back even further to the end of the eighteenth century, when the emergence of Federalist militarism made the insurrectionary black threat an essential component of a racially homogeneous national identity. The victory of Jefferson and the Republicans only solidified the reunification of a white nation. Even more than the post-1812 period, the late 1790s established in public consciousness, once and for all, that the United States was a *white* nation weakened by the defiant slave population it harbored.

7. For the standard history of the movement, see P. J. Staudenraus, *The African Colonization Movement, 1816–1865* (New York: Columbia University Press, 1961). In addition, the annual reports from the American Colonization Society, as well as Garrison's manifesto denouncing their agenda, help round out one's understanding of the colonization movement.

8. For the standard history of the Missouri Compromise, see Glover Moore, *The Missouri Controversy, 1819–1821* (Gloucester, MS: Peter Smith, 1967). For an extended discussion of the relationship between the Missouri debates and American nationalism, see George Dangerfield, *The Awakening of American Nationalism, 1815–1828,* New American Nation Series (San Francisco: Harper & Row, 1965). More recent studies have interpreted the controversy as a discourse on national expansion and a growing market economy in the early nineteenth century. See Charles Sellers, *The Market Revolution: Jacksonian America, 1815–1846* (Oxford: Oxford University Press, 1991).

9. James Fenimore Cooper, *The Pioneers* (New York: Penguin Classics, 1988). There are five Leatherstocking novels, in the following sequence: *The Pioneers* (1823), *The Last of the Mohicans* (1826), *The Prairie* (1827), *The Pathfinder* (1840), and *The Deerslayer* (1841). The series tells the life story of Natty Bumppo (also known as Hawkeye, Leatherstocking, Pathfinder, and Deerslayer), who prefers the natural laws of the wilderness and the companionship of American Indians to the rules and miscreants of American civilization.

10. Brook Thomas examines the novel in relation to the 1821 New York Constitutional Convention. See Thomas, "*The Pioneers,* or The Sources of American Legal History: A Critical Tale," in *Cross-Examinations of Law and Literature* (Cambridge: Cambridge University Press, 1987). Steven Watts finds Cooper's own financial ineptitude and worries the most useful context. See Watts, "'Through a Glass Eye, Darkly': James Fenimore Cooper as a Social Critic," *Journal of the Early Republic* 13 (1993): 55–74. Alan Taylor points to the Republican "revolution" of 1799–1801 as the historical source of *The Pioneers.* See Taylor, *William Cooper's Town: Power and Persuasion on the Frontier of the Early American Republic* (New York: Vintage, 1995). For a host of other critics, including those mentioned, the Cooper family drama, especially the novelist's relationship with his father, becomes the interpretive frame for the novel. These critics, including Stephen Railton, suggest that the figure of the father, William Cooper, looms largest in the novelist's "mental life." See Railton, *Fenimore Cooper: A Study of His Life and Imagination* (Princeton, NJ: Princeton University Press, 1978). The Missouri controversy affected Cooper's "mental life" in ways previous critical approaches to the novel have been unable to assess. D. H. Lawrence and Richard Slotkin, by arguing

that racial conflict between the United States and American Indians was the primary influence on Cooper's national vision, initiated a vast mytho-psychological industry related to Cooper. See Lawrence, *Studies in Classic American Literature* (New York: Viking Press, 1964); and Slotkin, *Regeneration through Violence: The Mythology of the American Frontier, 1600–1860* (Middletown, CT: Wesleyan University Press, 1973). I have benefited from such a wide range of approaches to *The Pioneers*, which helped me focus on a critical absence: the pressures instigated by the Missouri controversy and the colonization movement.

11. See Eric Cheyfitz, "Savage Law: The Plot against American Indians in *Johnson and Graham's Lessee v. M'Intosh* and *The Pioneers*," in *The Cultures of United States Imperialism*, ed. Amy Kaplan and Donald Pease (Durham, NC: Duke University Press, 1993), 109–29. For an equally insightful reading of dispossession in relation to Native subjectivity and nationhood, see Priscilla Wald's "Terms of Assimilation: Legislating Subjectivity in the Emerging Nation," in the same volume, 59–85.

12. Saidiya Hartman examines how seemingly harmless concepts—like reform, patriotism, or love—conceal methods of white domination in nineteenth-century American literature. I also study this imperial power, although I am less focused on "defamiliarizing the familiar" in narratives of terror and slavery. See Hartman, *Scenes of Subjection: Terror, Slavery, and Self-Making in Nineteenth-Century America* (Oxford: Oxford University Press, 1997).

13. Noble Cunningham, *The Presidency of James Monroe* (Lawrence: University of Kansas Press, 1996), 1–41.

14. Cooper, *The Pioneers*, 15–16.

15. According to Brook Thomas, "the legal system that had come down intact from 1793 had allowed the wilderness to be transformed into a romantic, picturesque, and productive landscape" ("*The Pioneers*, or The Sources of American Legal History," 230). For another reading of Cooper's historical tableau, particularly in the way Cooper uses this passage to "declare his historiographic intentions," see William Kelly, *Plotting America's Past: Fenimore Cooper and the Leatherstocking Tales* (Carbondale and Edwardsville: Southern Illinois University Press), 4.

16. *American Colonization Society Annual Reports*, 7 vols. (New York: Negro Universities Press, 1969), 1: 18; hereafter referred to as *ACS Annual Reports*.

17. Ibid., 1: 10.

18. Ibid.

19. Jane Tompkins, *Sensational Designs: The Cultural Work of American Fiction, 1790–1860* (New York: Oxford University Press, 1985).

20. Cooper, *The Pioneers*, 204.

21. *ACS Annual Reports*, 1: 15.

22. Cooper, *The Pioneers*, 205.

23. Ibid., 151.

24. Ibid., 24.

25. Ibid., 153.

26. Kelly, *Plotting America's Past*, 22.

27. Since critics have overlooked the plight of the African-American characters in *The Pioneers*, there has been little commentary on the ways in which white power,

working through terror and domination, contributes to identity formation in the novel. This is also a focus of Hartman's, although she might consider this a spectacle of white power in which the violence is inflicted with an alarming ease. The "casualness" of such violent scenes, she suggests, "rather than inciting indignation, too often immune us to pain by virtue of their familiarity" (*Scenes of Subjection,* 3). Consequently, she chooses to "look elsewhere and consider those scenes in which terror can hardly be discerned—the dancing in the quarters, the outrageous antics of the minstrel stage, the constitution of humanity in the slave law, and the fashioning of the self-possessed individual" (4). Like Hartman, I look elsewhere, at episodes in which violence is only residue, but I also have no desire to distinguish these moments from more terrible spectacles. For some texts, such as Cooper's *The Pioneers,* in which this type of cataloging of racial violence has not been done, it is important that both the familiar and the unfamiliar receive critical attention.

28. Cooper, *The Pioneers,* 53.

29. Ibid., 55–56.

30. Ibid., 56.

31. Hartman, *Scenes of Subjection,* 23.

32. Jefferson quoted from Sellers, *The Market Revolution,* 141, 274. Sellers makes an important link between the Missouri debates, expansion, and the fear of racial violence.

33. Historical studies of the Vesey affair—now, once again, the Vesey controversy—include Joseph Carroll, *Slave Insurrections in the United States, 1800–1865* (1938; repr. New York: Negro Universities Press, 1968). For my discussion of the recent controversy surrounding the Vesey conspiracy, see chapter 1.

34. In chapter 5 of this book I take up the subject of Garrison and the issue of racial justice in the writing of the American Indian writer William Apess.

35. William Lloyd Garrison, *Thoughts on African Colonization* (New York: Arno Press, 1968).

36. Cooper, *The Pioneers,* 171.

37. Ibid., 173.

38. Representing the Middle Passage was a staple of abolitionist writing, and as Cooper demonstrates with the oracle Pump, a manner of exploring the depths of national consciousness. For a memorable study of the iconography of the international abolitionist movement and how art constructs slavery, see Marcus Wood, *Blind Memory: Visual Representations of Slavery in England and America* (New York: Routledge, 2000). "The Middle Passage was initially the primary site for the depiction of the trauma of slavery in terms of the problems it posed for the art and collective conscience of European and American societies" (14).

39. Cooper, *The Pioneers,* 176, 169.

40. Several studies discuss this dynamic of white racial formation, particularly David Roediger, *The Wages of Whiteness: Race and the Making of the American Working Class* (London: Verso, 1991); Alexander Saxton, *The Rise and Fall of the White Republic: Class Politics and Mass Culture in Nineteenth-Century America* (London: Verso Press, 1990); and Eric Lott, *Love and Theft: Blackface Minstrelsy and the American Working-Class* (Oxford: Oxford University Press, 1995).

41. Cooper, *The Pioneers,* 194.

42. Ibid., 18.

43. Garrison, *Thoughts on African Colonization*, 4.

44. Here I am alluding to Philip Gould's study of New England historical litera-ture. He highlights the ways in which historical novels "do not merely make analogies between past and present but actually inscribe *contemporary* history" (Gould, *Covenant and Republic: Historical Romance and the Politics of Puritanism* [Cambridge: Cambridge University Press, 1996], 5). Recognition of this narrative strategy is fundamental to re-cent studies of historical fiction, including Eric Cheyfitz, "Savage Law"; Jared Gardner, "Alien Nation: Edgar Huntley's Savage Awakening," *American Literature* 66 (1994): 429–61; and Priscilla Wald, *Constituting Americans: Cultural Anxiety and Narrative Form* (Durham, NC: Duke University Press, 1995).

45. Cooper, *The Pioneers*, 195.

46. Cooper, *The Last of the Mohicans* (New York: Penguin, 1986), 295–306.

47. Cooper, *The Pioneers*, 135.

48. Ibid., 313.

49. Ibid., 195.

50. Ibid., 196.

51. Ibid., 338, 334, 355.

52. Ibid., 373, 380.

53. Cooper relies on this logic of Natty's bondage in other novels of the Leather-stocking series. In *The Last of the Mohicans*, Natty must use his skill with the rifle and mimicry to regain his freedom. Philip Fisher defines Natty's break from captivity in *The Deerslayer* as symbolic for an "essential American freedom. No longer surrounded or tied down, his freedom has been won." See Fisher, *Hard Facts: Setting and Form in the American Novel* (Cambridge: Oxford, 1985), 70.

54. Cheyfitz, "Savage Law," 123–24.

55. Wald, Constituting Americans, 61, 59.

56. Cooper, *The Pioneers*, 347.

57. Ibid.

58. Toni Morrison, *Playing in the Dark: Whiteness and the Literary Imagination* (New York: Vintage Books, 1990), 68.

59. Angus Fletcher, *Allegory: The Theory of a Symbolic Mode* (Ithaca, NY: Cornell University Press, 1964), 193.

60. Cooper, *The Pioneers*, 456.

61. Quoted in Staudenraus, *The African Colonization Movement*, 29.

62. *ACS Annual Reports*, 1: 95.

63. Cooper, *The Pioneers*, 44.

64. Ibid., 60.

65. Anthony Vidler, *The Architectural Uncanny: Essays in the Modern Unhomely* (Cambridge: MIT Press, 1992), 141.

66. The "composite order" invented by Jones and Doolittle adheres to no prece-dent or standard, and its populist vision rebukes the aristocratic authority of Judge Temple that was being challenged in the early nineteenth century. In 1814 Pennsylva-nia Supreme Court Justice Henry Brackenridge decried the emergence of what came to be known as utilitarianism—popular legal reform that departs from the standards

of common law—by constructing an unstable house. Only a wise and discerning judge, "no one but a *skilful architect* . . . who can have the whole edifice in his mind," should attempt legal reform. "The legislature can act only in detail, and in particulars," Justice Brackenridge continues, "whereas the able judge can remove at once, or alter, what was originally faulty or has become disproportionate in the building" (quoted in Morton Horowitz, *The Transformation of American Law, 1780–1860* [New York: Oxford University Press, 1992], 24).

Untutored and brazen, Jones and Doolittle are blinded by the details and cannot envision the whole edifice—just the type of legal architects whom Brackenridge dreaded. After finally viewing the edifice that stands as the symbol of Templeton's sociopolitical order, one reacts to a structure lacking all the classical ideals that usually constitute a suitable metaphor for a balanced and coherent body republic: "It was lucky for the whole fabric, that the carpenter, who did the manual part of the labour, had fastened the canopy of this classic entrance so firmly to the side of the house, that, when the base deserted the superstructure in the manner we have described, and the pillars, for the want of foundation, were no longer of service to support the roof, was able to uphold the pillars" (*The Pioneers*, 60). The classical elements that still exist, the "classic entrance" and the pillars, no longer represent the "whole fabric," and are overwhelmed by the "lucky" measures of the two amateurs. Jones and Doolittle meet none of the requirements described by Brackenridge: neither one is a "skilful architect" who could "alter [a] disproportionate" structure, precisely because their "composite order" is based on the principles of utilitarianism that cancels out stylistic precedence.

67. Peter S. Onuf, *Jefferson's Empire: The Language of American Nationhood* (Charlottesville: University Press of Virginia, 2000), 117.

68. R. D. Madison, "Gib a Nigger Fair Play": Cooper, Slavery, and the Spirit of the Fair," *James Fenimore Cooper: His Country and His Art* 8 (1991): 37–47. In their interpretations of *The Pioneers,* Gardner, Levine, and Ezra Tawil also position the novel within the historical context of slavery. See Gardner, *Master Plots: Race and the Founding of American Literature* (Baltimore, MD: Johns Hopkins University Press, 1998); Levine, "Section and Nation: The Missouri Compromise and the Rise of 'American' Literature," *REAL: The Yearbook of Research in English and American Literature* 14 (1998): 223–40; Tawil, "Romancing History: *The Pioneers* and the Problem of Slavery," *James Fenimore Cooper: His Country and His Art* 11 (1997): 98–101.

69. Cooper, *Notions of the Americans: Picked Up by a Traveling Bachelor* (Albany: State University of New York Press, 1991). For material on Cooper's political character, critics often look to *The American Democrat* (1838), considered to be a minor classic in nineteenth-century American political science, and while nobody has made the point as far as I know, its adherence to strict construction evolves out of the constitutional defense presented in *Notions of the Americans*.

70. Cooper, *Notions of the Americans,* 244; emphasis added.

71. Ibid., 235n.

72. Cadwallader's journey into the Southern slaveocracy serves a different purpose than two other travelers, Brown's Arthur Mervyn and Royall Tyler's Updike Underhill. For these two protagonists the trip exposes the fatal contradictions of the American system, and they bear witness to white-on-black violence that marks the South

as an inferior national space. For example, Underhill discovers the true meaning of hardship and moral hypocrisy when he encounters a Southern minister, late for church, beating his slave.

73. Cooper, *Notions of the Americans,* 242.

74. Ibid., 471–72.

75. Ibid., 4.

5. WILLIAM APESS AND THE NULLIFICATION OF EMPIRE

1. In addition, the Adams-Onis treaty ceded Florida to the United States in exchange for U.S. assumption of $5 million in damages claimed by U.S. citizens against Spain. Official U.S. occupation took place in 1821 with Jackson appointed military governor.

2. Like the Puritan emigrants who came to the colonies, slaves who escaped into Florida desired religious and cultural freedoms. Some unfortunate slaves fell into virtual slavery in Spanish settlements, but others founded autonomous communities in which they developed a complex Pan-African nationalism, despite being forced to elude both the U.S. military and slave raiders. See Tolagbe Ogunleye, "The Self-Emancipated Africans of Florida: Pan-African Nationalists in the 'New World,'" *Journal of Black Studies* 27, no. 1 (September 1996): 24–38.

3. Clark Reynolds collapses the conventional categories of first and second wars and sees them as part of a "continuous war" waged by the United States against American Indians. The Seminole conflict initiates a stage of American empire in which the military expands across the continent in order to dispossess Natives and protect white settlers. See Reynolds, "American Strategic History and Doctrines: A Reconsideration," *Military Affairs* 39, no. 4 (December 1975): 181–91. On the Second Seminole War, see John Mahon, *History of the Second Seminole War* (Gainesville: University of Florida Press, 1967); and John Sprague, *The Origin, Progress, and Conclusion of the Florida War* (Gainesville: University of Florida Press, 1964).

4. On Andrew Jackson and "Jacksonian America," see Edward Pessen, *Jacksonian America* (Homewood, IL: Dorsey, 1969); Robert Remini, *The Age of Jackson* (New York: Harper and Row, 1972); Marvin Meyer, *The Jacksonian Persuasion* (Stanford, CA: Stanford University Press, 1957); and Charles Sellers, *The Market Revolution: Jacksonian America, 1815–1846* (Oxford: Oxford University Press, 1991).

5. All of these texts are collected in Barry O'Connell, *On Our Own Ground: The Complete Writings of William Apess, a Pequot* (Amherst: University of Massachusetts Press, 1992). See O'Connell's remarkable introductory essay about Apess's life and career (xiii–lxxvii). I am indebted to O'Connell, who popularized Apess, as well as other insightful contributions that position Apess in complex historical and political contexts. See Renee Bergland, *The National Uncanny: Indian Ghosts and American Subjects* (Hanover, NH: University Press of New England, 2000); Daniel K. Richter, *Facing East from Indian Country: A Native History of Early America* (Cambridge: Harvard University Press, 2001); Roumiana Velikova, "'Philip, King of the Pequots': The History of an Error," *Early American Literature* 37, no. 2 (2002): 311–36; Maureen Konkle,

"Indian Literacy, U.S. Colonialism, and Literary Criticism," *American Literature* 69, no. 3 (September 1997): 457–86; Theresa Strouth Gaul, "Dialogue and Public Discourse in Willam Apess's Indian Nullification," *ATQ* 15, no. 4 (December 2001): 275–92; Scott Michaelsen, *Limits of Multiculturalism: Interrogating the Origins of American Anthropology* (Minneapolis: University of Minnesota Press, 1999); Robert Allen Warrior, "William Apess: A Pequot and a Methodist under the Sign of Modernity," in *Liberation Theologies, Postmodernity, and the Americas*, ed. David Batstone (London: Routledge, 1997); Jill Lepore, *In the Name of War: King Philip's War and the Origins of American Identity* (New York: Vintage Press, 1998); Arnold Krupat, *The Voice in the Margin: Native American Literature and the Canon* (Berkeley: University of California Press, 1989); Bernd Peyer, *The Tutor'd Mind: Indian Missionary-Writers in Antebellum America* (Amherst: University of Massachusetts Press, 1997); Kim McQuaid, "William Apess, Pequot: An Indian Reformer in the Jackson Era," *New England Quarterly* 50, no. 4 (December 1977): 605–25; David Murray, *Forked Tongues: Speech, Writing, and Representation in North American Indian Texts* (Bloomington: Indiana University Press, 1991). Karim M. Tiro, "Denominated 'SAVAGE': Methodism, Writing, and Identity in the Works of William Apess, a Pequot," *Journal of the Early Republic* 48 (December 1996): 653–79.

6. Warrior, "William Apess," 188.

7. Ibid., 201. In the first stages of the critical recovery of William Apess, shortly over a decade ago, critics defined Apess as the sum of his Christian conversion narrative. This "commonsense" approach to American Indian autobiography, the most attractive to critics, located the roots of the genre in a precontact tribal tradition. Thus, one of the first important studies to address Apess's work, Arnold Krupat's *The Voice in the Margin*, concludes that *A Son of the Forest* deploys Protestant rhetoric and a fervent belief in Christian salvationism that effectively erases all indigenous traces from his life story. This position on Apess's cultural identity typified early interpretations of Apess, perhaps best represented by Krupat's final assessment: "If there is a Pequot dimension to Apess' [texts], they are not apparent to me. In Apess' case, indeed, there is the implication that when the native lost his land, he lost his voice as well" (*The Voice in the Margin*, 147). In addition to Krupat, scholars like David Brumble and Hertha Wong claim that closeness to the orality and spirituality of tribal tradition is the defining element of American Indian autobiography. See Brumble, *American Indian Autobiography* (Berkeley: University of California Press, 1988); and Wong, *Sending My Heart Back across the Years: Tradition and Innovation in Native American Autobiography* (Oxford: Oxford University Press, 1992). As Scott Michaelsen observes in a recent interpretation, even the best studies during the first stages of the Apess recovery were compromised for "passing judgment on the 'Indianness' of texts" (*Limits of Multiculturalism*, xii). This perspective no longer dominates Apess criticism.

8. Apess, *A Son of the Forest*, in O'Connell, *On Our Own Ground*, 19.

9. Bergland, *The National Uncanny*, 128.

10. Apess, *A Son of the Forest*, 9.

11. Ibid., 10.

12. Ibid.

13. Ibid.

14. Ibid., 11.

15. Bergland, *The National Uncanny*, 127.

16. Apess, *A Son of the Forest*, 11.

17. Karim Tiro observes how people of color chose Methodism because of its opposition to practices of Euro-American power and privilege: "During the nineteenth century, as larger numbers of Indians moved off their reservations into the dominant culture, they shared with increasingly disaffected whites and blacks a quotidian existence as wage laborers, servants, and whalers. Methodism, like Baptism and other 'enthusiastic' varieties of Christianity, articulated the grievances they all shared against the classes responsible for their situation and promoted understanding across racial lines" ("Denominated 'SAVAGE,'" 654–55).

18. Apess, *A Son of the Forest*, 4.

19. Ibid., 11.

20. Ibid., 51.

21. Ibid.

22. There are other sources, too, such as the Cherokee response to Indian removal. Refuting the dominant belief in the Indian's inevitable passing, Cherokee leaders argued that the State of Georgia was bringing about removal by violating their civil rights. See Brian Dippie, *The Vanishing American: White Attitudes and U.S. Indian Policy* (Middletown, CT: Wesleyan University Press, 1982), 71. On the case of Cherokee removal, see Theda Perdue and Michael D. Green, eds., *The Cherokee Removal: A Brief History with Documents* (Boston: Bedford Books, 1995).

23. Paul Goodman, *Of One Blood: Abolitionism and the Origins of Racial Equality* (Berkeley: University of California Press, 1998), 57.

24. Throughout this chapter I refer to democracy, Jacksonian democracy, and Jacksonian America in order to indicate the political transformation occurring over the course of the 1830s. The 1828 presidential election was the first decided by popular vote, hundreds of thousands of new voters voted during the 1830s, an evolving market economy promised increased opportunities to ordinary Americans, working men and women gained rights in the workplace, and literacy levels rose across the country. Nevertheless, these advances took place within a U.S. imperial network that was committed to protecting the institutions of slavery, deporting free African-Americans to Liberia, and removing American Indians to the western territories. While a significant democratic transformation occurred in the 1820s and 1830s, the period's democracy was also shaped by the violence of national expansion. See Thomas Hietala, *Manifest Design: Anxious Aggrandizement in Late Jacksonian America* (Ithaca, NY: Cornell University Press, 1985).

25. Goodman, *Of One Blood*, 57.

26. Henry Mayer, *All on Fire: William Lloyd Garrison and the Abolition of Slavery* (New York: St. Martin's Griffen, 1998), 138. See also James Brewer Stewart, *William Lloyd Garrison and the Challenge of Emancipation* (Arlington Heights, IL: Harlan Davidson, 1992); and Christopher Castiglia, *Bound and Determined: Captivity, Culture-Crossing, and White Womanhood from Mary Rowlandson to Patty Hearst* (Chicago: University of Chicago Press, 1995).

27. Garrison, *Thoughts on African Colonization* (1832; repr. New York: Arno Press, 1968), 143.

28. Ibid., 146.

29. Ibid., preface.

30. Peter P. Hinks, ed., *Walkers Appeal, in Four Articles: David Walker's Appeal to the Coloured Citizens of the World* (University Park: Pennsylvania State University Press, 2000). On the history of American abolitionism, see James Brewer Stewart, *Holy Warriors: The Abolitionists and American Slavery* (New York: Hill and Wang, 1976).

31. Apess, *A Son of the Forest*, 60.

32. Apess, *An Indian's Looking-Glass for the White Man*, in O'Connell, *On Our Own Ground*, 155; hereafter page numbers are cited in the text.

33. David Roediger, *The Wages of Whiteness: Race and the Making of the American Working Class* (London: Verso, 1991), 21.

34. Garrison, *Thoughts on African Colonization*, 14; emphasis in original.

35. Ibid., 43.

36. Ibid., 37.

37. Goodman, *Of One Blood*, 42.

38. Quoted in Mayer, *All on Fire*, 138.

39. The Mashpee revolt exists in a historical field well marked with other notable episodes of class and labor struggle. For example, during the 1830s in nearby Rhode Island, a populist movement against property qualifications for voting began with Seth Luther's manifesto in 1833 and culminated with Dorr's Rebellion almost a decade later. See Marvin Gettleman, *The Dorr Rebellion* (New York: Random House, 1973). In Boston, the Trades' Union, perhaps borrowing from Apess's work in the newspapers, appealed to the Declaration in their fight for protection. Other significant labor battles occurred in the 1830s, including the intense battle for a ten-hour workday and the 1834 strike by female factory workers in Lowell, which also utilized the American language of equality and rights. Similarly, in the influential general strike in Philadelphia in 1835, laborers unfurled a banner proclaiming "Liberty, Equality, Rights of Man," the very same rhetorical platform Apess used so brilliantly the year before in Mashpee. Finally, the Mashpee revolt actually precedes by five years the more touted anti-renter movement in the Hudson Valley. White laborers fought against their landlords, and they struggled to protect their right to timber, a similar battle fought by the Mashpee. These working-class struggles, however, generally did not incorporate the aim of racial justice.

40. The pursuit of civil rights has frequently been considered at odds with the pursuit of Indian self-determination and tribal sovereignty. I do not think Apess understands this decision as a choice between an inclusive civil rights model and a separatist tribal sovereignty model. In the 1830s, this historical problem had yet to acquire its twentieth-century connotations. In their specific case, the Masphee succeeded in gaining limited self-government in which civil rights meant protection from the board of overseers, local authorities, and the State of Massachusetts. The Mashpee saw their civil rights movement as inseparable from their desire to protect their land, which is characteristic of the historical struggle for Indian civil rights and self-determination. As Vine Deloria and Clifford Lytle note, "as land is alienated, all other forms of social cohesion begin to erode, land having been the context in which other forms have been

created." See Deloria and Lytle, *The Nations Within: The Past and Future of American Indian Sovereignty* (Austin: University of Texas Press, 1998), 12.

41. James Clifford, *The Predicament of Culture: Twentieth-Century Ethnography, Literature, and Art* (Cambridge: Harvard University Press, 1988), 304.

42. Apess, *Indian Nullification of the Unconstitutional Laws of Massachusetts Relative to the Marshpee Tribe,* in O'Connell, *On Our Own Ground,* 178.

43. Ibid., 179; emphasis in original.

44. Ibid., 200.

45. Ibid., 167. Apess includes both of these examples from the *Boston Advocate* in his account of the events. For a reading of how the play *Metamora* shaped pro-Mashpee feeling in New England, see Lepore, *In the Name of War.* She also uses Hallet's reference to the Tea Party, claiming that "much of Hallet's rhetoric seems to have been inspired by Metamora itself" (216). I think this is a wonderful insight, although my use of Hallet's Tea Party takes a different angle, as my analysis of *Indian Nullification* will demonstrate.

46. O'Connell, *On Our Own Ground,* xv.

47. Sandra Gustafason, "Nations of Israelites: Prophecy and Cultural Autonomy in the Writings of William Apess," *Religion and Literature* 26, no. 1 (Spring 1994): 49.

48. Lepore, *In the Name of War,* 216.

49. Bernd Peyer, *The Tutor'd Mind: Indian Missionary-Writers in Antebellum America* (Amherst: University of Massachusetts Press, 1997), 157.

50. On the nullification crisis, see William Freehling, *Prelude to Civil War: The Nullification Controversy in South Carolina, 1816–1836* (New York: Oxford University Press, 1992).

51. Apess, *Indian Nullification,* 211–12.

52. Ibid., 214.

53. Ibid., 191, 219.

54. Ibid., 201.

55. Ibid., 240.

56. Ibid., 222.

57. Lepore, *In the Name of War,* 206.

58. Apess, *Indian Nullification,* 177.

59. Michael Rogin, "'Make My Day!': Spectacle as Amnesia in Imperial Politics [and] the Sequel," in *The Cultures of United States Imperialism,* ed. Amy Kaplan and Donald E. Pease (Durham, NC: Duke University Press, 1993); David Spurr, *The Rhetoric of Empire: Colonial Discourse in Journalism, Travel Writing, and Imperial Administration* (Durham, NC: Duke University Press, 1993); Michael Taussig, *Shamanism, Colonialism, and the Wild Man: A Study in Terror and Healing* (Chicago: University of Chicago Press, 1987).

60. Historically, New England attempted to guard against "colored people," since American Indians and African-Americans occasionally joined forces against colonial authority. The white fear of a joint insurrection, as Peyer notes, became codified over time, as American Indians were included in New England's prerevolutionary slave codes (*The Tutor'd Mind,* 144).

61. Apess, *Indian Nullification,* 227; emphasis in original.

62. Ibid., 180–81.

63. In his conversion narrative, one might remember, Apess related in a "tale of blood" how white fears of the American Indian afflicted him in the cherry orchard; the terror he experienced upon mistaking two "dark" women for "savages" is a memory that has now become integral to his literary practice and collective memory.

64. I am drawing on Michael Rogin's larger point that "racial and political demonology define the peculiarities of historic American empire"; one effect of this production of political culture is a willful forgetting of historical crimes, particularly racial domination ("Make My Day!" 503).

65. Apess, *Indian Nullification,* 182.

66. Ibid., 183; emphasis added.

67. Ibid.

68. Ibid., 224; emphasis in original.

69. Ibid., 186.

70. Ibid., 172.

71. Ibid.

72. Garrison, *Thoughts on African Colonization,* 6.

73. Ibid., 8.

74. Ibid., 6; emphasis in original.

75. Ibid., 7.

76. Ibid., 27.

77. Ibid., 31.

78. Apess, *A Son of the Forest,* 30.

79. Ibid., 31.

80. Castiglia, *Bound and Determined,* 38.

81. Apess, *Indian Nullification,* 239–40; emphasis in original.

82. Quoted in ibid., 195.

83. Incorporated as an Indian district, the Mashpee did not receive full civil and political enfranchisement, as did other towns in the Commonwealth. In 1870, the State of Massachusetts, citing the new Fifteenth Amendment to the Constitution, passed acts that established the town of Mashpee and granted its people citizenship and suffrage. See Jack Campisi, *The Mashpee Indians: Tribe on Trial* (Syracuse, NY: Syracuse University Press, 1991), 99–118.

84. Lepore's distinguished study of King Philip's War traces how interpretations of the event change at particular moments of crisis in American history. "Through plays like *Metamora,*" Lepore writes, "white Americans came to define themselves in relation to an imagined Indian past" (*In the Name of War,* 193). For another incisive analysis of how the symbol of Philip may have shaped Apess's narrative practice, see Velikova, "Philip, King of the Pequots."

85. O'Connell, *On Our Own Ground,* 276.

86. Apess, *Eulogy on King Philip,* in ibid., 297.

87. Ibid., 305.

88. Ibid., 279.

89. Ibid., 281.
90. Ibid., 304.
91. Ibid., 290.
92. Ibid., 297.

EPILOGUE

1. Gabriel García Márquez, *El Otoño del Patriarca* (Sudamericana, 1992).

2. "[L]as vértebras enormes de los Andes"; "la América nuestra"; "Crees que la vida es incendio / que el progreso es erupción / que en donde pones la bala / el porvenir pones." Rubén Darío, "A Roosevelt," in *Voces de Hispanoamerica: Antologia Literaria*, ed. Raquel Chang-Rodriguez and Malva Filer (Boston: Heinle & Heinle, 1988), 267–68.

3. There are many outstanding readings of "Benito Cereno" and the domestic crisis of slavery. I am indebted to the following: Carolyn Karcher, *Shadow over the Promised Land: Slavery, Race, and Violence in Melville's America* (Baton Rouge: Louisiana State University Press, 1979); Michael Rogin, *Subversive Genealogy: The Political Art of Herman Melville* (Berkeley: University of California Press, 1983); Eric Sunquist, *To Wake the Nations: Race in the Making of American Literature* (Cambridge: Harvard University Press, 1993); Dana Nelson offers two terrific readings of "Benito Cereno," in *National Manhood: Capitalist Citizenship and the Imagined Fraternity of White Men* (Durham, NC: Duke University Press, 1998), in which the story figures a "democratic melancholy of white manhood," and in *The Word in Black and White: Reading "Race" in American Literature, 1638–1867* (New York: Oxford University, 1992); Wai Chee Dimock, *Empire for Liberty: Melville and the Poetics of Individualism* (Princeton, NJ: Princeton University Press, 1989); and Allan Moore Emery, "'Benito Cereno' and Manifest Destiny," *Nineteenth-Century Fiction* 39, no. 1 (1984): 48–68.

4. For a wonderful reading of the tale's narrative structure, a "carefully unified spatial and temporal structure," see Edgar Dryden, *Melville's Thematics of Form: The Great Art of Telling the Truth* (Baltimore, MD: Johns Hopkins University Press, 1968), 200.

5. C. L. R. James's reading of *Moby Dick* as figuring the power of an expansive American state has long been fundamental to my own understanding of Melville's fiction: James, *Mariners, Renegades, and Castaways: The Story of Herman Melville and the World We Live In* (London: Allison & Busby, 1985). I am also drawing on conversations with Ed Dryden and his observation in *Melville's Thematics of Form* on the similarity between Spanish and U.S. imperialism.

6. Melville, "Benito Cereno," in *Norton Anthology of American Literature*, 5th ed., ed. Nina Baym (New York: W. W. Norton, 1998), 1: 2399.

7. Ibid., 2414.
8. Ibid., 2415.
9. Ibid.
10. Ibid., 2416.
11. In *Blake, or The Huts of America* (1859), African-American novelist Martin Delany

located U.S. imperial power in Cuba and in the visions of Southern imperialists (ed. Floyd Miller [Boston: Beacon Press, 1971]).

12. Ibid., 2415.

13. Ibid., 2413.

14. Michel Foucault, *Society Must Be Defended: Lectures at the Collège de France, 1975–1976* (New York: Picador, 2003), 47.

15. Melville, "Benito Cereno," 2390.

16. Ibid., 2416.

17. Ibid., 2427.

18. Ibid.

Index

Andy Doolen is assistant professor of American literature and American studies at the University of Kentucky.